BER SERK

Berserk. Written in Darkness
by Quentin Boëton
published by Third Éditions
32, rue d'Alsace-Lorraine,
31000 Toulouse, France

contact@thirdeditions.com
www.thirdeditions.com

Follow us:
: @ThirdEditions
: Facebook.com/ThirdEditions
: Third Éditions

Publishing Directors: Nicolas Courcier and Mehdi El Kanafi
Editorial Assistants: Ken Bruno, Ludovic Castro and Damien Mecheri
Texts by: Quentin Boëton
Proofreading: Zoé Sofer and Anne-Sophie Guénéguès
Layout: Julie Gantois
"Classic" and "First Print" covers: Nicolas Côme
Cover Creation: Steffi Girinon
Translated from French by Michael Ross, ITC Traductions

This educational work is Third Éditions' tribute to the *Berserk* manga series. The author aims to
explore part of the story of the *Berserk* manga series
in this unique collection by deciphering the inspirations, context, and content of the manga
through original analysis and discussion.

English edition, copyright 2020, Third Éditions.
All rights reserved.
ISBN 978-2-37784-276-6
Legal submission: November 2020
Printed in the European Union by TypoLibris.

Quentin "Alt 236" Boëton

WRITTEN IN DARKNESS

03rd.

THIRD
éditions

TABLE OF CONTENTS

WRITTEN IN DARKNESS

PREFACE

T HE PERSON crazy enough to endeavor to analyze *Berserk* must embark on a journey almost as painful as Guts' quest: a solitary one without respite or room for error. The series' author, Kentaro Miura, has created a saga that is wild like a bucking bronco. Trying to tame that animal is a lost cause: your only hope is to try to get close by showing you mean no harm, abandoning the idea of controlling its complex gait. Miura is the only person capable of riding that charger, as if he were the Skull Knight in the dim nights of Midland. Like the Knight of Skeleton, Miura holds the keys to a deep and cryptic tale that encompasses myriad myths and elements of fantasy.

To dare to analyze *Berserk* is to commit sacrilege: you risk impinging on the personal interpretations of millions of readers, each one positing their own theories about this or that point of the plot. I do not purport to hold the truth; in this book, I am simply trying to share with you my wonder for this series. The beauty of it is that each and every individual can find something unique and personal in it. Then there's the fact that, when it comes down to it, a story must stand on its own. If you have to explain it for it to work, then you're missing the subliminal power of the tale. That said, *Berserk* is constructed so densely and with so many references that it's impossible to resist the temptation to hunt down its secrets. As you explore the series, you discover various ways of interpreting it and numerous symbols peppered throughout, left as a trail for anyone who cares to search for them... For those who open their "third eye," a critical eye.

Berserk is a manga written in Japanese and there are surely certain passages of dialog whose meaning changed when they were translated. That is inevitable in any adaptation. As I have not mastered the Japanese language, I based my analysis on the French and English versions. But in the end, although there may have been some small changes, they are part of how the series has been read in our corner of the world and it's through these versions that I came to know and love *Berserk*.

One of the risks that I'm taking in this book is analyzing a work that is still in progress. Can you really claim to have understood a story without knowing how it ends? It's true that this book could end up with a pie in the face if the author decides to deceive everyone by coming up with some incredible twist, catching us all off guard. There's always the slightest possibility that Miura could decide to reveal that Guts is actually a creation of artificial intelligence from the future who dreams of having chivalrous adventures, just as an example. In that case, yes, we would certainly have to reread the entire manga in light of that revelation... But even if such a far-fetched conclusion did occur, no matter. The 40 volumes that we've read to this point have taken us on the most ill-fated and memorable journey in dark fantasy imaginable. All of the twists and turns of the story given to us by Miura, all of the symbols he's laid out, there's so much there that you could write a book about it... like the book you're holding right now. It doesn't much matter what Miura might decide to do as his story continues. There's no reason for us not to venture onto the winding paths of interpretation that he has invited us to walk down.

There exists another danger: overinterpreting, finding meaning where there is none, or worse yet, building a theory that doesn't hold water. But as long as our analysis of the manga relies on specific, coherent elements found in the text, then all interpretations are fair game. You could even argue that the *mangaka* does not hold all the answers to all that he has revealed to us: part of *Berserk* comes from the unconscious mind, from its buried past, its dreams, its fantasies, and its nightmares.

As such, this book does not in any way aim to prove anything whatsoever and does not claim to hold the word of God, like the unyielding Mozgus. On the contrary, this book invites you on a journey. It is the fruit of many hours of passionate reading and research by a fan of imagery, art, and fiction who would like to share with you his findings and feelings, laying out the clues that Miura has left for us. In this book, I'd like to explain what I think I've seen behind the images and words of the *mangaka*, a man whose secrecy made this quest for interpretation that much more difficult. My goal is not even to "reveal" the creator's intentions, but rather to shed light on the universal complexity of his work, in both his story and his drawings. On all that can be found there if you just pore over it with curiosity and good intentions.

After all, a work of art no longer entirely belongs to its creator once it's been given over to the public. We should be able to enjoy the work without having to know the artist hiding in the wings or his intentions. Even if we try to decipher some of Miura's choices based on scant clues he has revealed in interviews, when it comes down to it, one of the most important things is our own relationship with the work. What's important is what we, the readers, feel when we turn the last page of a chapter of *Berserk*, before devouring the next.

This manga belongs to each and every one of us. I am just one of you. I am writing this book because this story leaves me awestruck by its depth and masterfulness. That is the true magic of the saga of Guts: it allows you to immerse yourself in its depths. An entire universe comes to life on these pages, and that universe in turn is surrounded by several layers of interpretation that are at once coherent and diverse. *Berserk* is not just an adventure story. It's a work of art, philosophy, and symbolism, an ode to the dark side of human nature, a declaration of love for fantasy. You can feel that Miura tries to offer us a tale that is much greater than even him, a parable to serve as a milestone in the ultimate story...

The author: Quentin Boëton

After abandoning a master's degree in law and an ill-fated "career" as a musician, Quentin Boëton found light in the universe and meaning in his life when he enrolled at Beaux-Arts (the National School of Fine Arts) in Paris at the age of 25. He graduated in 2009 and entered the job market having taught himself video editing and Photoshop. He was finally able to dedicate himself to his almost pathological love for the strange, the arts, and creativity. After three years working as an editor on an obscure feature-length film called *Sorgoï Prakov* (US title *Descent into Darkness: My European Nightmare*), and after years of struggling to make it, out of an irrepressible need to turn his ideas into reality, without really believing it would succeed, he launched the YouTube channel "ALT 236" at the age of 35. Thanks to a miracle, and the support of his subscribers, he now works on this channel full-time as a video creator. He avidly explores the dark corners of the human imagination and tries to invite everyone in, including neophytes. He has worked on the program *BiTS* and also has a column for the magazine *Canard PC*.

WRITTEN IN DARKNESS

INTRODUCTION

B EFORE we launch with reckless abandon into the thorough autopsy of *Berserk*, I should briefly summarize the structure, events, and important characters of the story up to volume 40, the latest volume as of the publication of this book.

The timeline of *Berserk* is unusual: the first three volumes feature Guts as an adult busy exacting revenge, without the reader knowing exactly why. From the end of volume 3, Miura radically rewinds the story and takes us back to the birth of Guts, then leads us back to where we were at the start of volume 1. The story's events then follow a chronological timeline up to the most recent episodes published. The manga is divided into parts called "arcs," which in turn consist of several chapters. These story arcs are of different lengths: the "Black Swordsman" arc has eight chapters, but is followed by the "Golden Age" arc with 86 chapters. Next is the "Conviction" arc with its 82 chapters, then the "Falcon of the Millennium Empire" arc, the longest to date with 131 chapters. The current story arc, "Fantasia," is now on its fortieth chapter.

Summarizing over 9,000 pages of manga comprehensively would take up another book entirely, but to give you the keys needed to understand, and to jog your memory, we need to briefly cover the most crucial points of each story arc.

THE BLACK SWORDSMAN

This story arc, while quite enigmatic, nevertheless reveals many of the essential elements of canon, whose origins and meanings we will understand later in the story. We follow a mysterious, solitary warrior named Guts, who is accompanied in spite of himself by a kindly little elf named Puck. Guts appears to be on a quest for vengeance, as we see him tracking two prominent figures who are apparently hiding their monstrous nature. He first kills the Snake Lord, then heads off in pursuit of the Slug Count. Along the way, he discovers a strange object, one that was used to turn the Count into an "apostle," a sort of monstrous demon that serves a group of evil beings. These beings are in fact the object of Guts' vengeance: they are called the Guardian Angels of the God Hand. The object used to summon them is egg-shaped and called a "beherit" (or "behelit" in some editions). The Slug Count finds his beherit and summons the God Hand in the presence of Guts. When the Black Swordsman sees one of them, whom he calls "Griffith," we understand that all of his hate is directed at this one evil being... The God Hand ask the Count to sacrifice his own daughter in exchange for the death of Guts, but when he refuses, the Slug Count is dragged into the abyss and the God Hand disappears.

THE GOLDEN AGE

This is where the story resets to the very beginning. We see the birth of Guts, his extremely difficult childhood, and his flight from the group of mercenaries that took him in after he killed his adoptive father, Gambino. Guts then encounters the Band of the Falcon (or "Hawk" in some editions), a group of mercenaries led by the cunning and captivating Griffith, who happens to wear a beherit as a pendant. In the group, Guts also meets Casca, for whom he first has conflicted feelings, before falling in love with her. This entire story arc sees the Band's rising power, as they achieve victory after victory and finally end the Hundred-Year War that had plagued the Kingdom of Midland. Griffith even begins courting the king's daughter, but due to strong feelings of jealousy and possessiveness, the relationship between Guts and Griffith becomes complicated. The Black Swordsman then decides to leave the Band to find his own way and, out of spite, Griffith sleeps with the Midland king's daughter. Enraged, the king imprisons Griffith, a.k.a. "the Falcon," and tortures him until the former knight's spirit is broken. When the Band rescues him, he is but a shadow of his former self and, in a bout of despair, he activates his beherit, causing the Guardian Angels to appear. It is at this moment that the Eclipse ceremony takes place. Griffith sacrifices all of his friends to the Guardian Angels in order to become one of them, being reborn as Femto and becoming the fifth member of the God Hand. Intoxicated with a thirst for violence, he rapes Casca and drives Guts mad with pain, ripping out one of his eyes and cutting off one of his arms. However, the two lovers escape at the last minute thanks to their timely rescue by the mysterious Skull Knight. Just after the Eclipse, Casca, who had been carrying Guts' child, gives birth to a demon child who disappears as the sun rises, although we see him again later on, at key moments in the story. It's at this time that Guts is equipped with his cannon arm by Godot the blacksmith, and that he receives his legendary sword, the Dragon Slayer. Instead of staying with Casca, who remains listless and broken from her trauma, Guts leaves her with the blacksmith and Rickert, one of the few members of the Band of the Falcon to have escaped the Eclipse.

CONVICTION

This story arc focuses mainly on Mozgus, the Chief Inquisitor of the Holy See, and his henchmen. Mozgus leads the Inquisition and tracks down pagan cult members and sorcerers who, according to him, are a scourge on Midland. We also meet Farnese and Serpico, who are in the employ of the order of the Holy See and are searching for information about a prophecy announcing the return of a legendary being. At the same time, we follow the solo adventures of Guts, who, as a bearer of a cursed mark branded on his skin during the Eclipse, attracts all the monsters and apostles around him. The Black Swordsman is captured by Farnese's band of knights, but manages to escape by taking Farnese hostage. Because of this, she is faced with monsters for the first time in her life. Attracted to Guts and shaken by the abominations that she's seen, Farnese begins to evolve... to the point that she eventually joins forces with Guts. Meanwhile, Midland is invaded by the Kushan Empire, led by the terrible Ganishka, which wreaks havoc on the country. During this time, Casca, who has fled her refuge, is first captured by a pagan cult, then finds herself in the clutches of Mozgus, who wants to burn her for heresy because of the Brand of Sacrifice that she too bears, attracting monsters and earning her a reputation as a witch. Guts has a dream announcing the death of his beloved, so he heads off to find her. During a complex, apocalyptic battle where all of the various adversaries find themselves in the same place at once, the Guardian Angels take the opportunity to reappear for a new ceremony, a second "Eclipse": this one allows Femto to reincarnate in his original human form, Griffith. As the Kushan army arrives at the battlefield and further complicates the situation, Zodd, a winged demon working for Griffith, carries his master out of harm's way. Mozgus and his underlings, transformed into demon-like creatures, are finally felled, and Guts and his friends flee.

THE FALCON OF THE MILLENNIUM EMPIRE

The Kushan army continues to take the country by force and the oppressed people of Midland place great hope in a prophecy that came to all in a dream, promising the advent of a Falcon of Light. At this time, the newly reborn Griffith is working to form a new band, this time composed of demon knights who, thanks to their fight against the Kushan invaders, are seen as a resistance force rather than a threat. Guts, accompanied by Isidro, a young man who wants to become Guts' disciple, by Casca, who has amnesia, and by Farnese and her servant Serpico, finds himself in the home of a friend of the Skull Knight, the witch Flora. Assisted by the young Schierke, she reveals many pieces of information that help us understand the complex universe of *Berserk*.

She offers weapons and powers to the entire band and, in particular, gives Guts the Berserker Armor. The band then leaves to rescue villagers under attack by horrible, bloodthirsty trolls. This arc ends with a huge battle pitting Ganishka against Griffith. The defeat of Ganishka, who is an apostle, brings about his transformation into a giant, luminous tree that completely changes the world. Reality and legend intertwine and the world is invaded by fantastic monsters and creatures. At the same time, an enormous city named Falconia magically appears. Because of this, Griffith is seen as the Falcon of Light from the prophecy and he becomes the ruler of this new city, where all the humans in Midland take refuge.

FANTASIA

This final story arc begins as the real world and fantasy world are fusing together. Guts and his band embark on a journey to the island of Elfhelm, Puck's homeland. It is said that Elfhelm possesses a way to treat Casca and restore her strength and memory. What follows is a long and perilous crossing of the sea, with combative pirates, sea monsters, and mysterious islands. After all these hazards, the band reaches Elfhelm and meets the queen of the elves. She reveals to them that the only way to treat Casca is to delve into her mind and find the pieces of her psyche, which was shattered by her trauma. It's up to Farnese and Schierke to try their luck and forge a path through the terrible thoughts keeping Casca prisoner. In volume 40, the young woman regains her memory... What will happen next? How will Casca put her life back together? Will Guts succeed in exacting vengeance against an ultra-powerful Griffith?

While we've had to skip over a thousand fascinating characters and adventures, you now have the key pieces of this fantastic story...

BER SERK

W R I T T E N   I N   D A R K N E S S

PART ONE
Antihero Quest

AT THE INTERSECTION OF GENRES

The plot of *Berserk* forms an epic, operatic saga presenting the destinies of numerous protagonists in a vast and rich story, where each person has their own special role to play. The manga's basic structure, which was covered in a fairly simple manner in the introduction, mainly follows the adventures of Guts, the Black Swordsman; Griffith, the Falcon; and Casca. Their intertwined fates lead the world to its destruction and rebirth. They are propelled by a divine force that goes beyond their individuality and against which Guts, especially, tries to fight back, leaving a bloody wake of monsters and misfortune behind him.

Of course, this summary glosses over the immense richness of the story and, for the time being, pushes aside evidence of the legendary nature of the story. That said, here is the essence of the saga: *Berserk* is a story of love, ambition, and vengeance. It has all of the ingredients of a tragic adventure story: a band of friends, a hero, betrayal, monsters by the hundreds, an evil threat hanging over the world, a love triangle between three strangers to leave us with bated breath... Miura lays out all the elements for one of those stories that pulls us in and keeps us forever captivated.

What this synopsis fails to capture is the macabre and Dantean backdrop that Miura establishes for all of his seemingly classic narrative devices. The *mangaka* throws us headlong into a dark and violent story, one that is deliberately immoral and ruthless. However, *Berserk* is not all darkness. It is a sensitive, poetic, and often funny work that takes on so many different facets that the reader is left with a burning question: what genre does this manga belong to anyway?

Answering this question is more complicated than you would think. When Miura describes his own style, he refers to "dark fantasy." This rich sub-genre of fantasy, in general, establishes a dark universe over which there is very often an apocalyptic threat brewing. The reader meets broken, pessimistic, sometimes monstrous protagonists who often struggle to distinguish between right and wrong. The dark fantasy genre results in works that are violent and hopeless, psychologically oppressive, in which combat is featured prominently to give the story a certain degree of brutality. The genre frequently flirts with

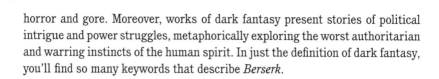

horror and gore. Moreover, works of dark fantasy present stories of political intrigue and power struggles, metaphorically exploring the worst authoritarian and warring instincts of the human spirit. In just the definition of dark fantasy, you'll find so many keywords that describe *Berserk*.

"I've been working on the concept of my own fantasy world since I was in high school and college. Like I mentioned, I got ideas from *Guin Saga*, and from films, like *Excalibur* and *Conan the Barbarian*. I came up with the dark fantasy concept from those movies[1]."

Conan. Created by the pen of Robert E. Howard in 1932, the Barbarian became a global hit when played by Arnold Schwarzenegger in the 1982 John Milius film. While *Conan the Barbarian* is not immediately classified as dark fantasy, it shares many themes and similarities with *Berserk*. Like Guts, Conan is driven by vengeance. He is a peerless swordsman and listens only to his anger and ardor because, like the Black Swordsman, his loved ones were killed. There are numerous elements in the film that must have, we can imagine, made an impression on Miura: the violent fights of Conan, who decapitates entire tribes of cannibals; the duels with Dagoth and Thoth-Amon, who are reminiscent of the Apostles. Of course, the historical ages evoked in the two *Conan* films differ from *Berserk*, which is also more somber. However, in both cases you find the same love for quests and gear, strong characters, and that special ingredient that makes a story epic, as if there were a brutal and bestial air flowing through the story. When Miura gives *Excalibur*, a film by John Boorman (1981), as an influence, the homage is more apparent: epic sieges by armies on castles, a fascination with armor, with medieval decorum and chivalry, their codes and values. However, as a manga artist, you're not limited by numbers of extras or money. As such, Miura does not hold back his medieval visions from reaching a degree that the film does not. While today the manga enjoys definite, well-deserved renown, when Miura began the story, was the choice of a dark fantasy aesthetic one that was sure to meet success in Japan? Not necessarily.

"At first I didn't have any advanced plan. I just thought to do a shonen fantasy manga with a dark hero because the manga of mine that had received a prize was published in a shonen magazine. A hero that suited shonen[2] magazines. And well, there weren't many fantasy manga at that time. If I had to name

1. Interview given for the American release of the *Berserk* anime series, as an audio supplement for the zone-3 DVDs. See Bibliography.
2. *Berserk* has since been classified in the *seinen* manga genre because of the violent, adult tone the series has taken on since the beginning.

any... just *Bastard!!* So I thought about going for a niche genre... But that's all. I couldn't see further than that[3]."

"Explore the dark side..." So, there's the intention that led Berserk into the "dark" fantasy genre. And that's what characterizes Miura's work: a fascinating exploration of the artistic architecture of the dark side. The degree of physical, sexual, and emotional violence in *Berserk* has rarely been reached in any work of dark fantasy. For example, some people on the internet have amused themselves counting the precise number of people and creatures killed by the "hero" throughout the manga series. As of volume 37, the body count was around 1,190 victims... That goes to show how prominently death is featured in *Berserk*. It is constant: in battles and duels, but also in scenes of torture and public executions. Other manga that share this dark fantasy classification, such as *Bastard!!* (Kazushi Hagiwara), *Übel Blatt* (Etorouji Shiono), and *Claymore* (Norihiro Yagi), do not push the visual insanity and morbid realism nearly as far. It's not enough to have knights and monsters to earn the distinction of "dark fantasy masterpiece." You must set yourself apart with a very "credible" and detailed style, even when it comes to creating improbable creatures. You have to pay almost pathological attention to the aesthetics of the misfortune and violence. Incidentally, some of the most ambitious works of dark fantasy of the early 21st century are *Dark Souls* and *Bloodborne*, two video games from the Japanese studio From Software. The brains of the studio, Hidetaka Miyazaki, is open about his deep love for Miura's epic, even hiding "Easter eggs" from the manga in his games. A number of other works of dark fantasy have achieved critical success, including *The Witcher III*, a video game in the universe created by novelist Andrzej Sapkowski, and *Game of Thrones* by George R. R. Martin. All of these examples show that the public is eager for this type of bloody and romantic story with an epic and "historical" flair. While in the beginning when he launched *Berserk*, Miura may have felt a little lonely with his somber, medieval style, it's fair to say that, today, audiences are more familiar with this type of story. And they've certainly gotten to know *Berserk*. However, it's worth noting that *Berserk* has evolved over time and its *mangaka* has not held back from exploring other genres. What's more, as the manga has progressed, Miura has expanded its universe to be a more "classic" fantasy universe, verging on magical. Throughout the story, the author has explored sub-genres such as high fantasy, heroic fantasy, and medieval fantasy, with *Berserk* ultimately fitting into all of these categories. And that's part of Miura's genius: his ability to mix so many styles while remaining strangely consistent.

3. Interview given in December 1996 in Kentaro Miura's studio, published in *Berserk: Illustrations File*. See Bibliography.

He draws from fairy tales, stories of knights and pirates, folkloric and religious fables, mythology, films, and literary works. His inspirations come from such varied and distinct works, from science fiction to the Bible, from painting to literature. Finally, the liberties he has taken with the historical eras represented in the series make it even more difficult to define *Berserk*'s "genre."

THE PILLARS OF FANTASY

Miura was not content to just insert a few fights, a pair of trolls, and a dragon to fit with the codes of a pre-established style. He is a creator who seems obsessed with the art and cultural force of fantasy in our societies. Never forget that Kentaro Miura is a Japanese author who uses a form of fantasy that actually has its roots elsewhere in the world. Japanese culture has its own codes, history, and bestiary. By writing about a culture with mercenary knights and court nobility in a Europe of his dreams, Miura puts himself in a position that must be uncomfortable in the challenge that it poses: taking ownership of a style of fantasy that is so foreign to his own culture... And yet he seems to approach this with a carefree attitude.

"So, European readers might say, 'what the hell is this?' Well, I think the way foreigners see us, Japanese people, matches this case perfectly: 'hey, ninjas!' It's OK because I just draw my work to please Japanese people. I don't have any strategy for the global market[4]."

We can take Miura at his word, but I suspect that he doesn't actually take this issue so lightly. When reading the manga, I am absolutely blown away by the level of research and the degree of detail infused in each "historical" element. Although the artist creates his own armor, we see many examples that actually existed. The depicting of thousands of armed soldiers in very detailed battles reveals a meticulous and scholarly artist who has a masterful understanding of his subject. You can tell that he spent many hours designing and researching inspirations for medieval garb to attain such a level of detail and credibility. His architectural design is also mind-blowing: from the foggy, Gothic paved passages of Wyndham to the bustling streets of the metropolis of Falconia, Miura shows that he has deep knowledge of medieval Europe, its cities, and its artistry. The same can be said for the faithfulness with which he tries to depict the medieval environments, whether they be landscapes, living spaces, customs, or even faces. At times, it's astounding to see how an artist

4. *Ibid.*

from a culture so faraway and distinct is capable of capturing with such mastery the visual and artistic ethos of an era that we Europeans don't always represent accurately. Interestingly, Miura has admitted that he would be curious to hear what Westerners think of his anarchistic vision of "our" history.

"What do Westerners think of this fantasy world created by a person from the Eastern tradition? Many of us in the East feel that the fantasy worlds created in Hollywood... or believed in by Westerners are more genuine fantasy worlds. And I think *Berserk* is strongly influenced by Western culture. I'm trying to create something from what I learned from the West. So, I'm curious about what people in the West think of *Berserk*[5]."

It's a safe bet that the choice of an anachronistic Middle Ages was not a random one (Miura mixes periods ranging from the High Middle Ages to the Renaissance). Indeed, the Middle Ages offer many useful attributes for any author looking to write a story in a fantasy universe. It was an era that saw many major events in human history, both in terms of barbarism and beauty. As we see throughout this text, Miura explores our collective unconscious through the pages of his manga. He aims to draw monsters and magic straight from the source of our imagination. The Middle Ages become the most obvious choice for a setting because it was during that time that the first "modern," post-mythological fantasy stories were written. For example, it was in the Middle Ages that Arthurian legends flourished; and incidentally, it would not be much of a stretch to imagine finding in *Berserk* Knights of the Round Table on a quest for the Holy Grail or for the legendary sword Excalibur, which, like the Dragon Slayer, held a mythical place in the epic tales of King Arthur. Like *Berserk*, the Arthurian legend is centered on Christian themes, such as evil, sin, and a quest for perfection, symbolized by the Holy Grail, seen as the ultimate relic for having held the blood of Christ. The romantic relationships, like that of Tristan and Iseult, which most likely inspired the romance between Lancelot and Guinevere, marked the beginnings of courtly love, of which Miura delivers a sort of diabolical mirror image.

The Middle Ages were also a period of wars and conquests, court intrigue and conspiracies. It was a period that saw the spread of plagues and famine, but also subjugation by Machiavellian lords, keeping the dying masses in abject poverty. The Middle Ages were the time of the Inquisition and super-stition. That right there is probably one of the most important reasons behind

5. *Ibid.*

Miura's choice to set his odyssey in this medieval context. In the Middle Ages, people still believed in the existence of hell and demons. Entire books were written about fantastic beasts that were assumed to be real. Some even continued certain forms of pagan cult worship, with sorcery developing in parallel. The Middle Ages offer the perfect palette for a *mangaka* wishing to paint a tableau of biblical proportions, who wants to subject his characters to unthinkable dilemmas in a merciless time period... To top it all off, from a Japanese viewpoint, the Middle Ages offer so many fantastic elements for both plot lines and visuals. Miura was able to perfectly choose a slice of history that would take his Japanese readers by surprise and deliver to his Western audience a stunning view into his imagination. In short, if Miura has placed his story in the time of the Vikings, he would have had to limit his references to Nordic mythology. By situating it in the fantasy Middle Ages, the *mangaka* opened up a treasure trove of possibilities. And he has taken full advantage of that: *Berserk* encompasses practically every genre of fiction. It is an adventure story, a fairy tale, a medieval epic, a legendary odyssey, an homage to H.P. Lovecraft, a biblical parable, a "rape and revenge" story, and so much more, and yet all this variety does not detract from the originality or coherence of the story. The more the story of *Berserk* unfolds, the more it appears to be a perfect synthesis, the quintessential fantasy epic.

GROUP DYNAMICS

With *Berserk*, Miura delivers a mosaic that ties together the fates of many characters with all sorts of relationships. The author explores horizontal relationships: those between individual humans. He also explores vertical relationships: those between God, his servants, and humans. What's more, in the manga, no one goes it alone. Each person has their ban, henchmen, whatever sort of group with which they share interests, even if only for a given time. Even Guts, Casca, and Griffith (the three beings who seem to have fairly individual fates) are inextricably linked to the secondary characters who accompany them. Their decisions are crucial because they directly influence the fate of those close to them and humanity as a whole. Before we even get into the nature of these relationships between characters, I would like to applaud Miura for his ability to create "gangs" that are strong and coherent, making them immediately iconic. And it's not totally off-base to call them gangs because each band evokes some form of fear and fascination, has its own style of combat, has strong personalities, and has a coherent, easily recognizable look. Even if we set aside all the different armies and militias, there are other unforgettable groups that stand out: the seven inquisitors that are Mozgus and his band of torturers, the five Bakiraka, the Four Kings of the World, Silat and his four bodyguards, and last but not least, the five Guardian Angels of the God Hand. These groups are at once both disparate and consistent: each of the members of a band is most often very different from their associates, but together they form a quite homogeneous whole. Incidentally, in general, when these gangs appear for the first time, Miura likes to dedicate an entire page to them. The reader gets to see all of their outfits, weapons, faces, and appearances. The gang adopts an iconic pose to accentuate the aura that they always project. However, initially, one group stands head and shoulders above the rest: the Band of the Falcon in The Golden Age. The Band gets the whole story going. It's a heroic group with a perfect ascent to power, from the bottom of the totem pole as an anonymous mercenary group to being inducted into the official army of Midland. And yet, this motley crew was in no way predestined to achieve such glory. A sociological examination of the members that make up the Band of the Falcon reveals social outcasts rather than gallant knights: "We've got escaped prisoners, street urchins, sons of blacksmiths, and even second sons of poor aristocrats in ours! Yup!" By choosing fragile or marginalized characters as his protagonists, Miura offers figures we can identify with because their flaws evoke empathy in us. We want to know why Pippin is always closing his eyes and seems so mute; we want to understand why Casca is such a secretive fighter; why Griffith seems so unapproachable... The entire Band of the Falcon, in spite of all of its shows of bravery, is beset by complex internal dynamics that reach their zenith during the Eclipse.

This team is a case study on the concept of friendship and the processes that can transform it into hatred. At the beginning of the story, the Band of the Falcon serves as an adoptive family for Guts and makes him more human. In the group, he finds all that friendship can provide: human warmth, overcoming difficult times together, shared victories, laughter, arguments, memories, affection, and sometimes more... But as in any group of friends, there's also jealousy, ambition, and selfishness. These flaws ultimately lead to the worst thing that can happen in a friendship: betrayal. While in the beginning the group seems close-knit, it soon proves to be dysfunctional because all of its members are essentially dependent on a charismatic leader who totally hypnotizes them and leads them to their destruction. As Guts clearheadedly tells Griffith: "Right, everything's in the palm of your hand, like it's always been," as if to foreshadow the advent of the God Hand that will crush each and every one of them. Although he is admired, Griffith shines so brightly in his arrogance that he eventually creates an inferiority complex in all of his comrades, like Corkus, who feels this most strongly and isn't afraid to say it: "Without Griffith, the Band of the Falcon's just a rabble anyway..." And as if by chance, Guts comes along and disturbs the adoring relationship between Griffith and his band, exposing all of their dysfunctions, particularly due to

Casca's jealousy. Intimate relationships are not exclusive to the love triangle between Guts, Casca and Griffith, and several complicated liaisons develop throughout the story. Judeau develops a crush on Casca, but dies when he was on the verge of telling her. Initially, Casca is in love with Griffith, who in turn only shows interest for Guts. Casca's jealousy ramps up when, to add insult to injury, the Falcon weds Princess Charlotte. Post-Eclipse Griffith goes on to generate more jealousy, as seen in the relationship between the naive Charlotte and the devoted Sonia. However, while the Falcon unleashes such passion, Guts is also a heartbreaker in his own right. As is often the case in *Berserk*, these are cases of forbidden love, like Schierke's attraction to Guts. Schierke is beset by waves of feeling for him when they're together, but the young witch refuses to let her emotions run wild, perfectly aware that she's too young, since the object of her affection is twice her age. Her relationship with Isidro, although they seem to be constantly at odds, is closer to a "liaison" appropriate to her age, more abstract and juvenile. Another case of love that wasn't meant to be is Farnese's feelings for Guts. As he only has eyes for Casca, the commander harbors some jealousy towards the young amnesiac. Farnese also wins the award for greatest tragic romance for her brief affair with Serpico, who discovers that their nascent attraction must be nipped in the bud because they share blood. As I list all of these romantic plots, you might get the impression that *Berserk* is just a soap opera. That couldn't be farther from the truth, as Miura develops these story lines over many volumes and often plays on what's not said. All of these plots offer dynamics that enrich the human relationships. What's more, the story itself crosses into horror due to a matter of tradition: Griffith is thrown in jail for sleeping with the daughter of the king of Midland without his approval. This marks the beginning of Griffith's descent into evil.

Much of the drama that troubles the Band of the Hawk comes from the duality of the conflicting, and almost romantic, relationship between Guts and Griffith, with Casca in the middle of this complicated connection. The two male protagonists have diametrically opposed personalities: while Guts is "rough around the edges," doesn't mince his words, which can be harsh, and seems to have no qualms about using violence, deep down he's actually big-hearted and faithful. Conversely, while Griffith seems peaceful, shrewd, and strategic, giving off an angelic air and fighting with the lightness of a feather, deep down he's actually a demon in the making, willing to betray all those he seems to care about. Having two such antagonistic profiles going head to head within a group keeps us with bated breath all the way to the terrible tragedy of the Eclipse, and then well after. As for the Eclipse, it's actually quite a daring choice by the author to eliminate so many characters in one fell swoop, characters that readers had come to love over a dozen volumes. The journalist who conducted the interview for the *Berserk Official Guidebook* asked Miura if drawing this part of the story had been devastating for him:

"I was emotionally invested in each character, so I felt more depressed than scared. And the story went way down in popularity with the readers around the time of the Eclipse [laugh]. Many readers were furious that I'd do such a thing to the characters they liked. My editor at the time was concerned but also of the opinion that we'd just have to follow it through to the end. The point I had to pay attention to was making sure the flow of the story wasn't completely severed with the Eclipse. That's why I spared Casca. If she had died and the serialization had continued for a long time, I feared the reason for revenge would become something of the past; and if Guts were to establish new relationships, then his incentive would waver. It may seem calculating and unpleasant, but it's because Casca's by his side that he can never forget the Eclipse[6]."

In this way, Miura uses the Eclipse tragedy as the origin of a new dynamic: after watching a group of friends come together, fight, care for each other, and win, we now see them fall apart and open themselves up to revenge, hatred, and pain. In the end, *Berserk* is a manga filled with action and intrigue: jealousy, power struggles, moral and religious strife, stories of love and friendship. The story puts human behavior under the microscope, often exploring its most unsettling aspects. Furthermore, having so many free radicals come together and collide with each other makes the series feel ample and dense. Via the complex interactions between the characters, Miura presents a broad spectrum of feelings ranging from the lightest of comedy to the darkest of tragedy...

GUTS: A PATCHWORK OF INSPIRATIONS

While readers may sometimes find themselves torn between veneration for Guts and fascination for Griffith, we have to acknowledge that the story mainly focuses on Guts' point of view. The Black Swordsman is at the heart of this story. We can even argue that he is the backbone of *Berserk*. There are even parts of the story where Casca and Griffith are totally absent for long periods. Meanwhile, Miura never lets our dark protagonist out of his sight. Guts is the common denominator for all of the characters; their shared fate and the coherence of the narrative rest on his shoulders. As such, it's no surprise that his character is intricately detailed at all stages of character development:

6. In *Berserk Official Guidebook.* See Bibliography.

Miura digs into his background and depicts him from every angle. We know all of the important people who made an impression on Guts' life. We witness his feelings, his most intimate dramatic moments, the reasons behind his anger... Few fiction characters have received such in-depth character development, likely out of fear of revealing too much of the character. And yet, Guts remains a mysterious individual who keeps his deepest thoughts and emotions to himself. Although Kentaro Miura has given very few interviews, he has nevertheless been quite generous in sharing information and revelations about his creative process. Reading between the lines of these statements reveals the fascinating nature of the artist: he is an alchemist of imagination. He doesn't create things out of nothing. He draws inspiration from other creators, then transforms anything that speaks to him to make it his own. He transforms and transcends his references using the machinery of his own creativity. He uses existing "materials" and, once he has broken them down in his creative laboratory, he changes them into a new, even more precious substance. I use this imagery because, with *Berserk*, Miura offers a work of art packed full of references that often transcends its models. The author demonstrates extensive knowledge of the mechanisms of fiction and knows how to take advantage of the necessary borrowing that takes place between artists. The reason why I stress this point is that this idea will be a common theme throughout this book. In a detailed interview he gave for the manga's official guide[7], Miura admitted that Guts was born of "a style." His initial idea was simply to invent a dark and gloomy hero. The number of influences that he cites is impressive. He is very comfortable revealing them and they reflect his personal tastes, showing that Guts is a sort of composition: the perfect blend of all that the *mangaka* admires in fiction heroes.

Before I list these influences, it's important to underscore that Miura provides us with an opportunity to debunk some old beliefs that people have maintained about artists: originality. When we think of an artist, we often imagine a person cut off from the world, solitary and tormented, who stays up until the wee hours of the morning to finally seize that divine power that gives him talent and originality... The truth is, an author is never alone. They are always a part of the history of art and techniques. This image of the artist who creates something out of nothing is linked to another cliché: one has to suffer in order to create; they have to play the part of the tortured artist. Miura is the antithesis of this: he is a creator who has built his reputation on endless hours of work, practice, doubts, failures, and attempts. However, his work is also the product of his cultural and artistic influences, because it is by learning from others that he paints his own masterpiece; it is by borrowing concepts

7. *Berserk Official Guidebook*, see Bibliography.

from kindred works that he can transcend them. Where would *Berserk* be if *Devilman* had never existed? Under no circumstances should this be confused with plagiarism, which is identically copying an idea from another without giving credit or respect. As such, it is crucial that we bear in mind that Miura is an artist with tremendous cultural knowledge from both art and literature. He consults hundreds of documentary and historical works and has excellent command of the codes of fantasy. This disposition can be seen from the very beginning of the manga, when the author laid the foundation for his main character. The Black Swordsman is a veritable patchwork of references. The gloomy and nihilistic side of Guts? An idea that comes from Hakaider, an antihero from the manga *Jinzo Ningen Kikaider* by Shotaro Ishinomori. This masked, enigmatic supervillain gave Miura the idea for a solitary, tough, and hopeless character. It's interesting to note that this same character served as inspiration for George Lucas while creating Darth Vader, the emblematic antagonist of his *Star Wars* saga. To bring it all full circle, Kentaro Miura himself has admitted that *Star Wars* is his favorite movie. And yet, Hakaider's universe would be categorized as science fiction and is in no way related to medieval fantasy. Miura explains that the fantasy genre was "grafted" onto this idea of the nihilistic antihero. The imagery of a "graft" is interesting, as Guts is a sort of "Frankenstein's monster" cobbled together from various parts by Dr. Miura, if you will. In regards to his fantasy inspirations, he again cites *Conan* by Robert E. Howard, but also, in particular, *Guin Saga*, a series of heroic fantasy novels by Japanese writer Kaoru Kurimoto, a story stretching over more than 130 volumes... It's at this crossroads of genres that he got the idea for the "Black Swordsman." Miura confesses that when he first created *Berserk* in the 1980s, Hollywood and its genre films were at their peak and were a major influence in the development of the manga. While Guts' face comes from the *mangaka*'s sketches as a teenager (Miura says that he would instinctively create this same head whenever he would draw a character), the aura that he projects is inspired by the work of one of Miura's favorite actors: Rutger Hauer. When asked who was the inspiration for Guts, here's what he said:

"But if you're only talking about his looks and not about his personality then I guess Rutger Hauer was the model. I saw him playing a mercenary in a medieval movie, *Flesh & Blood*, and I really liked him in that movie. He also played the lead in *The Blood of Heroes*. It was a sci-fi movie, but I thought the character he played was similar to Guts. And the main character from *Highlander* kind of reminds me of Guts. I think it had a lot to do with those cool, collected-type heroes I admired when I was in college[8]."

8. Interview given for the American release of the *Berserk* anime series, as an audio supplement for the zone-3 DVDs. See Bibliography.

From the inception of his hero, Miura has been aware that he is creating a sort of ideal monster. While the author confesses that when he began *Berserk*, he had no clear ideas about the direction his manga would take, he very quickly realized that he needed to create a complex, colorful, highly detailed protagonist who would be memorable due to both his appearance and his abilities. To achieve this, his character needed recognizable physical and personality attributes. In addition to having one eye shut, Guts is disabled: he's missing an arm. This fact was an opportunity for Miura to set his character apart by creating a weaponized prosthetic, a mechanical and deadly appendage that would be immediately iconic. It was also a nod to two works that Miura admires. One is *Dororo* by Osamu Tezuka, in which the protagonist can remove the fleshy envelopes of his arms to reveal razor-sharp samurai swords; the other is the fantasy manga *Cobra* by Buichi Terasawa, and more specifically the hero's Psychogun, a plasma cannon hidden in a false forearm. This sort of gimmick becomes emblematic for a hero: readers come to identify them with their prosthetic weapon; it becomes their trademark. Guts wouldn't be Guts without his cannon-crossbow arm. As *Berserk* takes place in a medieval universe, this cannon is a good way of making the main character stand out from the rest because Miura knows that equipping Guts with a sword as his main weapon makes him a more classic hero. The protagonists in *Guin Saga* and *Pygmalio* by Shinji Wada, two works that Miura admires, are both swordsmen. Guts' sword itself needed to be distinguished from its forebears, so Guts needed to carry a weapon like no other, a sword so big and unusual that no man other than him would be able to handle it. The legendary Dragon Slayer was conceived out of the *mangaka*'s desire to create his own mythical sword. To lend credibility to such an absurd blade, Miura spent hours imagining the physical consequences of wielding such a weapon. What muscles would Guts work? How would he have to move his body to maneuver such a big hunk of steel? To draw his hero's body, the artist worked off of real-life images to add realism to the musculature in order to make the handling of this improbable weapon more credible. In the manga, there are countless bits of dialog where characters wax poetic about Guts' sword and its lethal capabilities in order to add extra emphasis to its extraordinary nature.

Being a perfectionist, Miura also works hard on his protagonist's facial expressions, again drawing inspiration from Hollywood. Fascinated by the work of actors playing RoboCop and the Terminator (humans playing the roles of machines), he used those portrayals as models to give Guts that superhuman look, with the face of an unflappable tough guy.

Miura opted for such an archetypal model for his hero to make sure that his creation would last over time. Although *Berserk* has been around for 30 years now, a reader could pick it up today and become enthralled by the values that Guts embodies and the dilemmas that he deals with, without feeling like they're reading something that's dated. The Black Swordsman is so iconic that he never ages. Miura first depicts a hero who's hardened and violent, who seems rigid, but we soon realize that he has a complicated backstory. The reader is then pulled into the tale, eager to see how Guts will evolve. However, in order to build that anticipation, from the beginning, Guts needed to have the glimmer of a diamond in the rough, that aura of a character who immediately stands out from the crowd, even if he was first distinguished for his violence. It was notably Miura's love for Japanese writer Buronson and his hero Kenshiro (*Hokuto no Ken*, or *Fist of the North Star* in English) that inspired him to style Guts as a badass from the very first chapters. While in the first three volumes, published by Hakusensha, Miura succeeded in creating a character with an iconic look and legendary strength, something happened that would change everything and push the author to dig down deeper into the character development of his hero. Publication in *Animal House* was suspended and Miura had to start anew. At that very same time, the *mangaka* was working with the creator of Kenshiro on a manga called *King of Wolves* and so he had to choose which series he wanted to continue... To everyone's surprise, he abandoned his collaboration with Buronson after two volumes and dedicated himself to *Berserk*, the series that he hoped would finally prove him to be a fully-fledged artist. Starting with volume 4, Miura thus decided to go back in time to the birth of Guts so as to not limit our perception to the violent and amoral man of the first three volumes, and instead show us how he got there. So, Miura came up with a true origin story capable of making Guts a memorable hero. To get out of Buronson's shadow, he infused his story with a Renaissance spirit and more subtle human interactions, inspired by the works that made an impression on him as a younger man. Notable among these influences is the protagonist of *The Rose of Versailles* by Riyoko Ikeda: Griffith's look is a vibrant visual homage to the mysterious character that is Lady Oscar. In spite of this clear patchwork of influences, which are both purposeful and numerous, we should note that Miura again had to avoid all accusations of plagiarism, not to mention criticisms about a lack of originality. While he freely admits that he takes inspiration from various places, he always manages to make these ideas his own. That's the real crux of his talent: citing hundreds of works and references without his originality being called into question. Berserk is totally unique and, today, it "shines" in the history of manga just as much as the many works that inspired it. What's more, as chance would have it with creativity, sometimes similar ideas pop up around the same time in two very distinct places in the world, without having influenced each other. This is famously the case with *The Evil Dead.* In an interview with the master, available on the bonus DVDs for the anime series, Miura expresses his fear of being accused of even the slightest bit of plagiarism due to troubling similarities.

"Back then I was still in college, it was the day I finished the first episode of *Berserk* and there was *Evil Dead 2* playing in theaters. So, after I mailed the episode to the publisher, I went to see the movie. It was so similar to *Berserk*, I was really surprised by myself. In *Evil Dead 3*, I also know it as *Captain Supermarket*... the main character had his arm cut off and he had a chainsaw attached to his arm and had a shotgun on his back. I was like, 'What the?' Because Guts has a gun on his arm and a huge sword on his back. It was just like Ash. I remember getting worried that I might get sued. I had just finished my very first manga, but I was already nervous[9]."

When it comes to creation, it's not unusual to find coincidences, both happy and troubling, as if certain concepts just happened to be in fashion. Similarly, Miura was troubled to learn several years after starting *Berserk* that a real-life German knight named "Götz" von Berlichingen had lived in the 16th century, had been the big-hearted leader of a band of mercenaries, and in 1504 lost his arm in combat. His forearm was replaced by a prosthetic, very similar to Guts' own, that is on display at a museum in Jagsthausen, Germany. He was nicknamed "Götz of the Iron Hand"...

No matter what the influences may have been, Guts' appearance was set and Miura then had to flesh out his hero's past in order to give him substance and explain the events that made him so angry and violent. When it came to creating Guts' backstory, we can say that Miura did not skimp on darkness and despair, making Oliver Twist's childhood look like a walk in the park.

THE STORY OF A CURSED CHILD

Guts' path in life was paved with suffering from the time he took his very first breath. To have his character born into a life of pain, Miura came up with what must be one of the worst origin stories in the history of fiction. Guts was born to a woman who was hung while pregnant. As such, he was technically born from a corpse. The infant Guts survived thanks to the liquids leaking from his deceased mother's uterus until Shisu, Gambino's lover, discovered him in the mud, believing that the newborn had already passed away. From the very beginning, Guts' fate is tied to death. After all, he was born of death. The primal cry of the baby who would be named Guts (because he was born from his mother's "guts") is thus that of the perfect antihero. This archetype, first found in literature, is a protagonist who, although "central" to a story, lacks all of the qualities that define a classic hero. An antihero is a mediocre,

9. *Ibid.*

or even sometimes bad, person who demonstrates a certain lack of empathy and altruism. The antihero is no Adonis: his features are unsightly or covered in scars; he suffers from some sort of disability; he is most often tormented, troubled by moral dilemmas. The antihero lives neither for glory nor justice. He is a hero in spite of himself, a protagonist without a purpose or cause. Even Guts' birth has an antihero nature to it. He is no Moses, saved from the waters of the Nile to guide his people to the promised land. Instead, he's a child who is predicted, from the very beginning, to bring misfortune to all those who cross his path. And we must admit, he does not leave sunshine and rainbows in his wake. Having lost his mother and father (who we can imagine was hung tragically alongside his wife), Guts brings no more luck to his adoptive parents. Shisu dies when Guts is just three years old, her face ravaged by some sort of plague. Gambino is left to raise the child on his own and ultimately trains him more than actually raising him, turning him into an attack dog. We can tell that Gambino makes Guts bear the burden of his own pain and convinces himself that the young boy indeed brings bad luck. The child is thrown out onto battlefields from the time he's only six years old. His education comes purely in the form of military training. His childhood is neither loving nor carefree. As if all of that despair wasn't enough, Miura has Guts live through an atrocious and traumatic event: in exchange for a few pieces of silver, Gambino "sells" the child's body for a night to Donovan, a burly brute in Gambino's band of mercenaries. Guts is raped in a tent in their camp, plunging him into suffering that will continue to plague him for a very long time. This toxic relationship between Guts and Gambino reaches its climax one night when Gambino shows up drunk at his adoptive son's tent and reveals that he knew all about the rape. Gambino then becomes violent and the adolescent, in a move of self-defense, unintentionally skewers his adoptive father. Guts flees the camp to escape the vengeance of Gambino's underlings and begins his solitary journey. In spite of the horrors perpetrated by this ersatz father, the Black Swordsman will carry with him the macabre weight of this involuntary parricide. The outcome of this terrible origin story is that death surrounds Guts. To accompany him is to live with Death. He was born of death, he deals death, and death follows him wherever he goes. By providing us with his protagonist's entire backstory, Miura aims to make his antihero more credible and to explain his immense suffering. The result is that the reader ends up really empathizing with Guts, the same character who had been so detestable in the first three volumes because of his hardened, individualistic personality. He is now humanized. Consequently, we feel sad for him; we're much more forgiving with this person who has known nothing but misfortune, and we even end up cheering for him to carry out his revenge. In his place, would we not be just as hardened, angry, and vengeful? He was raised on the battlefield, which makes him a child soldier, and few of us can imagine the psychological damage caused by such a

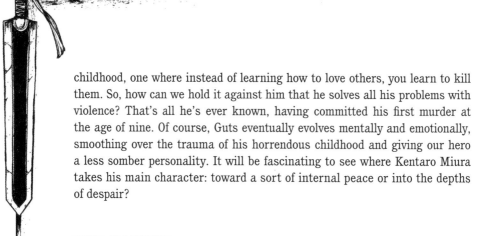

childhood, one where instead of learning how to love others, you learn to kill them. So, how can we hold it against him that he solves all his problems with violence? That's all he's ever known, having committed his first murder at the age of nine. Of course, Guts eventually evolves mentally and emotionally, smoothing over the trauma of his horrendous childhood and giving our hero a less somber personality. It will be fascinating to see where Kentaro Miura takes his main character: toward a sort of internal peace or into the depths of despair?

WAR MACHINE

To stick in people's minds and become iconic, a good "hero" can come in a number of different forms, employ all sorts of magic and powers, use weapons or tools designed specially for his mission. But above all, the hero must impress with his abilities and accomplishments. In this regard, Guts is a veritable war machine. According to approximate information provided by the official guide, after the first Eclipse, Guts is supposed to be around 24 years old, a little over six and a half feet (2 m) tall, and weigh in at 253 lbs (115 kg). So, he's a big guy who, even without weapons, can be pretty formidable in a fight. He has impressive physical and muscular capabilities, but never goes for a bodybuilder aesthetic, as can be found in other contemporary manga series. Guts is fairly realistic in his physical description, but it's his strength, his resistance to pain, and his endurance that seem superhuman. He learned from a very young age how to handle a weapon, likely having trained on adult swords that were much too big for him, which explains his ability, as an adult, to handle a sword "as big as a man," the Dragon Slayer, and to use it in a manner so impressive and lethal. This improbable meat cleaver is not his only asset: Guts also has an entire set of gear, first designed and forged by Godot, then by Rickert after the death of the old blacksmith. First, there's the artificial steel hand, made to be magnetic so that it can hold a sword and which hides a cannon that saves Guts' life in quite a few deadly situations. Guts can also use the hand to shoot crossbow bolts thanks to a contraption attached to the forearm. He also has throwing knives, ideal for felling bandits or poking out the eyes of apostles. Guts always has with him a little purse used to hide the beherit, store his gunpowder, and, especially, serve as a home for Puck, a little elf able to produce a powder with healing and restorative powers. As such, Guts has an excellent way to heal, ideal for dealing with his many fatal injuries that he barely survives from each time. Guts is often referred to as the "Black Swordsman," a nickname that is interestingly similar to the "Dark Knight," the nickname for Batman. There are intriguing parallels between these two superhero-like figures; Guts could even be the long-lost medieval twin of Gotham's defender. Indeed, Batman has no supernatural or magical powers, just like Guts. Both of them have a large number of gadgets available to them and physical strength that allows them to triumph over trials and tribulations. They're both cloaked in mystery and a black cape. Then there's the fact that they both lost their parents and are driven by a thirst for vengeance. So, Guts and Batman are both heroes who are certainly formidable, but who are ultimately realistic because they don't have any actual supernatural powers. This was intentional on the part of Miura from the inception of the manga, as he explains in *Berserk: Illustrations File*, using another similar superhero as an example:

"I think it's an interesting balance, the way it's more incredible than reality, but not so much that it demolishes reality. For example, there's an American comics character named Captain America in the Marvel hero movies. In terms of abilities, he's a little more incredible than an Olympic athlete, making him a lot weaker than the other heroes."

In the second part of the manga, Guts receives the Berserker Armor. A fantastic treasure from Miura, this practically living armor is a double-edged sword: it allows Guts to fight evil minions, but it also destroys him physically and psychologically. Once the helmet closes, in a movement and shape reminiscent of the jaws of a wolf, Guts transforms into a true wild beast. Showing its ugly side, the suit of armor ultimately overrides Guts' humanity and he becomes a living, breathing killing machine. The armor becomes a weapon of blind destruction that mows down all those who cross its path, whether friend or foe. Eventually, help is even needed from the witch Schierke to go look for Guts in the Astral World and bring him back to reason. The Berserker Armor even allows the Black Swordsman to continue fighting with broken limbs because the metal goes through flesh to attach to the bones. This armor is a twist on the classic magical artifact that solves all problems. In this case, there's a danger in using it, a heavy price to pay. Moreover, it enters the story at a moment where Guts is becoming more human and demonstrating more reason and emotion. In this way, it allows Miura to show his hero in ultra-violent, insane situations, even as his soul seems to be soothed. In the end, if Guts hadn't had the advantage of the armor's powers, he would no doubt have succumbed to one of his many battles.

THE BERSERKER ARMOR'S DEADLY TRANCE

There's a good reason why the manga is called *Berserk*. It's an adjective representing one of Guts' key traits: his ability to enter a superhuman battle fever. Indeed, Guts, capable of singlehandedly defeating a hundred men at once, occasionally enters a different state of mind, a murderous, animalistic trance. The etymology of the word "berserk" is from Old Norse, tied to Nordic and Germanic traditions. A "berserker" was a warrior who, "by the power of Odin," could enter a sort of spiritual fury giving him incredible strength and insensitivity to pain. While historians and linguists still debate certain interpretations, the mythology of the berserkers forged an entire category of fantasy, loosely based on historical facts, that spread through pop culture in the 20th century, resulting in our image of the heroic fantasy warrior. The term "berserker" even became an adjective in English, with the expression "to go berserk" meaning to "to go crazy with rage."

In the *Old Norse King's Sagas* (*Heimskringla*), a collection of sagas compiled around 1225 by an Icelandic poet, it says:

"His [Odin's] men would go in first, without armor, enraged like dogs or wolves, biting their shields, strong like bears or bulls, and killing people in a single blow. But neither iron nor fire affected them. They were called *berserkers*."

Originally, *berserk* could mean either "bear skin" (*ber särk*) or "without protection" (*berr särk*, literally "shirtless"). This lack of protection could refer to the fact that these warriors would fight without shields, holding their swords with both hands, as a brave man facing danger must fight... Just like Guts wielding his Dragon Slayer. As for the "bear skin" meaning, it seems the most plausible explanation and reveals folklore attached to these warriors: in battle, the berserkers would enter a trance induced by their warrior "spirit animals." According to legend, three totem animals would lend their strength to the fighters: boars, bears... and wolves. It's hard not to draw a parallel here with Guts and his Berserker Armor, which literally contains a powerful, savage beast, a raging wolf that takes over the human controlling the armor. Whether consciously or not, Miura makes Guts the purest incarnation of the mythical berserker. Over the centuries, the aura of the berserker warrior has evolved, from soldiers protecting their sovereign to savage pillagers... All sorts of crazy explanations have been proposed, like the idea that they used drugs or practiced shamanic rituals. While today these theories have been dismissed, a more recent one fits perfectly with Guts psychology. In 1990, a book by Richard A. Gabriel entitled *No More Heroes: Madness and Psychiatry in War* advanced the following theory: berserkers could be fighters rendered mad and violent by the traumas of war. Basically, they could have been affected by post-traumatic stress disorder, which put them into a state of murderous rage. Guts' terrible past offers a devastating number of personal and physical traumas in a violent, aggressive context. So, there's a potential explanation for the Black Swordsman's fighting trance. Many of us have experienced something so unjust and so harsh that we begin to fantasize about violence as a liberating force. Thankfully for all of us, as violence doesn't solve anything, and as it goes against societal norms, we keep our frustrations in check. Guts, on the other hand, when he transforms into a berserker, unleashes all of the hatred and anger that he has kept bottled up behind his clenched jaws since his childhood. He demolishes all of the boundaries of his humanity and lets his destructive impulses run wild. He calls on the well of hate that lies within and lets it pour out. That's what gives his violence that desperate, almost suicidal aura. As it was Death that brought him into the world, Guts latches onto this violence and gives himself over to it. It is the only thing that has never left him, the only constant in his life.

To come full circle with the animal metaphor, if Berserker Guts had a spirit animal that represented his personality, it would be a canid, a creature somewhere between a dog and a wolf, just like the one hiding in his deadly armor. This comparison reappears constantly throughout the manga, as if Miura intended to push this metaphor. On the night of his death, Gambino tells Guts: "You killed Shisu. And then you followed me around like some lonely puppy!" Later, Casca excoriates Guts for his individualism, calling him a "rabid dog" who only takes pleasure from the idea of fighting. What's more, during certain fights, the Black Swordsman uses his jaws, like a dog biting its prey. Later, Farnese and Schierke go on a "journey" into Casca's mind in hopes of helping her. In Casca's dream, there appears a dog riddled with lances and dragging a coffin. The dog is missing one paw and one eye, so it's no big mystery who this animal represents in Casca's mind; the coffin, meanwhile, bears a falcon emblem. Thus, Guts is the stray dog, faithful to those who walk with him and becoming rabid when someone messes with his companions, like a wolf protecting its pack... Unlike the untouchable falcon who glides over all, surveying his prey and soaring towards the sun, Guts is this earthbound animal trying to sink his fangs into Griffith, carrying within him the totemic power of the berserker.

PSYCHOANALYSIS OF THE BLACK SWORDSMAN

Preparing a psychological profile of Guts would drive any psychiatrist mad. In his narration, Miura pays careful attention to the characters' psyches, their personal histories, their private struggles, their shameful fantasies, and since the manga is a long-term endeavor, the author can take the time to develop his protagonists and give them true psychological depth. However, in this regard, Guts is a special case: he is the only character for whom we know the entire backstory. We literally witness his birth and we never lose sight of him throughout the story. This is Miura's dream scenario for offering us a near-perfect psychological case study: a person for whom we see every episode in his life, from the most terrible moments to the happiest. In this way, the reader witnesses the development of the mind of a man who grows up in a violent, pitiless world. We know that many of a person's personality traits form in childhood and are tied to events that occur during that period. In this regard, there is a scene that is absolutely crucial, and yet very understated, that really reveals Guts' emotional distress in his youth: one evening, young Guts is injured on his face and then overhears the guards talking about him. They wonder aloud if Guts bears bad luck and if that same curse caused Shisu's death. Devastated and feeling alone in the world, Guts appears to be overcome by a bout of despair. While we can tell that he's in need of support and warmth, suddenly, his eyes fall on his sword lying near the bed. He grabs it and pulls it in close to him, lying in the fetal position, as if the sword were his mother. All is said without a word in just a few frames: his weapon becomes his surrogate family, his only source of affection. In this context, it's no surprise that Guts lives for this sword, the only thing that has given him comfort when he was at the bottom of an emotional chasm. As Guts never knew his biological parents, he has to live with this total ignorance of where he comes from, and even of the name that they'd chosen for him. As such, Guts as a newborn has no ties. He is more accident than miracle. This person, with no known ancestry, no identity, is given a crude nickname rather than a worthy first name, and that nickname, by nature, is a reminder for him of the tragedy of his birth. Playing the role of parental figures, he has a couple of mercenaries, Shisu and Gambino. Sadly, Shisu, who actually seems loving and human, dies when Guts is just three years old. Young Guts is thus condemned to relive the death of his maternal figure. He is then just left with Gambino, who turns out to be a catastrophic substitute for a father: he places responsibility for his wife's death on the boy Guts. Their only connections are through swords, whether in training, in battle... or in a duel. Gambino raises, trains, tames Guts by and for violence. Because of this, their toxic relationship inevitably leads to the tragic end described previously, when Guts learns that Gambino sold his young body to Donovan. This rape explains why Guts hates being touched, an idiosyncrasy that recurs without explanation in the first few volumes. What was interpreted as social aversion and misanthropy turns out to be a chink in his armor, a trauma whose consequences are still felt acutely by the Black Swordsman as an adult. Here we get to the heart of Guts' trauma. This rape that he suffered explains the destructive rage that he feels when faced with situations that remind him of his painful past. When he sees a child being mistreated or a person about to be sexually assaulted, Guts is blinded by rage, to the point where he is so out of his mind that he almost decapitates Farnese just after saving her from rape. We can only imagine the repugnance he must feel when his own sword takes the lives of children. After the young Colette transforms into a demon, she manages to stick Guts with her sword because he feels incapable of doing her harm. As he fights for his own life, he ends up killing the young girl, but immediately after, he pukes his guts out: this scene is one of the rare moments where Guts is so greatly repulsed by killing. Similarly, when Guts accidentally deals a fatal blow to the young Adonis, he is devastated and holds the child's hand until his soul departs. Because of the suffering he lived through as a child, Guts is particularly sensitive to the issue of stolen innocence. This wound deep inside him is, in a way, his Achilles' heel because there is a dark place in his heart where an abused child resides. This makes Femto's actions that much more atrocious: not only does he rape Casca in the most brutal way possible, he also forces Guts to watch, making him relive his own trauma. Guts' sex life is also impacted by his trauma. While we don't often see our hero indulging in carnal pleasures, on the rare occasions where he does, Guts demonstrates a certain level of sexual violence, falling victim to visions of his past trauma. This emotional insecurity, which has affected the Black Swordsman since his childhood, has made him a mistrustful and distant individual. It takes time to get close to him and he deadbolts the doors to his inner self.

On the list of hero archetypes, you'll find the "hero with a dark and troubled past." Indeed, certain protagonists have origin stories that make them tortured individuals filled with doubts and dark feelings. They have to work with their inner darkness in order to triumph over evil. This produces heroes with greater depth, but also a more skewed moral balance. This archetype can be identified by the tragedies that mark the hero's life. So, if you want a hero to meet this definition, they have to have, for example, been betrayed by a person they love, have lost a loved one (parent, spouse, child), or have been abandoned. Sexual abuse obviously counts, as do experiences of torture and war. These horrors can also be experienced by someone close to the hero to turn them into that dark character, the person seeking justice in the shadows, ready to exact revenge for their loved one. This type of hero can sometimes be the cause of his own sorrows, which adds a whole other layer of despair. A "savior" can be motivated by values, an ideal, or a noble cause, but they can also be driven by vengeance, anger, or hatred brought on by past suffering. Certain heroes with some of these personality traits come to mind: The Punisher, Batman, The Crow, Max Payne, Darkman, the list goes on. However, it's worth noting that Guts blows them all out of the water: he checks every single box of misfortune. He was born to parents who died before his birth, saw his adoptive mother die, was raped as a child, unwillingly killed his adoptive father, witnessed the rape of his lover by his closest friend while all of his companions were dying around him... When it comes to dark, troubling experiences, the Black Swordsman sits on the throne in the palace of tears. One might think that, having lived such a life, Guts would have become a purely nihilistic individual who believes in nothing. But in fact, that's not the case. Even as he goes through the worst trials and tribulations imaginable, Guts is quite the opposite: he never abandons a fight and always gives the impression that he'd rather die than flee. On this point, we see what makes him a peerless and legendary warrior whose reputation precedes him: his wild determination. This impressive iron will is, nonetheless, due to feelings that are more negative than positive, and it's this negative energy that makes Puck writhe with pain when he touches Guts: "Not... Not again! Like before his emotions are pouring into me. It burns! Dark and violent emotions, pounding into me! Self-hating, destructive... Burning like black magma. Is this the source of Guts' strength?" The Black Swordsman is not motivated by life; he runs on hate... However, he uses these dark feelings, this black oil that runs through his veins, as his adrenaline, as his fuel, the very same fuel that makes his war machine run. This point is illustrated in all of its macabre glory during the Eclipse when Guts, with his left arm stuck in the jaws of an apostle, cuts the arm off himself to try and save Casca as she grapples with Femto. When pain no longer holds us back, preventing us from hurting ourselves, that's when we become truly dangerous. To ourselves, yes, but especially to others. That's what makes Guts such a formidable adversary.

CASCA: A WOMAN'S FIGHT

The character of Casca, a central figure in the leading trio, makes us explore the complexity of being a free and respected woman in this fantastical, ultra-macho, medieval setting where survival of the fittest is the only law of the land. She is a strong character who definitely faces adversity because of her personality, her rank, her sex, and her life choices, which are unusual for the Middle Ages. While women knights did indeed exist—some of them even fought in battle and led troops in the Crusades—they were an exception to the rule. Women were most often relegated to whatever role the men deigned to assign to them. Although this physical trait is not emphasized in the manga, we should note that Casca is also a woman of color, which makes her even more unusual in the eyes of the people of Midland. She is a character whose fate sees major, unexpected twists, to the point where readers have debated about her character development. However, before we analyze the story that Miura is trying to tell with this character, we should briefly examine what it means to be a woman in Midland. In the manga, women often hold secondary positions in power structures or in society. As a rule, they are excluded from the clergy. It's always men who rule, from the Kushan Empire to Midland, whether they're kings or emperors. Other than Casca, it's very rare to see a woman on a battle-field. Some are aristocrats, like Theresia and Charlotte, but they seem to be distanced from the realities and decisions concerning them, subjected to the will of their fathers or brothers. Furthermore, even on the part of Griffith, there's a disdain for supposed "women's issues," which are considered, by nature, to be more frivolous than men's. After a long tirade in which he describes his worldview and his ambitions, the Falcon says to Princess Charlotte: "Forgive me, I've chattered on so. It must have been a boring topic for a lady." As if women at that time weren't allowed to dream of more than a good marriage. The women we come across in the manga are mostly courtesans, or simply prostitutes, like Luca and Nina. They are also mothers and wives, and most of the time are left to deal with life's vagaries on their own, as their husbands are most often off on the battlefield. For example, when Shisu dies of a disease in her tent, Gambino is summoned to be with her in her final moments, but he's off at war. "Shameful. You'd think a man would be with his woman in her dying moments." Being a woman in Midland leaves very little room for freedom, but if a woman wants to play an important role in this patriarchal order, then she has to hide or disown her femininity. In the beginning, Farnese is the closest you can get to a fundamentalist monk, immaculately following the precepts of the Canon and burning untold numbers of heretics. She denies herself all emotions and lives in strict obedience. Even her sexuality appears to be stifled by the dogma that she lives by. It's only after she's shown herself to be hard and indifferent that the Church grants Farnese a position of respon-sibility, a status reserved for a young virgin (thus a woman sufficiently pure for her religious superiors). However, when a woman fails, which is ultimately what happens to Farnese, men have no compassion or pity and the woman is disgraced and deprecated, even by her own father. In the end, there are only two statuses that offer relative freedom for women: walk in the footsteps of men or live on the margins of society. Casca chooses the former, taking up a sword in a group of mercenaries, while Schierke opts for the latter, becoming a witch and thus setting herself up as a heretic in the eyes of moralists... (Incidentally, Farnese starts with the first choice and moves to the second.) What's more, Casca has a "tomboy" appearance, with her short hair and her armor hiding her feminine attributes. This is probably done to imitate the men she spends most of her time with, but also to blend in with the masculine crowd. As Judeau says about her: "It's only natural... Our Casca gave up being a woman so she could be a mercenary long ago." At the Midland ball, Casca even refuses to dance, feeling alienated from a practice that she associates with femininity. It's worth noting that Casca has always been accustomed to the company of men: she was the only daughter in a family with six children. She reproduces this same set-up as an adult, being the only woman soldier we know of in the Band of the Falcon. Additionally, in this regard, I should add

that no other woman in armor appears in *Berserk*'s armies. According to Guts, if a woman stands up to you and asserts herself, then she's a tomboy... After taking a hit from Casca, he implies as much with very little subtlety: "That hurt. This girl must have a pair on her." The young woman, who looks like the odd one out among all this testosterone, deals with a heavy load of sexism on a daily basis. First, she gets it from her enemies, who view her femininity as a weakness, as is the case when she faces off against the knight Adon, a burly brute who makes degrading remarks against her: "So you're her... The only woman who commands a thousand of the Band of the Falcon. I can't stomach it. A woman playing at being a knight." According to Adon, a woman must "stay in her place," i.e. being subservient to men and not fighting alongside them. He then makes what he thinks is a knockout argument by saying, "Women are inferior to men in strength. What use could they be in a battle?" He also claims that nature didn't "intend" for women to fight. Finally, for Adon's sexist coup de grâce, he insinuates that Casca must have used her feminine charm to get into the band: "You might have a use as a nighttime plaything for your fellow soldiers. [...] Perhaps you even achieved your rank of commander by sneaking into that man Griffith's bedroom?" After Casca sharply invites him to take back his words, Adon more or less tells her that women are too delicate and frivolous for the battlefield. "The battlefield is the sacred ground of men. I shall teach you the folly of your frivolity in setting foot upon it!" After hearing such nonsense, Casca is overcome by menstrual cramps and faints from her suffering, falling from the top of a waterfall. After Guts saves her, one would expect him to offer the young woman some words of comfort, or any other awkward form of support. But no, Guts does not rise to the occasion: "Going to the battle with a fever? This is why women don't have any sense." He undresses her to stop her from dying of cold and discovers that she's bleeding, finally understanding that Casca is on her period. Still no more understanding, Guts adds insult to injury and reproaches the angry Casca: "You're always so damn ready to be pissed about somethin'... This is why women ain't cut out to be warriors." The worst part about this sexist harassment, whether coming from friends or foes, is that it leads Casca to apologize for being herself: "I wasn't born a woman because I wanted to be." Casca is truly alone in her position, stuck in between. Men don't understand her because she is of the opposite sex and women don't understand her any better, strangers as they are to the bloody, manly world that she faces on the daily. Casca's view of men and authority figures must be quite dark, and we can understand why: at just 12 years old, she was sent by her own parents to work for a nobleman who tried to rape her as soon as she set foot on his land. We can only imagine the terror that the young girl must have felt towards this other world, this world of power-hungry, lecherous, bestial men. The worst part for Casca is that the only time she meets two men who seem a bit less brutal and chauvinistic than most, she ends up with an even more morbid result, as we see with her rape during the Eclipse. What's more, she is raped solely for the purpose of hurting Guts, doubly dehumanizing poor Casca. In a twist of fate, the man who rapes her is actually the man who saved her from such a situation as a child. She is the one who pays the greatest price in *Berserk*. She is destroyed because of the jealousy between the two men, sacrificed on the altar of male egotism. The most infuriating thing in this outrageously chauvinistic universe is its injustice, because Casca constantly demonstrates her strength, courage, value, and faithfulness throughout the story, making her a better knight than most of the men we encounter in the series. As Judeau puts it: "In truth, she's a much better swordsman than the men here." Before Guts joins the Falcons, Casca is described as the best fighter in the band, surpassed only by Griffith. She is described as an intrepid warrior with sharp reflexes, agile and fearless. It's not unusual for her to take on men twice her size. She knows how to be resourceful, even in the worst physical conditions: an exhausted Casca manages to parry the deadly blows of an unrelenting Silat. She is not just a proud fighter; she is also a peerless leader of her band, even though she had to take on that role in an emergency as a replacement for Griffith. Judeau recognizes her true value because she saved the band in the midst of a crisis: "If Casca hadn't become our leader, by now a Band of the Falcon without Griffith would have scattered to the winds... The band itself wouldn't exist." In her darkest moments, she manages to bring the Falcons together behind her, particularly during the Eclipse, when she tries to command the mercenaries to the very end. In spite of her difficult past, Casca is a fighter. Even when she regresses to a child-like state after the events of the Eclipse, she manages to fight instinctively to escape from a band of rapists, rediscovering her warrior reflexes, as if this combativeness is part of her, even as her consciousness lies dormant. The Casca that Miura creates after the Eclipse is even more surprising: in a way, the author hits the reset button on his character, erasing her memory and personality. The contrast is striking: she goes from a strong, combative young woman with a hard outer shell to a wild child who must be watched constantly in order to protect her from others, as well as from herself. Some readers have expressed their frustration with seeing such a strong and credible female character—which is not the norm in *seinen* manga—be erased and replaced with a sort of damsel in distress. This is not the first time that Miura makes a risky bet with his storytelling and endangers the popularity of his manga, as we mentioned before. However, when you see the impetus that this dramatic departure lends to his story, it seems that the *mangaka* knows exactly what he's doing. Indeed, in volume 40, when Casca finally regains her memory, we can tell that her reawakening will have enormous consequences for the story, as if forcing Casca's true personality to go into hibernation was a necessary evil to make her "return" that much more powerful. Finally, it would probably be a misreading of the story to accuse Miura of sexism. While the momentary frustration caused by the young female warrior's state may disappoint, it enables the emergence of some of the strongest, most positive and important female characters in the manga. In addition, these women end up being the ones who watch over Casca and eventually help her get better, showing a sort of female solidarity. For example, there's the young, and yet maternal, prostitute Luca who disguises Casca as a syphilis patient to protect her from her clients and the world around them. Besides Luca, who is presented as one of the few good people in the manga, Schierke is also an iconic character: she has tremendous powers that she inherited from another central matriarchal figure, Flora, an elderly witch who is the only person capable of protecting Guts from his bestial power. Finally, there's Farnese, who embodies a model of female liberation that's almost anarchical. She goes from a rigid, aristocratic, traditional life to that of a mystic, new-age witch, a figure rich in feminine symbolism. So, we can't accuse Miura of bad intentions on this point, even if he never misses a chance to show just how hostile this world is to women. And then, on the flip side, the image that the author presents of the various men in the story is not particularly positive. His way of writing the story most often puts us on the side of the person being oppressed rather than the person doing the oppressing. To evoke this empathy in the reader, the *mangaka* relies on the fact that the characters' psyches are constructed in reaction to the violent world around them. We like Casca; witnessing the horrors that she suffers is dismaying for us. It makes us want to see her succeed, exact revenge, and rekindle the flame that drove her before. Miura works off of the principle that damaging his characters gives them depth. In sum, he does not hold back with the brutality of the emotional ups and downs that readers may feel. On that point, I'm sure that Miura has more in store for us: what will be the effects of Casca's restored faculties? How will she put her life back together? Alone, far from everyone? Will she turn to Guts or Griffith? Will she choose to seek vengeance or to forget the whole thing? All of Casca's misfortune and suffering have been caused by her connection to these two men, Guts and Griffith. What if she decided to banish them both from her life? Maybe we'll find out what the young woman's dreams are, her goal in life, as she's always lived to serve others' ambitions. Using medieval fantasy as a vehicle, Miura harshly explores the constant strength that a woman must demonstrate in a ruthless world led by men, whether the situation be psychological, social, or sexual.

GRIFFITH, THE BIRD OF PREY

Out of all of the characters in *Berserk*, Griffith is probably one of the most difficult to define. Behind his almost angelic facade hides unimaginable darkness. Correspondingly, he shows very different sides of himself, like an iron fist in a velvet glove. Griffith knows that in order to be fascinating and mysterious, you have to be inscrutable. You have to be able to muddy the waters to hide who you truly are. Judeau understands the complexity of this two-faced mask that vacillates between good and evil: "How can I put this? Just when you think he looks like he's got some strange wisdom, he seems just like a kid... Just when you think he has a spine-chilling look on his face, he smiles innocently like a baby. Is he a child or an adult, a good guy or a villain?" Although Griffith is a murky figure, Miura gave him a destiny, a goal... a dream. He filled him with ambition that is so all-consuming that the Falcon ends up embodying in the worst way possible the common saying "the end justifies the means," the idea that when you want something, you have to be willing to sacrifice everything for it. Where Miura once again demonstrates subtlety is that instead of creating a detestable, despicably greedy character, he creates a radiant, magnetic Griffith who readers are initially quick to admire. What interests the *mangaka* is writing a story that shows how a person can lose their humanity and do horrible things out of pure individualism. Instead of creating a character who is evil right off the bat, Miura chose to show a figure who slowly changes from apparently good to truly evil. However, was Griffith ever really good? To his credit, we can say that he was an underdog and singlehandedly climbed to the pinnacle of power. Born to a family so poor that they struggled to afford even a bit of bread, Griffith appears to have been a street urchin like any other. Still, from the low-lying, narrow streets zigzagging through the center of town, he could see the magnificent castle. This symbol of power, reaching toward the sun, inspired in him a wild dream: to one day sit on the throne of his own kingdom. Seeing such a grandiose dream in a child so far from realizing it, Fate must have tipped the scales in favor of the young Griffith. Via a fortune teller, Fate bestowed on him both a gift and a curse: a beherit. Not only did Griffith not know what it was, he had no idea that the one he received, the Crimson Beherit, marked him for a singular destiny: to become a demon lord of the God Hand. Without knowing it, the ambitious Griffith's entire life would be a succession of choices leading up to one particular event. All those who would cross his path would also be sucked into a sinister machine to be used and disposed of. However, for Griffith's betrayal to really make an impression on readers, Miura made every effort to ensure that the Falcon would advance undercover, so that he would at first be taken as a heroic figure and then fall way down from that high pedestal. Indeed, although Griffith is a warlord capable of ending the thorniest of conflicts, there's nothing brutish about him. He is a paragon of refinement, from his delicate features to his calm, measured words. We should note that this haughty aspect of him is thrown into relief by the presence of Guts, who contrasts with Griffith due to his much more brutish, tormented energy. The

two characters act like mirror images and Griffith would not be Griffith without Guts there to provide cover for him. While Guts is "black," solitary, asocial, and constantly living in the moment, achieving his aims by force, the Falcon is "white," sociable, and rubs shoulders with the upper class, constantly strategizing and planning. Even in combat, Griffith distinguishes himself from the Black Swordsman: he uses speed, knows how to break through his adversaries' defenses, and targets vital points to win his fights expeditiously, with surgical precision. He is a shrewd fighter, tactical and calculating, whereas Guts tends to give the impression of striking with a hammer rather than a sword. However, the Falcon did not wait for Guts' arrival to make a name for himself. He gives off a particular aura that he knows exactly how to use to achieve his goals, whether that be by selling his body or by simply charming the people he meets. He seems to have a magnetic attraction for his followers, as Judeau confirms: "Whether you desire to follow him from the bottom of your heart or you are attracted by his reputation... We've all been seduced, that's what unites us." Griffith is the common denominator, the light bulb that blinds and attracts flies lost in the night. He's like the Pied Piper playing his flute and leading a horde of faithful rats behind him. His feats of arms and his magnetism give Griffith natural authority, ideal for leading troops. "Ordinary people like us don't understand Griffith... It might take him longer than a lifetime to achieve it, but I guess he must have some kind of conviction... in everything. It's not whether he's a good guy or a bad guy. It's not whether we really know him or not. Isn't that just how it is when a man gathers other men together?" So, he can certainly lead troops, but toward what? That's the heart of it... Griffith had a "dream," one that, on the whole, was quite vague and totally hackneyed: to rule the world. The fact that those close to him don't suspect a thing shows just how lowly the Falcon thinks of them, just there for him to walk over. Here's how he talks about people willing to give their lives for him: "They are excellent troops. Together we have faced death so many times. They are my valuable comrades, devoting themselves to the dream I envision... But to me, a friend is something else." In his dream, Griffith only has room for one person, and that's him. Even before he betrayed and eliminated his people, the Falcon was already on a slippery slope of troubling individualism, a direct consequence of his unbridled ambition. A master manipulator, when he meets the Black Swordsman, he comes face to face for the first time with someone who he is unable to control. It's for this simple reason that Guts shatters Griffith's plan to smithereens. Used to no one being able to resist his charms, he finds in Guts an indomitable alter ego who stands up to him and who becomes his obsession. Griffith's inability to take hold of Guts drives him mad. He is incapable of managing his feelings toward someone who does not succumb to his serpentine charms. Of course, Guts is more fascinated by the fact that Griffith has a dream, a goal in life, and that's even, at least in part, what drives him to leave the Band of the Falcon, as he wants to discover his own purpose in life. Mirroring their first meeting, a duel takes place that drives them apart. However, this time it's Griffith who loses. In a fit of pride and jealousy following Guts' departure, the Falcon loses his precious control and commits the unforgivable by sleeping with Charlotte, leading to the chain of events that we all know. I wouldn't go so far as to say that he was in love with the Black Swordsman, but there's no doubt that Griffith fell under the spell of the only person who ever resisted his powers of attraction and the only man to have equaled him in combat. This love and hate stick with Griffith permanently from the moment Guts abandons him. He thinks of him while sleeping with Charlotte and throughout the year of torture he endures because of this act. He remains obsessed with Guts. Let's not forget that, as Griffith has had the beherit since he was young, the demons have long watched his comings and goings, preparing the ceremony for many years. They chose a young man willing to do whatever it takes to succeed and they sent him Guts to be a thorn in his side to push him over to the dark side. That's the truly Machiavellian genius of the God Hand: they had foreseen this fall from grace from the very beginning. So, when the Falcon leaves the Tower of Rebirth, there's nothing left of him. He's nothing but skin and bones. He has no more tendons or tongue, and his face appears atrociously mutilated. When he sees his friends again, he realizes that all those who admired him before now only feel pity for him. Griffith is at his lowest: he will never achieve his dream and his legendary magnetism no longer works. Thus, it's the ideal moment for the beherit to come to life. At the time the ceremony begins, Griffith has nothing left to lose and is angry enough with Guts, Casca, and his band that he's willing to sacrifice them. At the end of the vision of his childhood that Griffith has during the Eclipse, he understands that to reach the castle of his dreams, he must walk over numerous bodies, including those of his friends. Still, he forges ahead, accepting that he's prepared himself for this moment. He crosses a bridge made of corpses that takes him to the infamous castle and he says this: "This is the path I have traveled. To get what I wanted... I can't apologize. No. I won't apologize! If I apologize, if I repent, everything will come to an end. I'll never get to reach that place." Willing to do whatever it takes to achieve his dreams of grandeur, Griffith understands that he's being called by the devil to rule the world. After sacrificing his people to keep up his end of the bargain with the Guardian Angels, he is reborn for the first time. He leaves behind the wreckage of his human form to become a demon lord. This is the perfect moment to highlight the resemblance, which Miura has recognized, between Femto/Griffith's helmet and that of Winslow Leach, the tragic protagonist of the Brian de Palma film *Phantom of the Paradise* (1974). There are certain parallels between the two characters: they are both disfigured, left for dead, and hungry for revenge. Both also make a deal with the devil. However, the resemblance stops there. While, in spite of his actions, we may feel a certain empathy for Leach's tragic fate, Griffith has crossed a line that makes us immediately hate him. In his new demonic form, Femto can finally lay the groundwork for his future return to "earth." With his reincarnation, Griffith is finally able to realize his dream. He brings an end to the domination of the Kushan Empire with the support of his underlings and takes the helm of Falconia, an unbelievable city that appears upon the death of Ganishka. Finally, Griffith embraces the greatness of his destiny. The worst part of it is that he manages to deceive everyone. He succeeds in fooling Charlotte and getting her under his control so that their marriage gives him access to the royal bloodline... On top of that, the Falcon gains a hold over the old, senile pope, who blesses the ascension of this bird of prey. A final subtle move, Griffith, by "projecting" a dream announcing his advent to everyone in Midland, succeeds in passing himself off as a sort of messiah. Having killed virtually everyone who witnessed his terrible betrayal, there's no one left to foil him and prevent him from presenting himself as a savior. If Guts were to go to Falconia and publicly denounce Griffith, there's little chance that anyone would give credit to this dark, sinister looking knight... That's the real subversiveness of the new Griffith. In terms of characterization, every effort is made for him to be perceived as a demigod. Miura peppers his dialogs with elements that support this "deification" of his character, indicating to us that Griffith is a superior being. This is true even before he is actually transformed into an evil deity. Casca had already guessed early on that her boss would go on to accomplish big things: "Back then I idolized Griffith. He was like some prophet or saint." She even adds that Griffith was "a miracle." The usage of this biblical language gives his character a divine aura, a "superbness" to which all feel compelled to bow down. The same thing that all of his admirers say is that Griffith seems unreal, that he's closer to a work of art than a human being. "It was as if the image of some saint adorning the wall of my village church had just come to life." While Casca was impressed, the young Princess Charlotte was completely enthralled, almost paralyzed. Like Casca, she brings up the idea that Griffith is like a work of art. Wanting to bring him a cake that she's baked, she declares, fascinated by the man she loves: "Almost like a painting, one cut from eternity. It feels like I mustn't touch him." This sensation is not one exclusive to women. Rickert finds himself practically in awe whenever the Falcon is near him: Griffith is "like some religious painting." The future demon gives off an almost divine aura. What's more, religion is not the only metaphor that Griffith evokes. As Gaston naively puts it: "Everything about boss Griffith as a person was just so different from us. There's just something about him. Just like he was someone out of a legend." To stand with Griffith is to accept a destiny that is greater than yourself and which will lead to a grand existence because "to live in service to Griffith is to live a legendary life." Miura's insistence on telling us that the Falcon is greater than the common mortal prepares us readers for his future divine transformation, for his legendary fate. The *mangaka* indicates to us that his character's life will be one of those that is talked about for centuries in heroic tales... When Griffith comes to the Hill of Swords, Erika describes him in this way: "He was so pretty I could hardly tell he was a man. More like someone out of a fairy tale." Mule also takes this point of view, speaking of Griffith's exploits as if he were a legend in the making: "I knew it by instinct. That what I had set before myself wasn't merely another war to be recorded in history." Miura, meanwhile, drew a shooting star in the sky at the same moment that Mule pronounced these words, as if to show that the universe itself was endorsing this analysis. Finally, the fact that the author chose the nickname "Falcon" for Griffith is likely not without meaning. The falcon is a gracious and powerful animal, stealthy and formidable. Falcons are skilled hunters and swoop down silently on their prey. But above all, falcons are celestial creatures, flying high above the ground where they can see everything. They look down on everything, flying above the rest of the animal kingdom. The fact that he is renamed as a Phoenix, which symbolizes his mythical resurrection while maintaining the celestial and flight-related dimension, is no coincidence. In this symbolic context, how could I not bring up the myth of Icarus? Locked away with his architect father, Daedalus, Icarus is held captive in the Minotaur's labyrinth. To escape their prison, Daedalus makes for the both of them wings made of wax and feathers, allowing them to fly away. Before taking off, Daedalus warns his son not to fly too close to the Sun, as its heat might melt the wax. However, overwhelmed by the altitude and the feeling of great power he gets from flying, Icarus fails to heed his father's warning and flies so high that his wings melt, causing the young man to fall into the sea. In a thinly veiled manner, the King of Midland implicitly evokes this mythical story: "You are young. No doubt your heart burned with dreams and ambition. If you had but known your place, you might possibly have attained them. No, this must have been because you're young... It's so disappointing. Who could have seen it coming? It's disappointing that the white Falcon of the Battlefield would destroy himself over such a worthless matter. The falcon has fallen to earth. It will never take flight again." When he transforms into Femto, Griffith gains magnificent wings, adding a little more to the Icarus reference. To conclude, although the Falcon has committed some true atrocities, we must be honest about one thing: from the moment Fate chose him, his future no longer belonged to him. No matter what choices he may have made, Fate would have found a way to realize what was written. For that reason, some readers say that "Griffith did nothing bad," and that he's just like anyone else, the puppet of a destiny he has no control over.

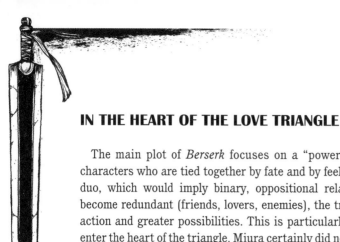

IN THE HEART OF THE LOVE TRIANGLE

The main plot of *Berserk* focuses on a "power trio," a trinity of strong characters who are tied together by fate and by feelings. Rather than a simple duo, which would imply binary, oppositional relations that rather quickly become redundant (friends, lovers, enemies), the trio offers much more inter-action and greater possibilities. This is particularly true if romantic feelings enter the heart of the triangle. Miura certainly did not hold back from exploring the potential of such a configuration. Indeed, it is the passionate and terrible relationship between Guts, Casca, and Griffith that carries this story. With subliminal messages, Miura indicates to us that these characters are special: for example, the three of them are the only ones in the Band of the Falcon that wear capes, subtly highlighting them as different. Furthermore, Guts, who unleashes a dark rage at the slightest physical contact, only lets two people touch his face: Casca, his lover, and Griffith, his former friend. Finally, Miura sows seeds of doubt with the appearances of his protagonists to facilitate this romantic back and forth: Griffith has delicate features and a fairly feminine hairstyle, while Casca sports a cropped hairstyle and armor that hides her feminine attributes. As the author is extending his story over the long term, he has plenty of time to make the relationships between his central characters evolve. Before Guts crosses paths with the Band of the Falcon, Casca and Griffith have a relationship that we assume to be passionately platonic and unilateral: the young woman seems to be head over heels with admiration and desire for Griffith, who is content to remain mysterious and hypnotic. When he joins the duo, Guts disturbs this balance. The Falcon seems fascinated by the Black Swordsman and confides in him, to the chagrin of Casca, who sees a stranger getting special treatment from her idol, right in front of her. Griffith offers Guts a spot in the Falcons, but the latter refuses and a duel ensues, with the outcome to decide the fate of the newcomer. He loses and thus remains with the Band, creating the web between this cursed threesome. After a swift rise through the ranks of the Midland army, Griffith shows that his ambition comes before all else. Disappointed to see that he's just a tool for the Falcon, Guts then decides to take back his independence. It's a choice that, as we've seen, brings about another duel, this time won by Guts, pushing Griffith to commit the unforgivable. However, it's interesting to note that Miura clearly shows that the true object of Griffith's desire is Guts, even as he holds the princess in his arms. In his miserable dungeon, the Falcon doesn't spare a thought for Casca: in his few moments of lucidity, he relives all of his conflicting feelings for the Black Swordsman. So, it is his passion for Guts that keeps Griffith from giving in to death.

In the meantime, Guts and Casca reunite and rekindle their intimate connection, then try to save their friend, who is temporarily "out of bounds," outside of the love triangle. After his liberation, the unrecognizable Griffith nevertheless aggressively tries to ingratiate himself with Casca, who overpowers him and gives him an empathetic, compassionate hug. He realizes that she is no longer in the palm of his hand. This is confirmed when he catches Guts and Casca in a display of affection. This is likely the trigger that turns this tragic comedy of manners into a terrible drama when Griffith summons the five Guardian Angels, who exact their ghastly price. Griffith takes this already turbulent romance in a dark direction. Indeed, after rendering Guts powerless, he decides to rape Casca. Letting his monstrous side run wild, the Falcon takes her against her will, then breaks her. He thus takes revenge on Casca for turning away from him and on Guts for never reciprocating his feelings. In doing so, Femto knows perfectly well that he is destroying any possible happy future between Guts and Casca: they will have to live with this trauma. The young woman's mind seems to be temporarily destroyed: she loses her memory and the ability to speak, and acts like a child. The triangle is blown to pieces. Guts, rather selfishly, abandons Casca to soothe his anger in the hostile countryside of Midland. But there again, it's when the Black Swordsman returns for Casca that the main plot line resumes. Guts now knows that he loves Casca. Unfortunately, she no longer recognizes him and, not long after, Griffith is reborn and passes himself off as a peculiar savior who will change the fate of Midland. In volume 40, when Casca finally gets her memory back, we are left with one burning question: what will become of this crazy love triangle? Miura clearly shows us all of the dramatic and dynamic possibilities that exist in this romantic "power trio." Instead of serving up a simple tragic romance, he manages to intertwine these affairs of the heart with the fate of the world, giving them an almost legendary dimension. What makes this hot and cold threesome so unusual is also the non-simplistic aspect of its overall balance, because Guts and Griffith each have both dark and light sides to them. While the relationship between Guts and Casca will be explored in detail in the next chapter, it's worth noting here the strong homosexual subtext that Miura injects into the relationship between his two male protagonists. Their relations are not simply friendly, they're romantic (although conflicted and never consummated). If the author hadn't set up this unspoken love between these two men, Griffith's motivations for sacrificing all of his friends out of jealousy would have seemed hollow. It is truly a love triangle that explores all forms of sexuality, not just Casca torn between two male suitors. These passionate, possessive, and violent relations can be explained, above all, by Griffith's frustrated desire for his friend. Throughout the manga, Miura peppers his dialogs with more or less subtle innuendos to show this sexual tension that exists between the two men. During their duel, Guts asks why Griffith didn't aim for his heart. The Falcon answers: "Because I realized I want you"; and then shortly after: "You're interesting. And I've taken a liking to you. I want you... Guts." The Black Swordsman later retorts that if Griffith wins: "Then you make me your soldier or fag boy or whatever!" After this rather direct beginning, Miura develops a turbulent friendship between the two men, even if Guts' fascination for his friend appears to be more platonic. There are little scenes that add to this subtext: the friendly, half-naked splash fights under waterfalls; the long, ambitious speeches from a bare-chested Falcon to Guts, who seems to devour him with his eyes. There's also that moment where Griffith shows Guts a version of the *Kamasutra* in the library. This romantic tension does not go unnoticed by Casca who, when she falls from the cliff with Guts, tells him that Griffith acts toward him "as if...". As if he were in love with the Black Swordsman. The despair and anger that Guts later expresses upon finding his friend's mutilated body in the Tower of Rebirth give off an air of tragic romance, as Guts sees his idol broken. Griffith, meanwhile, constantly feels possessive about Guts: "Now you belong to me," or, "Because you belong to me, I will decide the place where you die." As we know the horrific outcome of the Eclipse, we understand the full destructive potential of Griffith's dominating impulses, which have grown stronger over time. In the end, his love for Guts is the Falcon's only Achilles' heel, as Griffith even admits that Guts will be the only person to have distracted him from his "dream." His feelings distracted him to such a degree that he lost sight of his goal. What's more, to underscore this point, the first thing that Griffith does after being reincarnated is to go find Guts on the Hill of Swords in order to see if his feelings are still there. Realizing that they're gone, the Falcon is now free of all sentimental attachments and he can finally fulfill his destiny.

The American film *Ladyhawke* (Richard Donner, 1985) was one of Miura's many film inspirations. In it, Etienne Navarre (played by none other than Rutger Hauer) is in love with Isabeau of Anjou. Unfortunately, the nefarious Bishop of Aquila, mad with jealousy because he too is enamored with the young Isabeau, makes a pact with the devil to place a curse on the lovers: by day, Isabeau will transform into a hawk, and by night, Etienne will transform into a wolf... Besides the obvious similarities, there's also this golden idea: "If you won't love me, I'd rather kill you." As you can see, Miura wants to explore the dark side of sentiments and resentment. In *Berserk*, he depicts the torment of unrequited love and the deadly jealousy that can stem from it.

GUTS AND CASCA AGAINST THE WORLD

As the trials and tribulations of our cursed trio unfold, we can see that Griffith is on another "level" compared to Guts and Casca. As the Falcon climbs the aristocratic social ladder, his extravagant dreams get increasingly extreme and demonstrate that he is not as "human" as his two comrades. At the same time, Guts and Casca get to know each other well in spite of their fiery temperaments and end up uncovering weaknesses that bring them together. We can even say that, in the beginning, their relationship was electric, as we see from the arrow that strikes Guts during their first encounter (which, of course, was not shot by Cupid). In that scene, while Guts defends against attacks from certain members of the Band of the Falcon, Casca fires a crossbow bolt that strikes him in the bicep. A sword duel ensues: as such, Guts and Casca fought each other before ever exchanging a word. Even their first physical contact is complicated: Guts is unconscious after being beaten by Griffith and Casca is ordered to care for the fallen warrior while he's out cold. She makes sure to show her distaste for this by hitting Guts in the gut. The young woman starts by being jealous of Guts because of the effect he has on Griffith and she only takes an interest in him once she realizes that the Falcon is beyond reach. At first, their temperaments seem quite incompatible given that early on, Guts puts on the alpha-male act and adopts a "shoot first, ask questions later" mentality. He even shows a certain disdain for women, which he is not shy about expressing to Casca. Conversely, Casca is not the kind of person to submit to this kind of man: she is a female soldier with a hardened personality and hates being ordered around. Truly, in the beginning, nothing would indicate that these two would end up being the manga's main love story. Especially because Guts is helpless when it comes to showing feelings, awkward as he is and often too direct. As for Casca, her need to show a hardened, impenetrable facade is too overpowering for her to lay it all bare. However, the thing that brings these two warriors together is combat. As they fight side by side and march in the shadow of the same person, they end up granting each other a sort of mutual respect. Guts even says of her: "But less a woman, I see her as a comrade." The Black Swordsman is fascinated by Casca's zeal for winning, her valor in battle, and her way of empathizing with those she commands. We remember Guts who, as a boy, slept while hugging his sword, as if his life depended on it, as if it were his only source of comfort and affection. During the first night he spends with Casca in a tent, we see the young woman replace that sword, Guts' weapon being placed next to his bed, as if to show that a person has managed to finally bring him some true human warmth. As Miura has explained, Guts' sword represents his strength and determination, but it also symbolizes his virility (the sexual aspect of the sword is demonstrated by Farnese in another episode). As such, it is interesting that Casca manages to break through this misplaced virility to reach Guts' heart; the heart of a man who is much more sensitive than one would initially think. Even as their story does not exactly unfold under the best of circumstances, the more we get to know them, the more their coming together seems to have been inevitable. Guts and Casca share the fact of living with the crushing weight of unspeakable suffering. When the two lovebirds finally find themselves embracing each other, undressed, in the forest, they discover each other naked, without "protection." Guts runs his hands over Casca's many scars while she leans toward him and licks one of his injuries like an animal, saying: "Licking wounds is good enough." That says it all. It's their pain and their mutual solitude that unites them. Guts has found the only person who can understand what he's been through, and the same goes for her. The list of commonalities in their backgrounds is impressive. They both lived through difficult family situations tied to being rejected by a parent. Guts' adoptive father tried to kill him, while Casca was thrown away by her own parents to be used by a sexual predator. So, they were both children who felt alone in the world, unappreciated. Both had to find their own path from a young age without any help. In addition, Guts and Casca both took someone's life before the age of 13 and had to deal with terrible moral dilemmas even before their sense of self was fully developed. Both cling to what they believe to be the only remedies for so much tragic disappointment: anger and violence. The elderly Godot really sums this up on his deathbed: "The thing about hatred... It's the place where people who can't look sorrow in the eye without waverin' run off to. [...] I wouldn't blame you if you wanted to. You've got some huge nicks in your heart." Unsurprisingly, the second in command of the Falcons and the Black Swordsman have each shown almost suicidal tendencies. Indeed, we remember Casca letting herself fall from the cliff, as if abandoning everything... As for Guts, while there may not be a precise moment where we think he's going to end it all, every fight that he has is suicidal, as his chances of survival are near zero at times. He constantly braves death by facing off against adversaries stronger than him, such as gigantic or immortal monsters. In the end, Guts never stops to think about his own survival and, moreover, he often escapes death thanks to the fortuitous and miraculous intervention of the Skull Knight, who comes out of nowhere every time. So, even if he never says it, Guts also has this extreme nature, this fault that could suddenly make him give it all up to end his suffering. It's yet another flaw that draws these two characters together. Even sadder and more traumatizing, our two heroes have both been raped. Guts survived this as a child, and though Casca may have escaped it at a younger age, she faced that horror during the Eclipse. Finally, they both survived the Eclipse and went through the exact same nightmare. They share the same mourning and will always relive those tragic moments, unable to share that weight with anyone else. As Guts tells Godot: "No one... No human... can understand what took place..." Besides Casca. Because of this shared trauma, both have the same defensive reflex: since being raped, they refuse to let anyone touch them, locking down and barricading their personal space. After the morbid climax of the Eclipse, Miura had several options about where to go with Casca. He decided that she would be in such shock and so hurt that she would become an amnesiac. This hits the reset button on her relationship with Guts, breaking the bond that they had created. What will remain of the connection they spent so much time building? Let's not forget that while Guts knows there's a chance of restoring Casca's memory, that doesn't mean that their romantic relationship is saved. As the Skull Knight warns him, the restored Casca may not have the same expectations as him, and this seems to deeply affect Guts. This leads us to ask a question that is, on the whole, quite tragic: is the manga telling a story of star-crossed lovers? I'm sure we'll find out soon, but could their relationship simply survive what they've been through? Setting aside Guts, what Casca went through in the Vortex was so devastating that regaining that memory could re-inflict serious trauma on her. This time, she won't fall into a sort of waking coma; instead, she will have to face what happened to her: being raped by the man for whom she sacrificed everything. The mix of anger, injustice, and betrayal that Casca is likely to feel will have an influence on the rest of the story. Now that the quest is finished, that Casca is healed, what will Guts do? Will he stay with her this time and give her the support and comfort she needs, or will he keep following his thirst for vengeance and slake it by destroying Griffith? For that matter, there's another aspect that we haven't discussed, which is the potential danger to Casca that Guts represents. Miura has stressed this a number of times: during their first sexual encounter, he relives his rape and becomes violent, nearly strangling a powerless, frightened Casca. Later, the Black Swordsman finds himself possessed by the beast within that eats away at him when he puts on the Berserker Armor and he's on the verge of hurting Casca, to the point that he distances himself from her and charges Farnese with watching over his lover... and, without saying it outright, with watching out for him. In any case, the violence that Guts and Casca have fallen victim to is so extreme, so incredibly hard to bear, that it's hard to imagine them letting that injustice go unpunished and going off to live out the rest of their days in a cabin far away from it all. They're not the kind of people to "turn the other cheek." Guts and Casca are warriors; surely, blood will be spilled. Knowing Griffith's dominant position in Falconia and his firepower, what can Guts, Casca, an elf, a mermaid, and two witches really do against so much evil power? That's one of the thousand questions to which readers are eagerly awaiting answers.

THE SPECTRAL CHILD

One would think that the arrival of a newborn, sealing the romantic fate of Guts and Casca, would be a happy occasion. However, you would be wrong given Miura's vision of birth in *Berserk*. If there's any subject where we would expect him to tone down the horror, it would probably be the epitome of innocence: childhood. However, it seems that to establish a truly dark and hopeless universe, the author chose to make birth a source of terror. As we've seen, a textbook case of this is when Guts' mother gives birth to him: being born from a corpse is not exactly a happy entrance into the world. Still, we have to give Miura this: to bring new life into the world in the Middle Ages was truly to risk one's own. That said, Guts' birth pales in comparison to the reproductive process of trolls, which takes bodily horrors to new extremes. These violent creatures rape human women and, within a few seconds, baby trolls start growing in the women's wombs in a sort of spontaneous gestation. The infant trolls then pop out of their mothers' abdomens in a fatal spray of blood. If we wanted to do some armchair psychology, we could theorize that Kentaro Miura has, to say the least, a conflicted relationship with birth. Finally, Emperor Ganishka and his sort of prolific uterus with apostles brewing inside do nothing to give a happy impression of procreation. Nevertheless, there is a "being" who, after a tragic beginning, seems to escape the sad fate that Miura assigns to his fantasy children. Guts and Casca, through their passionate lovemaking, unknowingly kick off a process that will change the course of the world and of destiny: Casca is expecting. The *mangaka* remains faithful to his dark story and first gives this fetus the worst fate possible. During the Eclipse, while raping Casca, Griffith passes on to the fetus a bit of his evil, "poisoning" the unborn child. Because of this, Casca is forced to give birth under the worst circumstances, surpassing even the birth of Guts in terms of horror and despair. The young woman, in shock from what she's just suffered, gives birth prematurely to a tiny black embryo that creeps along the ground to flee. Guts recognizes the fetus that he has seen over and over in his nightmares and his first reflex is to try to crush it with a vengeful stomp. Casca has to intervene to stop this tragedy. The Skull Knight explains the evil nature of this creature: "It has taken on the nature of a demon. It's a cursed child." Mirroring what members of Gambino and Shisu's band said after they took in Guts, the Skull Knight predicts that the child carries in him a bad omen and he squarely advises them to kill it: "It would be best to kill it. That's no human child. Someday it will bring woe upon you both." Casca, out of maternal instinct, protects the fetus, which grows in her arms right before their eyes, seeming to continue its growth as if it would actually survive. Guts again tries to kill it, but as the sun peeks above the horizon, the child suddenly disappears into thin air. The Skull Knight confirms that the child is a ghost; like all the other ghostly demons in *Berserk*, it fears the light. The child supposedly went to hide away in "a place nearer the world of the dead." What's interesting is that, initially, every indication is that this child is the spawn of the devil, their progeny defiled by Femto. So, Guts learns simultaneously that he is the original father of the fetus and that Femto has ruined that as well. As such, Griffith's horrors and betrayal extend even to this unborn child who could have become the future symbol of their love, the personification of a promise of happiness for Casca and Guts. However, several scenes in the manga suggest to us that Guts was not necessarily ready to be a great dad. As he is heading to the Misty Valley, Guts is injured, stops for the night, and makes a campfire. He decapitates a snake and drinks its blood, apparently trying to heal himself, then he eats a coca leaf. The plant's psychotropic effects then cause hallucinations: he sees his child in its demonic embryo form emerging from flames, accompanied by dozens of flaming silhouettes of children. Guts realizes that the fetus has brought these children there. This scene is quite dramatic and really shows the tragedy that underlies this difficult father-son relationship. The fetus uses the ghosts to speak to his father because, as a demon, it's his only way of communicating. This directly echoes the words of the Skull Knight on the day of the demon child's birth: "Someday it will appear before you both again. All children yearn for their parents, as do demons in their own way." The sadness of this campfire scene reaches a climax when one of the innocent-faced specters walks toward Guts and says to him between two sobs: "Mommy... Where are...?" This question, so sad and so innocent, receives nothing but a big swing of a sword in response. Not to make excuses for Guts' flagrant inhumanity in this instance, but this violence is likely due to the fact that the fetus must be a living reminder for him of the atrocities committed during the Eclipse. And given the father figure that Guts had as a model, Gambino, who tried to kill him, it's unrealistic to expect anything other than violence from the Black Swordsman in this situation. However, in spite of his father's ungratefulness, could it be that this child is actually a miracle for our two betrayed warriors? Indeed, there are several instances where the mysterious child saves the lives of his parents. It's the child who, in a vision, alerts Guts that Casca is in danger and that he must return to her immediately. What's more, while Guts is on his way, it's again the child who protects Casca from various dangers, as if he were trying to defend his progenitors at all costs. The child also appears while Guts is in the midst of a murderous rage caused by the Berserker Armor to remind him of his goal and his reason for living: he must protect Casca, the child's mother. Finally, it's also the child who prevents his father from drowning after his fight against the sea creature. This is Miura's stunning and poignant way of showing us the innocent love of a demon child for his parents. The creature does not stay in this embryonic stage forever: when the Egg of the Perfect World swallows the child of Casca and Guts, it takes on the form of a "normal" newborn, showing that the fetus has continued its growth. However, that proves above all that the child remains demonic in spite of himself. As further proof, it's again this infantile body that Griffith uses for his own resurrection. In spite of it all, the child returns: later in the story, Casca comes face to face with a silent child who comes out of nowhere. Once again, the child lends them a hand by repelling the Kushan crocodiles before disappearing again. The child's features are a perfect blend of Guts and Casca, so much so that readers have given the child a nickname: "Gusca." Schierke expresses doubt about the identity of this apparition, but all indications are that it is indeed the spectral child grown up... Even if we should exercise caution with such an assumption, it's a strong bet that Gusca will play a decisive role as the manga continues. He could even bring some form of hope to this world that needs it so badly. First, in spite of Femto's "evil stain" on him, making him part demon, Gusca seems to have chosen the good side. The child could have become a servant of Femto, but instead he seems to have decided to help his parents. He may be the first demon ever to repent and choose the path toward humanity. What's more, his demonic powers give him a major advantage: he commands evil beings and is able to repel them, as if he holds a position above them in the infernal hierarchy (which is indeed the case). That's what happens when Casca is about to be sacrificed during the Eclipse: the fetus manages to expel the spirits from the bodies they had taken possession of. Even before he is born, he had this power to repel demons, which impresses even the Skull Knight: "The evil spirits aren't inflicting harm upon her. Yet so many are gathered. Why?" Having on their side an entity with such powers will likely prove to be as useful as the elf's powder. Furthermore, this child has a special bond with Griffith that expresses itself physically, as the Falcon remarks when he's in the presence of the child: "Throbbing. A faint throbbing. My blood should have been frozen. These feelings must belong to that infant that fused into my vessel." As such, Gusca is connected to Griffith, and this manifestation humanizes the cold-blooded reptile that the Falcon has become... That's what makes his heart beat. This spectral child likely possesses a key to the plot that will open doors in *Berserk*'s future. Will those doors take us finally to sunny, peaceful skies or to a dark hurricane straight out of hell? Like Anakin Skywalker, will this child choose the light or the dark side of the Force?

LANDSCAPES OF THE UNCONSCIOUS MIND

While we can make inferences about a character's psychology based on their past, their words, and their reactions, Miura uses various narrative devices that allow us to "travel" through the psyches of certain protagonists. The first such device is dream or nightmare episodes. At several points in the story, the *mangaka* takes us into his characters' dreams, with Guts being the most frequent subject of exploration. For example, in the very first volume, as he's dozing off in the cart, he has a dream (that the reader doesn't understand, but which will make total sense later on in the story). He's naked, in what looks like a never-ending passageway, with walls so tall that you can just barely see the dark sky looming over the scene. A gigantic eyeball is floating above this labyrinth, watching a weakened and lost Guts. Hearing a sound, he moves and his mark begins to bleed, indicating that a demon is approaching. Guts' feet are impaled by spikes emerging from the water and he can no longer move, literally nailed to the ground, as an enormous, monstrous fetus appears and causes him to awake with fright. At the point where the reader sees this dream, they know nothing yet about what happened to Guts during the Eclipse; however, Miura already gives us clues about his hero's psyche. He is traumatized by the Occultation and is angry at himself for having been powerless to save Casca, with his arm stuck in an apostle's mouth. The image of the fetus is very symbolic: it is the expression of his love for Casca, the life that they almost brought into the world, mixed with the stain left on the child by Femto, preventing it from being born normally. This nightmare from Guts, showing his conflicting feelings about fatherhood pursuing him even in his dreams, is particularly terrifying. When he awakes, Guts realizes that he was actually being attacked by a creature as he slept. Once he vanquishes it, the monster reveals its true nature: it is an incubus. By using this creature, Miura is alluding to a classic piece of demon lore and he shows once again his deep knowledge and ability to include consistent references. Guts describes the incubus: "They're evil spirits that give people nightmares and feed off their fear." The classic definition of incubus is slightly different: an incubus is a male demon who materializes to sexually abuse a woman as she sleeps. If you're a man, it's a succubus, the female equivalent, who will come pay you a visit. As depicted in the magnificent painting by Johann Heinrich Füssli entitled *The Nightmare* (1781), an incubus comes and sits on the chest of its sleeping victim and tries to suffocate her. This type of demon has been mentioned under various names since the Mesopotamian civilization but it was the Greeks who began to "theorize" about such creatures, blaming them for nightmares. In the Middle Ages, the incubus took on a demonic dimension. It was represented as a devil and symbolized impurity, "the heresy of sexual intercourse with the devil." Of course, this subject would later be studied by scientists, who have interpreted the incubus legend as coming from hallucinations tied to sleep disorders and anxiety. Still, in all the stories of incubi, there is a very strong sexual dimension. It was even believed that it was possible to have a child with such a creature. Mythology and folklore are full of children of incubi (like the wizard Merlin), to whom legend often attributes a unique destiny and magical powers. The fact that Guts' fetus perpetually reappears in his nightmares, the pervasive subtext of sexual frustration (Guts specifies that incubi are born of a mixture of blood and vaginal fluids, seemingly to accentuate this blending of sex and violence), these examples show that Miura does not bring up the symbolism of the incubus randomly. He is fascinated by the folklore of dreams, especially nightmares. Another interesting dream episode is the dream Griffith has just before unleashing the first Eclipse. Griffith has just escaped the tower where he was held prisoner, tortured, and mutilated. In this dream, we see Griffith, years later, sitting in an armchair while a ravishing, pampered Casca comes looking for him. They are together and even have a child who, lo and behold, is named Guts, and a dog named Pippin. In this "alternative future," Griffith has recovered from his injuries over time and with support from Casca. They lead a quiet, peaceful life with their family. This dream has several functions here. First, it evokes the romantic feud between the two friends for the heart of Casca and, in this case, it's Griffith who won; it also shows his need to dominate Guts, making him his kid. However, the most interesting part of this dream is the meaning it takes on retroactively after the Eclipse takes place. When Griffith chooses to sacrifice Casca and all his friends, he has already had this dream and thus knows what it could look like to have a happy future as a family man. In spite of this, he decides to become a demon and sacrifices everything to attain his goal. This dream from Griffith adds an even more demonic aspect to the choice he makes during the Occultation: he chooses evil even though he has glimpsed the good life. Griffith's other crucial "dream" is the one he has during the Eclipse. It's hard to say if this episode is a reminiscence, a dream, or a hallucination, but it is absolutely essential to understanding the Falcon's personality and the selfish pact he makes with himself: to do whatever it takes to accomplish his dream, even the unimaginable. To be more specific, Ubik informs us that this vision is not an illusion, it is "the reality within your conscious realm," the "you" being Griffith. Yet another mechanism that Miura uses to allow us to delve into the hidden psyche of his protagonists. In this vision, Griffith, as a child, gets lost in the streets of his hometown as he looks for his friends. He then encounters an old weaver woman whom he asks for directions to the castle overlooking the town. He follows her instructions and enters a big, dark room. He senses something strange beneath his feet: lifeless bodies. Griffith walks across a carpet of corpses. He understands that everyone is dead, and revenants then come at him from all sides, begging him to take them to the castle, which here symbolizes the young man's dreams of grandeur. The vision suddenly becomes a nightmare: the bodies heaped on the floor make up the beginning of a bridge that is supposed to take him to the castle. The metaphor is both simple and terrifying because it shows the selfish sacrifice that pathologically ambitious individuals make. They are willing to step on and eliminate other people to achieve their goals. This dream ultimately convinces Griffith to sacrifice his band as he understands that even as a child, he was willing to do the worst to get his way. Under the circumstances, this vision could definitely be a manipulation by the Guardian Angels to push Griffith into sacrificing his friends (the proof being the weaver woman mask that Ubik wears over his face, showing that he was the old woman in the dream, thus influencing Griffith's perception).

However, dreams are not the only way of exploring a character's unconscious mind. In volume 27, Guts puts on his Berserker Armor to fight Grunbeld, who is extremely powerful. The much-feared risk is realized: Guts lets the armor's "spirit" of hate take over him and override his humanity. He lets himself be washed away to let out the beast and Schierke is unable to connect with him via telepathy. However, thanks to her astral projection powers, the witch manages to penetrate into Guts' mind, where she discovers an enormous, fiery whirlwind, which represents the hateful power of the armor. Schierke then makes a reference to psychoanalysis: "If a typical human being were similarly consumed, their ego would shatter." This clearly shows that Guts' psyche is in danger and that the witch is delving into the depths of the Black Swordsman's mind. Schierke is faced with a huge, wild, flaming beast that symbolizes Guts' hatred. She realizes that he is a prisoner of that hatred. As if doing a psychoanalysis, she dives into the beast and finds herself in Guts' memory, where each remembrance is a bubble with an image of a moment cherished by the warrior. Schierke discovers images of Griffith, Casca, the Band of the Falcon, but also scenes of battles won. Below this flood of bubbles tinged with melancholy is a current of "darkness." This is Guts' memory of the Eclipse. Schierke is so terrified by what she sees that she becomes overwhelmed and is dragged down. In the end, the young witch discovers Guts' ego, a flaming silhouette that flickers delicately, still alive thanks to protection provided by Flora. Schierke tries to bring Guts' ego back to the land of the living so that it can once again tame the beast that has taken him over. She manages to do so by reminding him how much Casca needs him. This scene is no more nor less than a spatial representation of the unconscious, an almost map-like projection of Guts' mind. With this technique, Miura creates a scene that is both epic and intimate, peppered with particularly effective symbolism.

There is a final situation where Miura takes us to explore an illusion; this one is crucially important in terms of the plot (and symbolism). In volume 39, our heroes finally find Danan, the Flower Storm Monarch (the queen of the elves), and ask her how to bring back Casca's memory... and her reason. Danan tells them that there is a way, but it requires that they follow "the passage of dreams." Through a ritual, one can access a person's unconscious mind, "going to the bottom of their heart and deciphering the events etched there to find the solution." This time, the trip into dreamland is done with help from hallucinogenic drugs, though the manga is more subtle with its wording. Schierke and Farnese lie down on amazing, gigantic mushrooms that would fit in perfectly in *Alice in Wonderland*. Danan tells them that they must relax, breathe in the spores, and let the mushrooms "tempt them into a dream." The two young women enter a powerful, hallucinatory trance that allows them to explore Casca's psyche. The psychoanalytical approach to dreams is clearly alluded to here, as the elf queen tells them: "The signs and symbols of that which is engraved in her are gathered there in the passage of dreams." The hypnosis session led by Danan first takes our heroines into an absurd euphoria, as one might expect from the initial effects of a drug: Schierke is eating honey and Isidro is a little monkey who tries to steal it from her, incorporating into her vision the sexual tension that exists between them. Farnese, meanwhile, is doing laundry while talking to the Berserker Armor as if it were Guts; she uses Mozgus' head as a bar of soap. However, the two witches partially regain their senses in the dream and decide to leave their own hallucinations behind to penetrate into Casca's mind. Miura made fascinating visual choices to represent Casca's psychological state: in her hallucination, everything is illustrated to look like it was drawn by a child. That is indeed what Casca has become since the Eclipse: a careless child whose mind seems to be elsewhere, incapable of communicating, mute like a newborn. This choice of simplistic, naive, poorly proportioned drawings is the perfect way to depict the young woman's current state of mind. However, as Schierke puts it: "We are in the surface layers of her consciousness. We have to go deeper." Indeed, "deeper" takes them to a world of gloom and doom. "Just what could have happened? For her innermost being to birth something like this place." Miura doesn't really take us into a dream; he tries to depict the symbolic landscapes of the psyche with imagery. The artist takes on this challenge with masterful skill. From afar, Farnese and Schierke spot a dog riddled with lances and dragging a coffin. He's missing a paw and has a Brand of Sacrifice: it's the image of Guts engraved in Casca's unconscious mind. And in the coffin... A shattered doll bearing the sinister rune over its heart. It's Casca's broken ego, the corpse of her old personality, blown into a thousand pieces by Femto. So, the two witches then go off on a quest through the warrior's emotional memory in order to collect all of the fragments of her shattered memory. With the ingenuity we've come to expect from him, Miura manages to bring to life in a fantasy setting the psychological mechanisms theorized by psychoanalysis.

THE HUMOR OF MIURA-SAN

Although *Berserk* is a profoundly dark series and is most often devoid of hope, it is peppered with numerous bits of humor. This is probably also what gives it a more human, more realistic aspect. In this way, Miura incorporates into his story various gags that must have come to mind during his long hours of drawing and writing. Above all, this humor gives his story rhythm, dynamics, and a chance for readers to catch their breath... He especially likes riddling his text with more or less hidden references, particularly paying homage to the works of other writers. For example, we see this when Magnifico lifts the cover from a barrel and discovers Puck secretly eating an apple. Miura shows the elf with the face of Jim Hawkins, as drawn by Osamu Dezaki in *Takarajima* (1978-1979), an adaptation of Robert Louis Stevenson's *Treasure Island*. Seemingly to apologize for this mischievous borrowing, Miura writes "Sorry, Mr. Dezaki" at the bottom of the frame in question. The *mangaka* loves this kind of humor and borrowing, and *Berserk* is filled with this sort of reference, at times intended as an inside joke. When reading the manga, you can see that the author uses Puck as the main comic relief: Miura expresses all of his cleverness via this tiny elf. Puck is a quirky character who, through his actions, reactions, and humor, is able to cut the tension in certain situations. He also provides Guts with the opportunity to talk with someone when he's alone. While some readers think that *Berserk* has "gotten softer" over time and that too much attention has been given to Puck's intrusive antics, this touch of levity is no doubt welcome because it allows the reader, and perhaps more so Miura, to take a "break." It adds a little oxygen to a story that is often stifling. While the *mangaka* offers a few visual gags where Puck falls and hits his head, it's more of the elf's way of putting on an act that constitutes the manga's main source of humor. When Puck gets into jokester mode, he is drawn in his *chibi* form, which in Japanese means "little person," "baby," or "child," depending on the context. This manga technique involves illustrating one of the characters in a childlike, caricatured version, often with a head too big for their body and simplified limbs. Schierke, Isidro, Casca, and even the Guardian Angels of the God Hand have all been drawn in *chibi* form, but Puck really receives this treatment more than anyone else. When he decides to add a bit of humor or do an impression (which happens often), it's like a portion of the frame becomes a tiny puppet theater where a zany little Puck performs a satire of the situation. And I don't use the term "theater" gratuitously: the elf has thirty or so different "costumes" that he dons in a flash to create a comic effect. On top of these outfits, in which Miura takes all sorts of liberties with whatever anachronisms and craziness he feels like, Puck can also change his face and hairstyle at will when he gets on his imaginary little stage. We could make an almost unending, completely ridiculous list of these "side costumes" that the elf puts on for his comedy sketches, drawn in the corner of the frame: Puck is a samurai, then a knight, an army colonel, a wrestling referee, a pirate, a nobleman, a sports fan, a cashier, or an accountant. However, he also sometimes takes on the appearance of well-known figures, whether from the real world or pop culture. For example, while giving advice to Isidro, Puck suddenly appears as Master Yoda, and even adopts his inverted sentence structure: "And perhaps for now I'm his master, you'd say. Already deep into the Dark side, this young one is." The elf takes on the appearance of Bruce Lee and Devilman (Go Nagai), makes reference to *Gundam* (Yoshiyuki Tomino and Hajime Yatate), *Doraemon* (Fujiko Fujio), and *Saint Seiya* (Masami Kurumada), as well as other figures who are better known only in Japan. Even Puck's way of fighting is comical: he gives his attacks grandiose names like the "bloody needle," the "albatross death blow," and the "explodin' fire chestnut." However, because he is tiny, the impact of his moves is always negligible, which creates a comic effect that makes him inoffensive, ridiculous, funny and, in the end, heartwarming. When he's drawn in *chibi* form, it has an immediate comic effect. When Puck is serious or emotional, he is good looking, normally proportioned, and graceful, as you might expect from an elf. However, as soon as he starts saying or doing something silly, he transforms into a simplified version of himself, laughable and disarming. Even the lines are reduced to their simplest form, as one might do in a drawing for children. Above all, the *chibi* offers a comical contrast with Miura's "official" drawing. The *mangaka*'s extremely meticulous and realistic style gives an epic and Dantean flavor to his story. Miura's talent is at times reminiscent of the grandeur and gravity of the work of Gustave Doré... Suddenly using this style with a caricature aesthetic introduces an element of surprise that immediately defuses the seriousness of a situation. When used well, this can produce explosive comical effects. The most surprising thing in Miura's work is that he often manages to commingle comedy and tragedy without choosing one or the other, with the darkest of *seinen* taking on the inoffensive airs of a *shonen*. The fact that the *mangaka* first thought that *Berserk* would be a *shonen* (intended for a teenage audience), but was then published in *Young Animal* (totally devoted to *seinen*) is likely the origin of this very special blend. It's a fair bet that Miura saw in Puck an excellent way to "make Guts' conscience talk" in a humorous way, all with a specific goal: to humanize the Black Swordsman and support his psychological development. In the beginning of the story, Guts is a very difficult character to empathize with because although he is impressive and you can tell that he suffers in silence, he is absolutely contemptible in his individualism, showing no empathy whatsoever for the innocents whose lives he takes, like Colette and her father. When Puck meets this bitter and indifferent Guts, he puts all his energy into trying to bring out the tiniest bit of humanity in him. Initially, Guts is so full of darkness and anger that the elf can't bring himself to use any humor. As Rickert later says, if Guts hadn't met Puck, our Black Swordsman probably would have fallen into a sort of insanity mixed with depression. Miura quickly discovered that Puck could be a tool for bringing the warrior back to his senses and emotions. In this way, the elf humanizes Guts; but he also does the same for the beherit, which Guts hides in his bag and which Puck nicknames Betty. The fact that he gives a name and a backstory to this object immediately transforms it into a full-fledged character. That's the power of Puck.

It's a bit like *Mystery Science Theater 3000*, a show with three goofballs sitting in front of a movie screen and making fun of the film playing. With Puck's *mise en abyme*, he seems to break the fourth wall[10]. When used well, this technique is very effective and creates a sort of fascinating blurring of the line between fiction and reality that takes us by surprise, enabling comedic effects that play off of a metadiscourse. Although breaking the fourth wall is best known for its use in film, from *Breathless* (Jean-Luc Godard, 1960), to *Last Action Hero* (John McTiernan, 1993), to *Fight Club* (David Fincher, 1999), graphic novels can use this technique too. In *Berserk*, Miura himself speaks to us through his protagonists. Luca, suddenly conscious of being simply a side character, exclaims: "Well... Doesn't make much difference what I think of it. I'm not even a main character." Other passages suggest that the manga's protagonists may be aware that they're in a fictional story. In addition to the efforts made to convince us that Griffith is a character "straight out of a fairy tale," Puck's numerous cryptic comments support this theory of the "character who knows they're a character." For example, in volume 38, when Puck is talking about the days of his youth riding on the back of a seagull, he describes that time in this way: "That was the *Berserk* prologue." Besides the comedic effect, Puck reveals to us that he knows the name of the manga in which he is drawn and he even takes the liberty of rewriting the story to start from his own point of view. Sometimes the elf is also a sort of avatar for the reader, for example, when he tells Guts: "I figured if I hung around you, I'd get to see all sorts of neat things." We can add to this the constant comments he makes on the Black Swordsman's reactions. All together, we can see Puck as passing on to the hero the questions in the reader's mind. The height of this is when the little elf shows that he is perfectly aware of being the comic relief of this fictional story in which he appears: "Hey, don't say that. Without me, this story'd be way too dark." This character offers Miura a way to have fun, to occasionally relieve the dramatic pressure and show that he anticipates readers' criticisms and reactions. The elf is a great mechanism for him to not take himself too seriously and to not make *Berserk* an exclusively depressing story, for both readers and for himself. While, as we've seen, *Berserk* is an extremely dark read, we can only imagine how taxing it must be to come up with the story and illustrate it. For a gory frame that the reader views for five seconds, Miura spends several hours imagining and drawing the image. Carefully crafting every morbid detail; asking yourself how you can make a severed head or a showy bust convincing; with all that, you can end up being eaten alive by the darkness of your own work... So, if *Berserk* were just one long, continuous Eclipse, we would probably have lost Miura long ago... I'm sure he needed to give himself a little room to breathe in this hellish series. It also may be a

---

10. A technique, particularly in film and theater, but also in literature, that involves having the protagonist address the viewer/reader directly, thus breaking the imaginary wall that separates them.

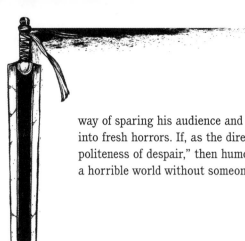
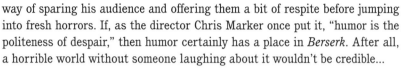

way of sparing his audience and offering them a bit of respite before jumping into fresh horrors. If, as the director Chris Marker once put it, "humor is the politeness of despair," then humor certainly has a place in *Berserk*. After all, a horrible world without someone laughing about it wouldn't be credible...

WRITTEN IN DARKNESS

PART TWO
Exploring the Darkness

A PITILESS WORLD

Midland is a world with magnificent, often pastoral, landscapes. It is far from Tolkien's arid, cursed lands of Mordor; it's mainly the humans that live there that have made this land a living hell. Though he admits that he borrowed from various periods of the Middle Ages quite liberally, Miura translates with brio all the horror that the medieval period was at times capable of delivering. Although the manga prominently features "supernatural" monsters, they are not necessary to make Midland a terrifying world. From the slums teeming with the "ordinary people" to the paranoid highest echelons of power, almost all of the humans in the manga are troubling or vile, each in their own way. However, before we explore these different profiles in detail, we should talk about the way in which Miura depicts the horrible harshness of this age. A "bloodstained, meaningless world": that's how the King of Midland describes his land... before trying to assault his own daughter. That sets the tone. Guts' personal history alone is pure misery. However, as we learn more and more about Midland, sadly, his life does not seem to be the only one with so many bumps in the road. His companions have nearly all faced trauma in their youth, to varying degrees. Coming from a family of oppressed peasants, Casca is no stranger to horror, having survived an attempted rape by a bigwig who hired her as a maid. Saved at the last second, she even kills her attacker when she gets the chance. So, that was young Casca's initiation into adulthood and the "real world." Her youth was thus a world of misery, tragedy, and injustice, with her parents selling her to a local fat cat. Of course, the aristocrats in the story are not depicted any more positively than the penniless peons. They are wicked, corrupt, and offer power to anyone who can gratify their desires, as we see in the encounter between the young Griffith and Lord Gennon, an old, lewd nobleman to whom the innocent Falcon offers his body in exchange for money to expand the Band. Often, Midland society does not function based on merit, and our leading trio, all three from modest backgrounds, struggles in their own ways in this unequal, inhuman, and often sad world. Indeed, sadness is not solely tied to social class: even if the level of comfort and problems are not the same for the rich as they are for the poor, everyone in *Berserk* is desperate and alone... For example, the "daughter of" characters, like Theresia and Charlotte, prove that even when you lead a comfortable, protected life, you can feel powerless. Wealth and education can't protect you from a lack of love. Farnese's

childhood (and, by extension, that of her secret half-brother Serpico) illustrates this perfectly. Farnese is the heir to an influential, rich family that neglects her throughout her childhood, although her parents shower her in toys to clear their consciences. As a little girl terrified by the world, Farnese becomes fascinated by the lights in the outside world that burn in the darkness of her childhood: the flames of heretics being burned at the stake outside her window. Not content to simply torture animals, she lends a hand to the executioners, personally throwing the torches that will take the lives of innocents. She becomes detestable and is even given the nickname "Devil Child" by her family's servants. In a twist of fate, Farnese is ignorant of the fact that Serpico, who she takes on as a bodyguard and confidant, is actually her half-brother, proving that her father is not simply absent, he is also an unfaithful, hypocritical, and cowardly man (who refuses to lift a finger as Serpico's mother dies), more concerned about his own reputation than the happiness of his two children. His decisions also deprive them of the bonds they could have formed as siblings. This terrible secret that connects Farnese and Serpico almost leads them to involuntarily commit incest. This is narrowly avoided thanks to Serpico, who happens to learn the secret of his birth. Thus, Mr. Vandimion's behavior and harsh words toward his daughter, who he considers unworthy, as we can plainly see, show that money does not necessarily bring happiness in Midland. It simply isolates and makes people bitter. Farnese is the perfect example of the damage that a lack of love and consideration can do to a child in the formative years for their personality. She doesn't discover the path to happiness until she finds a true adopted family in Guts and his band. Besides the main characters and their origins, Miura showers us with numerous facts that give substance to the era and people that he tries to emulate. To instill a certain fear in a reader's head, there's no need to make a big show. Sometimes, a small detail is enough to set up a background or inject a bit of fear. For example, Shisu, Guts' adoptive mother, dies of what seems to be some sort of contagious disease like the bubonic plague. This fact alone subliminally evokes one of the most devastating scourges in human history: while there were different massive outbreaks of the Black Death over several centuries, the second pandemic alone, around 1347, decimated over a quarter of the population of the Western world. Miura shows in great detail all of its devastating horror in volume 17, when Laban visits a village strewn with the bodies of people killed by the Plague. Thousands of rats cover the silent town and scamper through piles of corpses. The Plague may just be in the background, but its threat is real. Other illnesses can be found in *Berserk*, particularly the one that afflicts Nina, the young prostitute who has concerning symptoms ("The bleeding won't stop. It's mixed with pus too. And the inside of my mouth is swollen."). Midland is a dirty world without hygiene. Sewers seem to only appear with the advent of Falconia. In the manga, we even come across various mass graves, implying that Midlanders abandon anonymous infected corpses in the open air, creating veritable hotbeds for disease and beacons for scavengers. Tortured bodies are also left to rot on execution wheels mounted on poles. So, death and disease hang over everything, like impatient vultures. Miura doesn't accentuate it, but we can't deny the obvious: we just know that Midland gives off a stench of death. The *mangaka* also depicts harrowing cases of famine, particularly among the impoverished people camping below Mozgus' abbey. We even see a child who has died of hunger in his mother's arms, nothing but skin and bones. So, the author does not hold back with the tragic and merciless nature of the medieval period his story takes place in, and this is a crucial point because Midland is, in a way, a character in the story: it plays a subtle role, but one that is ever-present, spreading the idea that anything can happen, especially the worst. The society of Midland is as dark as the country it calls home. It is an unjust, violent game of chess, shaken by conflicts, wars, conspiracies, and all other sorts of quests for domination. The leaders–kings, bishops, and counts–are mostly vile people with borderline personalities, always on the verge of going mad. Power is most often concentrated in the hands of the few and the populace is simply subject to the whims of those who lead the country. To live in Midland is to endure a nightmarish existence that will turn you into either a victim or an executioner. This point touches on an aspect of the manga that is so flagrant that we almost forget about it: the ubiquity of violence. We can only imagine the psychological impact on the population of constantly seeing death and disease. Bodies disemboweled, burned, and tortured, heads rolling across the ground, bloody duels, savage wars, bodies on spikes along roads, the list goes on. So, it's no surprise that a population that witnesses this morbid spectacle on a daily basis is depicted as an amorphous, terrified, uneducated, and "vulgar" mass (in the original sense of the term, as vulgar comes from the Latin word *vulgus*, "the common people"), swift to submit and howl with the wolves. In the camp, they are drawn as forms huddled in the shadows, crushed by fear of the Inquisition and the weight of hunger. They are sometimes shown as a vengeful mob brandishing torches and pitchforks, ready to burn the first young girl suspected of being a witch. They might be people who would like to live in peace, but the social pressure that derives from fear makes them like this. The horrifying scene where a mother tells her child to throw stones at a person condemned to death so as not to stand out says a lot about this. In the Kingdom of Midland, you must kill or be killed. Even when certain people try to get around this dictatorial religious order, it's to secretly partake in Satanic orgies, which is not particularly reassuring. Truly, hope and joy are not commonplace in Midland... As for the "elites" who rule the commoners, the situation is hardly better: Mozgus is a passionate sadist who blindly tortures all those who he believes to be heretics. One of the worst scenes in the manga is probably the one in which Mozgus, with sickly sweetness and consideration, leads a poor woman to the torture chamber, having her skinned alive after convincing her that he was going to save her. Similarly, the Count also leads a witch hunt in order to get his hands on fresh human meat and assuage his evil-apostle cannibalistic impulses. Even the King of Midland, who initially seems to be a fairly enlightened monarch, falls into madness, torturing Griffith without boundaries and becoming almost brutal with his daughter. The wealthy Vandimions are depicted as a family of cold and calculating quasi-nobles, while the Kushan Emperor is a brutal and diabolical leader who pillages and destroys everything in his path. Even Griffith, who seems to offer Falconia a peaceful reign, is likely to eventually become authoritarian, as he seems willing to do absolutely anything to achieve his "dream." Midland is constantly at war, which adds to the spirit of "survival of the fittest" prevalent throughout these lands. However, it is not the "best" person who will come out ahead, but rather the most violent, the person with the ability to assert their point of view by force and coercion. Life is a battle, whether it's in the form of military strategy or a brutal, head-to-head duel; meanwhile, other people are simply seen as future adversaries. We can tell that there are very rigid social classes in Midland that are totally entrenched, and those classes feel disdain for one another. The scene in which Foss and Julius gripe about the sudden rise of Griffith into the aristocracy speaks volumes: "This nobody has the same rank as me? I'm supposed to treat this scum of lowly birth as an equal?" Worst of all, Miura brings this social injustice to the mystic realm: the Guardian Angels only fulfill the wishes of the vilest people who are willing to sacrifice innocent lives on the altar of ambition. Finally, one would think that all would subside in the next life, that at least death would bring rest, a sort of peace. But that's not how Miura works: either souls refuse to accept their natural deaths and wander aimlessly between life and death, or beings are killed by a demon and are swallowed by the Vortex of Souls, where all of the bodies are massed together in a tentacular spiral. If there is a heaven, Miura makes no mention of it. There is the mysterious Ideal World, which seems to be more "merciful," but only two lines of dialog are devoted to it and we've never seen it. Finally, you would think that good actions would lead to happier results, but once again, you'd be barking up the wrong tree: the episode in which Guts is picked up by Colette and the old monk in their wagon shows this well. After offering help to the Black Swordsman, they die at the hands of demons attracted by his Brand of Sacrifice. Even karma, which Miura mentions in the manga, does not come to their aid. Altruism is not rewarded. If the author wanted to make the darkest "dark fantasy" there ever was, he certainly did a good job. All sorts of threats are everywhere and spare no one. I should mention, however, that the manga does not only offer visions of horror. There are a few safe havens, hidden from the world. This is the case with Flora's tree, hidden in the Interstice, or Elfhelm, on the faraway island of Skellig. That said, even these few protected spaces do not last forever: Flora's tree burns down and Ganishka's transformation into the World Spiral Tree disturbs the Astral World, allowing it to spill over into the Physical World. In stunning fashion, Miura "resets" the Midland that we've known to recenter it on a place where all of Midland's inhabitants converge: Falconia. While this place seems to bring with it a certain modernity and everyone appears to be living there in peace, it's very possible that in the future, this capital will transform into a trap for its residents; after all, we should never forget that this city is under the thumb of a demon lord. Still, we have to admit, in volume 40, Falconia seems to be a less depressing place than we've come to expect from *Berserk*. But for how long?

THE MISERIES OF WAR

❃ *The Miseries and Misfortunes of War — 11 — The Hanging*

The very first image that opens the Golden Age arc, in volume 3, is a tree with bodies hanging from it. Crows, sitting on immense, skeletal branches, proudly guard the corpses of unfortunate souls who were executed. This particularly sinister image echoes a famous set of etchings by Jacques Callot entitled: *The Miseries and Misfortunes of War* (also called *The Great Miseries of War*). Etching number 11, *The Hanging*, bears strong resemblance to the image that Miura chose to kick off his most famous story arc. There's also a certain irony in placing the title "The Golden Age" on a two-page spread showing bodies swinging in the breeze. Callot's series, published in 1633, recounts the horrors of the Thirty Years' War and, in 18 panels, tries to depict the various scenes that an armed conflict can force us to reckon with. The series' etchings depict all of the themes that *Berserk* explores over its thousands of pages. Here are a few evocative titles: *Enrolling the Troops, The Battle, Pillaging a House, Looting a Monastery, Looting and Burning a Village, Highway Robbery, The*

Hanging, Burning at the Stake, Breaking Wheel, The Beggars and the Dying, Distribution of Rewards... While we can't say for sure that Miura is familiar with these etchings, though his vast knowledge would suggest that he may be, we can at least say that the author has stuck closely to a sort of authenticity in the vision of war that he offers us. We can tell that he has really dug down into the history of wars and knights and that real horrors of armed conflicts inspired the deep darkness that the *mangaka* chose for the ambiance of his work. Above all, a warring medieval world offers an author a vast range of plot devices. There are armies, mercenaries, and various other groups, each with interests and goals, powers, their own special looks, feats of arms, etc. And Miura does not hold back from exploring all of these possibilities. To create complex, multifaceted conflicts instead of simple, binary ones, the author created many armed factions, each with their own special characteristics. Most of the battalions in *Berserk* have a name that follows the same model: an animal and a color. So, Midland relies on Julius' White Dragon Knights, the White Tiger Knights, and, later on, the White Phoenix Knights. The Tudor Empire, meanwhile, has a predilection for longer names: the Black Ram Iron Lance Knights, the Blue Whale Ultra Heavy Armored Fierce Assault Annihilation Knight Corps, or the Holy Purple Rhino Knights. Besides these armed groups in the employ of kings, *Berserk* also has bands of mercenaries, falling somewhere between pillaging gangs and groups of independent soldiers. There's Gambino's band in which Guts was raised, the Band of the Falcon that Guts later joins, and the Black Dog Knights led by the ruthless Wyald. Although it is not supposed to fight, even the Church has its own order of knights, bearing the emblem of the Holy Iron Chain. Finally, the Kushans have an impressive human arsenal composed of clans such as the Daka, a normal army, and even magical assault troops. To round it all out, Miura also has other battalions garrisoned at Vritannis, further accentuating the implied size of this universe: there are soldiers from lands such as Balden, Randel, Paneria, and more. By listing all of the places represented by these armed groups, we can tell that Miura aimed to establish a world as complex as our own, with its struggles for influence, invasions, conniving schemes, and fratricidal disputes. In the manga (as in life), it is at times difficult to comprehend all of the factors at play in a conflict or to identify all of the players and their objectives. There are many forces and interests at work in the background, thus creating a sort of abstract geopolitics that expresses itself in the form of a massive, hazy, incessant war. However, curiously, all of this complexity operates with clarity, like a stage background in front of which more intimate adventures play out. You don't need to know all of the armies or the geography of the series to get wrapped up in the story. Above all, the large number of countries and armies are used to lend credibility to the universe of Midland and the events that Miura has take place there. Using this warring context, the *mangaka* presents duels, fights, and battles, as well as strategies, alliances, and conspiracies, moments of cowardice and heroism, and invading troops facing off against pockets of resistance. A world at war like Midland is a shifting universe where all of the forces present try to gain the upper hand and where safety is never assured. This creates constant suspense, an atmosphere where fear is always swirling around. It's interesting that Kentaro Miura makes direct reference to the Hundred Years' War: a slow-burning conflict, this war lasted longer than a human lifespan, giving the impression of an eternal battle, extending well beyond reason. One has to wonder, if Midland were at peace, what story could possibly be told given that everything revolves around battles and power struggles. *Berserk* is also the story of ascension through the ranks of the military to the pinnacle of power, a parable that shows what a person may be willing to sacrifice for domination. Miura also gives the impression that this world has never known anything but this violence. Indeed, our understanding is that the reign of Gaiseric, which long ago brought an end to the savage Age of Warlords, failed because he enslaved his people. After the fall of this empire, history seems doomed to repeat itself: present-day Midland has been plunged into chaos and it's only the rise of a leader, Griffith, that seems to put an end to it, as if he were a new Gaiseric. Will Griffith choose a different path or will he make the same mistakes? In sum, history is cyclical in Midland: it alternates between periods of chaos and authoritarian rule, as if only an iron fist is capable of bringing order to this general disorder. Miura shows us peoples with intra- and inter-group conflicts. They fight based on class, ethnic, and religious differences. When this hostile climate devolves into armed conflict, the worst aspects of human behavior come out. As such, it's no surprise that in *Berserk*, we come across pillagers, kidnappers, assassins, and rapists. The absence of social order prevents the protection of the weakest people and leaves things wide open for the worst deviancies. Each meeting between people is a potentially mortal threat. Wyald and his Black Dog Knights really represent all of the blind brutality of war. They parade around with human limbs stuck on the ends of their spears and are willing to carry out the worst atrocities for the highest bidder. Whether they're governing or fighting, it's men who lead Midland, with hypocritical honor, misplaced pride, and battles between egos thus coming into play. Conversely, Miura depicts the women as having more internal conflicts, like Casca or Farnese. He implies that war is a masculine trait, as Guts claims in a discussion with Casca: "What do you know [about battle]?! What would I know? I'm a man." This warrior's "honor" is directly correlated with his fighting abilities and the terror that he is supposed to provoke. In Midland, how violent you are serves as your resume. We see this with Bazuso: it's said that he once killed thirty men all at once. There's also Valencia, the mercenary nicknamed the "King of Massacre," a ferocious beast who slew 130 soldiers during the Hundred Years' War. Finally, there's Zodd:

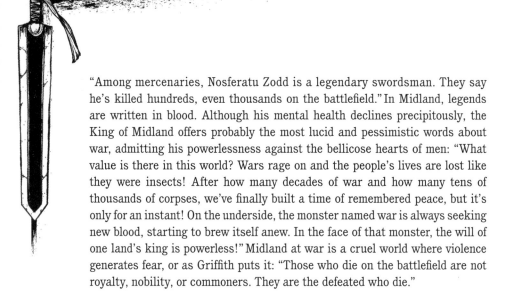

"Among mercenaries, Nosferatu Zodd is a legendary swordsman. They say he's killed hundreds, even thousands on the battlefield." In Midland, legends are written in blood. Although his mental health declines precipitously, the King of Midland offers probably the most lucid and pessimistic words about war, admitting his powerlessness against the bellicose hearts of men: "What value is there in this world? Wars rage on and the people's lives are lost like they were insects! After how many decades of war and how many tens of thousands of corpses, we've finally built a time of remembered peace, but it's only for an instant! On the underside, the monster named war is always seeking new blood, starting to brew itself anew. In the face of that monster, the will of one land's king is powerless!" Midland at war is a cruel world where violence generates fear, or as Griffith puts it: "Those who die on the battlefield are not royalty, nobility, or commoners. They are the defeated who die."

A MORAL VACANCY

Berserk sometimes seems like an ode to despair or like a fable warning about the folly of man. To establish a truly ruthless universe, Miura shows that every level of society is corrupted by evil and that innocence and goodness do not shelter you from a tragic end. Indeed, morality and good have deserted the country of Midland, leaving an unjust world to fill the void. The mythology of the Eclipse itself is based on an abandonment of values: the future apostle must "renounce" the good in him by sacrificing a loved one. It is by this very act that he becomes an omnipotent monster and achieves his most precious desire. Once a person is no longer encumbered by their conscience, they are much more capable of dominating others and surviving in such a universe. Once again, kill or be killed. While there are "good" characters in the manga, like Flora, Schierke, Luca, and Puck, we have to face the facts: *Berserk* is a gallery of characters, each one more troubled than the next when it comes to "values." According to Miura, the higher you climb on the ladder of power, the more the soul is corrupted. Ganishka, the almighty Kushan emperor, describes himself as the devil incarnate. In his defense, that's what happens when you're born into an amoral family: Ganishka's mother once tried to poison him because she liked his younger brother better. While once a victim, the young man turns into an executioner: barely surviving this assassination attempt, he takes revenge by killing his younger brother, which then pushes his mother to commit suicide. Because his father starts to suspect him, Ganishka also arranges his assassination. Once an adult, his only desire seems to be to dominate the whole world, pillaging, killing, and raping every living thing in his path. If he hadn't been transformed into a tree in a twist of fate, Ganishka likely would have achieved his goal, reigning supreme over all of creation. He is thus the ultimate proof that humanistic values do not get you to that level of dominance. Is it as Rousseau said, "Man is born good; it is society that corrupts him"? While we may initially think that the King of Midland proves this adage wrong, just look at how much he changes once he learns about Griffith and Charlotte. He transforms into an insane, bloodthirsty monarch in an instant, as if someone flicked a switch. He calls for Griffith to be subjected to the worst torture imaginable and, abandoning all sensible governance, he neglects his people and displeases his armies. Even worse, letting his incestuous impulses run wild, he ends up trying to rape his own daughter... So, Midland cannot count on its supreme leader to come restore even the slightest bit of moral order to this rotten world. While the emperors and kings are destined to lose their minds, their vassals don't fare much better. All of the members of the aristocracy we meet are, on the whole, quite contemptible and cold-blooded characters. The rich Vandimion patriarch seems to be more interested in his finances than in his daughter's happiness or his wife's love. As such, the elitism of the nobility does not come with the slightest moral superiority in Midland: it simply exposes you to more jealousy and scheming. All of these powerful men, not content with living the good life, immoderately take advantage of their status, abusing the "*droit du seigneur*" that they've given themselves. This is the case with Lord Gennon, the old pervert who shells out money for Griffith's young body, or the Baron in Koka's Castle and the Count, who both take advantage of their positions to feed their morbid apostle impulses. If Midland leadership is made up of evil beings, maybe the country's religions offer a little righteousness and good? Sorry, no such luck. The Pope appears to be senile, weary, and useless, and he blesses Griffith as a sovereign by divine right, even though he's a demon in disguise, revealing his incompetence and blindness. As such, the leader of the faithful is no moral compass either. As for Christly salvation, you certainly won't find it in Mozgus' torture chambers. While it's undeniable that the inquisitor believes he is instituting a sort of moral order, he is totally arbitrary, totalitarian, and hypocritical. Miura tries to show us that having "values" is not synonymous with righteousness, especially if those values involve things like torture or dictatorship. Although he is convinced that he is doing good by tracking down heretics, Mozgus has totally lost his reason and the meaning of justice. Since Miura likes to turn everything on its head, your logical reflex would be to think that these supposed "heretics" are actually good people because the awful Mozgus goes after them... Once again, you'd be wrong: Miura's depiction of them is just as troubling. Satanic orgies, sacrifices, kooky worshipers, crackpot gurus, and more: throughout the world of *Berserk*, we watch the darkest of human comedies unfold. What's more, no level of society is spared: the family unit, the last bastion of emotional connection in such an inhumane society, does not escape the *mangaka*'s darkness. Guts' first family is dead when he is born; his second is doomed from the start. Gambino's extremely toxic fatherhood is practically a textbook case. Indeed, he never shows Guts the slightest bit of affection. He makes Guts bear the weight of Shisu's death and sends him off to battle as a child. He fights Guts and hits him... and ultimately tries to kill him. Not exactly the kind of guidance you'd find in a parenting book. The worst part is, of course, that Guts ends up carrying with him the pain of killing his father, cherishing the memory of Gambino in a sort of Stockholm syndrome. While his familial relations were a source of sadness, Guts is not the only one to grow up in a hostile family environment. As Charlotte would tell us, being king does not make you a good father. Casca could go a step further and tell us about how parents can send you into the lions' den. And Farnese could add that you can have a father who's rich and powerful... but also absent. Before dying, the innocent Adonis probably would have told us how he would not miss the scornful bullying of his father, Julius, in the afterlife. Jill apparently prefers the company of evil elves over the beatings from her elderly father Zepek. Moreover, when Zepek hits her, he likes to tell her that she's probably not his daughter... So, clearly, in *Berserk*, family offers no warm and fuzzy protection. In fact, it is often characters' first contact with misfortune. The entire social and political hierarchy of Midland seems to be made up of disreputable people, from the greatest of emperors to the lowliest of peasants. The fact that Miura deprives most of his characters of the slightest sense of morality leads us to question his own ethics as an author. Even if they do so unconsciously, every creator places limits on what they're willing to show or tell. With Miura, it's hard to see where he's drawn that line. He seems to be willing to break down all the barriers of what's considered reasonable. Certain taboos are very difficult to broach because they often come up against our own limits as readers. Not everyone is ready to face certain topics, even if they're in a fictional setting. Besides the ubiquity of rape, which we will talk about more later, on several occasions, Miura breaks the ultimate taboo: having a child die in a story. The young and charitable Colette? Transformed into a demon and slashed to pieces. Poor Adonis? Skewered by our hero himself. Then there's the skeletal little bodies of children who've died of hunger, as well as those killed by the Kushans or by Wyald's troops. And what about the elf children in the Misty Valley who end up as a pile of ashes before their families' eyes? Absolutely no one is spared in *Berserk*. It seems that Miura has totally opened up all of the horrific possibilities of his manga. We get the message: Midland is a living hell where anything can happen and *Berserk* is the work of an author who knows no bounds. While people may sometimes feel that the *mangaka* goes a bit too far, he's not actually far off from certain real events of the past: the historical period that he emulates had its fair share of darkness and shattered child-hoods. What's more, the fact that Midland is constantly at war is the ideal accelerant for this moral destitution. What good are morals when death is waiting around every corner and doesn't give a hoot about how good your karma is? What is there to save? What good does it do to be good? Throughout the story, the image that Miura paints of humanity shows unparalleled misanthropy on his part. It seems that witches and prostitutes are practically the only people to get favorable treatment from him. That said, it seems quite unlikely that Miura is just a hateful author who enjoys spewing bile on humankind. While the author demonstrates a certain pessimism, we can tell that the total lack of morals is, above all, a plot choice. The reader has to understand that nothing is to be trusted in *Berserk*, that the story will not make the classic compromises, and that the worst is in store on every page. It's one of the means that Miura has chosen to get us to devour his story and anxiously await each volume. Some readers object to the fact that the *mangaka* has calmed down a bit since the Fantasia arc; they say that his turn toward the magical has distanced us from the story's dark origins. However, it is likely that Miura is trying to deceive us with this apparent enchanting shift in the story. It could be that he's letting us "breathe" a bit, that he's gently lulling us, all the better to grab us by the throat. It's like he's letting in a little bit of light so that the shadows can again swallow us whole. In addition, as the story has progressed, Miura has been "rehabilitating" Griffith, having him passed off as a savior in the eyes of Midland. Guts, meanwhile, is an untouchable, violent pariah... The manga's conclusion will deliver the final "moral of the story" that the author wishes to leave us with. It is likely–thankfully–that he will find a way to end his manga with a complex moral dilemma. If Griffith wins in the end, we will know for sure that Miura places no hope in justice and has abandoned all faith in morality. However, if the Falcon is vanquished, that does not necessarily mean that we will get a happy ending... In the end, the *mangaka* seems to ask a metaphysical question that could totally turn morality as we know it on its head: what if God were a "bad guy"? In the manga, a divine higher being certainly does exist, but it is the moral opposite of what we typically imagine. When we take into account the mythology of the Idea of Evil and its underlings, we get the impression that Miura has given form to this concept: Midland is a world ruled by an evil god who uses destiny as a spider uses its web. True, Miura has cut out the episode revealing the Idea of Evil; however, in a way, this episode revealed the author's plans for the story: to imagine a religion with inverse values and morality turned on its head. While the Christian religion calls on us to sacrifice and give of ourselves, the Idea of Evil encourages the sacrifice of others. The fact that the demonic hierarchy is made up of "Guardian Angels" and "apostles"–purely Christian vocabulary– shows that Miura purposefully based his dogma on the model of a classic religion. In this case, God is represented as a sort of human heart made up of the negative thoughts of humans. In place of a favorable destiny guided from afar by a benevolent god, the author imagines a fatal end orchestrated by this omnipotent and nefarious being. In place of a Christ crucified and risen from the dead to save humanity, *Berserk* offers us, in Griffith, a tortured egotist who is reborn by dedicating himself to evil. If you wanted to make an "evil" version of Jesus, there's no better way to do it. It will be fascinating to see if Miura officially reintroduces the Idea of Evil, if he decides to leave it behind the scenes, or if he decides to take the story in a different direction. How could there be a happy ending in a world where destiny is the instrument of evil?

ON THE EDGE OF THE ABYSS

With over 9,000 pages, the manga has all the time in the world to allow its characters to develop and go through all sorts of changes, whether psychological or emotional. Among the challenges that our protagonists face, keeping their sanity is one that recurs time and again. On numerous occasions, Guts, Casca, and many other characters face situations that are so horrible or powerful that their internal balance is disturbed, sometimes even destroyed. The protagonists' damaged psyches are also largely what defines them. The very name of the manga is the description of a trance-like mental state in which the individual "disconnects" from their conscience and becomes an invincible whirlwind of violence. When Guts goes "berserk," it's as if he is possessed by his murderous impulses. As such, the Black Swordsman's temporary insanity is a central element of the story. There is a strong emphasis on controlling—or not controlling—the fantastic wave of violence that overcomes him in this state. This is also reflected in Miura's drawings: when Guts goes berserk, the lines become more like hatch marks; we get the impression that his body is trembling and that he is about to explode. The *mangaka* sometimes draws him with his face totally black, with only his remaining eye left white and empty; the whole creates a striking, sinister effect. We get the impression that Guts' personality changes and that he is showing the darker side of his soul. It's interesting to point out that it's in this unstable mental state that Guts is most effective. In sum, his heroism goes hand in hand with his insanity. The Black Swordsman can have this condition unleashed by despair, hatred, or anger. Later on in the story, the Berserker Armor plays the role of psychological "switch." When that's the case, Guts no longer brings about his own insanity; it's an outside force that takes over him. Pushed down deep inside of himself because of the control the armor has over his mind, Guts even needs Schierke's magic to regain command over his conscience, like a psychiatrist trying to do the same for a schizophrenic person in the middle of a psychotic episode. We constantly get the impression that Miura has drawn a line in his characters' psyches that clearly separates a healthy mental state from madness. His goal is to get them as close as possible to this psychological border. While the Black Swordsman often crosses over to the other side, he always comes back. As such, Guts falls prey to what we call "borderline personality disorder." It is characterized by impulsive, unpredictable, and explosive behaviors, with tendencies toward suicide and self-mutilation, as well as precarious and contentious interpersonal relationships. People with this personality disorder alternate between idealizing and hating people. They have mood swings, going from sad, to rebellious, to despondent, to exuberant. Finally, borderline personality disorder involves difficulty managing emotions, particularly anger, with frequent bad moods, sudden bursts of rage, etc. The Black Swordsman is, in this sense, a textbook case: he seems to check all the boxes for this psychological condition. Guts' mental illness offers a meaningful contrast with the implacable, cold mind of Griffith, who manages to not let any of his internal turmoil show. Above all, Griffith shows obsessive persistence in pursuing his dream, depriving him of all empathy, even for those close to him. Griffith's case can be classified instead as narcissistic personality disorder: people suffering from this mental illness show a grandiose sense of their own importance. They see themselves as special and unique and think that they are entitled to everything. People with narcissistic personality disorder dream of boundless success, power, and brilliance. They see others as inferior, which translates to a lack of empathy and understanding of others. Narcissistic personalities, which Griffith represents quite well, also don't hesitate to use others to achieve their goals. One would think that Miura perused psychology textbooks to create archetypal characters with clearly identifiable person-ality disorders. Indeed, we could also mention Mozgus' obsessive-compulsive disorder, Corkus' passive-aggressive side, the list goes on. *Berserk* narrates the ups and downs of characters struggling with mental disorders. As Midland is a world that brings despair, all human feelings take a turn for the worse and are exacerbated. All of the people in the story are hypersensitive and moments of relaxation are rare because the fear of dying is overwhelming every day in such a universe. On top of that, in the Middle Ages, mental and behavioral disorders went untreated. As such, there's no consideration for others' psyches or for one's own mental well-being. If someone suffers from a serious psychological condition, you can generally bet that they will only get worse in such a hostile environment and will end up being thrown in the dungeons or burned at the stake. Incidentally, Miura seems to really like the moments where characters tip over into madness. While Guts' insanity is temporary, we can't say the same for the King of Midland, who suddenly slides into dementia. This is also expressed in the way that he's drawn, which changes radically: while initially dignified and reserved, the King transforms into a demented old man with wide eyes who belts out crazy orders, foaming at the mouth. Several scenes highlight the characters' reactions to tough psychological challenges: for example, Farnese, when she sees demons for the first time; Guts, when he accidentally kills young Adonis and then vomits in horror of his own actions; and Griffith, whose mind is slowly destroyed in the King's dungeons. Miura loves having his characters go from one extreme to the other. It seems that the interest of creating characters with dysfunctional personalities reaches its acme in critical situations. As for that, Mozgus is probably the person who swings the most between a peaceful state and fits of blind violence. *Berserk* analyzes human behavior when people are backed into a corner and madness takes control of the mind. Certain characters undergo a positive psychological evolution: this is the case for Farnese, who, after playing the part of an obsessive torturer, transforms into an altruistic, benevolent witch. However, not everyone is so lucky, and the damage is at times so brutal that the psychological devastation changes a character's nature. Miura explores this concept in greatest depth with Casca. Just after the abuse she endures during the Eclipse, the young woman is afflicted with dissociative (also called psychogenic) amnesia. This is a type of retrograde amnesia[1] caused by a traumatic experience or excessive stress. Casca's memory and identity are fragmented and her mental function regresses, bringing her back to a childlike state. It becomes impossible for a person suffering from this type of amnesia to remember various periods in their past. Those memories can be reactivated after treatment or events that trigger their recall. The mind suppresses the source of pain and puts the psyche on pause to limit its suffering. Miura "artistically" depicts Casca's illness using a shattered doll. Schierke and Farnese enter Casca's mind to pick up the pieces.

At what point does an individual cross over to the dark side of the psyche? What situations, tragedies, or actions push you into irrationality? This very question seems to resurface constantly throughout *Berserk*. How do you end up so paranoid that you sleep with your sword? How can you have killed over a thousand people and remain a psychologically healthy person? The Skull Knight launches into a tirade against Guts to warn him about the criminal sinkhole his mind risks falling into: "Black. Black. The beast of darkness. It thirsts while it's there. More and more. It thirsts. The more blood in which it bathes the more it does thirst. The beast has an insatiable appetite. As you kill it thirsts. As it thirsts, you kill. [...] And then the beast will consume you. It will take your place. You will come to feel nothing but hatred. You will become a monster in the form of a man. Perhaps, you can become a real monster." Guts is warned here about the damage to his mental health that he exposes himself to as he kills. He risks becoming nothing but a killer; a criminal without a

---

1. Retrograde amnesia: "Loss or alternation of information acquired prior to a pathological episode"; in other words, the amnesiac suffers from loss of memory of events that took place before the traumatic event, but they can remember perfectly events that occurred thereafter.

conscience. Several evil beings in the manga embody the most frightening of mental disorders: sadistic personality disorder. Wyald, the Slug Count, and the Snake Lord fall into this category. They put Hannibal Lecter to shame. The pleasure they take in causing suffering with a certain refinement sends shivers down your spine. It also shows the moral cliff Guts is heading over if he continues to be so destructive. At times, the Black Swordsman shows a terrifying face while fighting. Covered in blood, he sometimes bursts into fits of demonic laughter, as if he enjoys partaking in this spectacle of death. On other occasions, he has a disturbing, almost predatory, smile. Although you might not notice it at first, personality disorders are at the heart of *Berserk* and have direct consequences on the tragic events of the story. So many negative things take place in the manga because of a lack of understanding of psychology and psychiatry, sciences which, although first established in the 19th century, would have to wait until the 20th century to really mature. Before that, the medieval Western world was particularly severe with anyone suffering from mental health issues. This is one of the reasons why a medieval setting must have been so attractive for Miura: anyone living in the Middle Ages walked dangerously on the edge of the abyss...

FLESH AND BLOOD

We get the feeling that Miura aims to write a "visceral" story, one capable of giving us a gut punch, one that we can feel in our bones. The violence that the characters experience must be so realistic that we can feel their pain. To produce this effect, the author uses a device found in the greatest horror films: "body horror." Works that belong to the body horror genre are those that deal with alteration of the human body, most often in a repugnant and grotesque way. When it comes to suffering and distortion of the body, the human imagination knows no bounds, and Miura pays homage to this genre. Sex gone wrong, physical violence, monstrous mutations, all the diseases you can think of, torture, zombification, parasites, and numerous cases where the body's integrity is affected and altered, becoming no longer truly human: those are just some examples of what we mean by "body horror." It is a particularly popular genre in Japan: from *Urotsukidoji: Legend of the Overfiend* (a *hentai* manga by Toshio Maeda) to *Akira* (Katsuhiro Otomo) to *Tetsuo: the Iron Man* (1989 film by Shin'ya Tsukamoto), the country has generated many cult manga and films just as emblematic of body horror as the works of David Cronenberg or Clive Barker. In *Berserk*, violence is so ubiquitous that we *almost* end up numb to it; and yet, the fountains of blood are abundant, a man's members rarely remain attached to his body on the battlefield, and we see many a head roll. All you need is just one image of Wyald's band to capture all of the savagery of the period: they walk around with body parts stuck on the ends of their spears, like macabre trophies meant as a warning. Miura even aims to give a certain aesthetic to the dismembered bodies. This results in scenes that are both harmonious and morbid at the same time, during fights, for example. The scenes of butchery are so well choreographed and so brilliantly illustrated that he manages to make them almost "beautiful." On this point, the *mangaka* touches on one of the main characteristics of body horror: the undeniable fascination that it evokes. Fictional violence is a catharsis that has shown up in stories since the beginning of time. If we must deal with violence in real life, we can ponder and critique it through fiction. It's "just for pretend." As such, as we read, our mind confronts that violence and allows itself to consider it. This allows us to assess our values, understand the mechanisms that lead to conflict, etc. Once idealized by fiction, we can even take a certain guilty pleasure in the spectacle of violence. Of course, such scenes are disturbing at first, but it's hard to deny that they are one of the reasons why we choose to read a *seinen* manga. It is a significant part of *Berserk*'s DNA, a sort of macabre promise that we expect to be kept. The French edition even bears the warning "*Pour lecteurs avertis*" (For mature readers). People turn to *Berserk* when they want to read an adult manga that can offer horrible and disturbing scenes, ones that are not for all audiences. In this regard, Miura certainly does not disappoint. He has understood the attraction that a dark story with limitless violence can have. It's hard to think of any bodily horrors that the author has not included. Just among the most realistic tortures, we can list all of the things that happen on the battlefield: swords lopping off heads, arms, and legs, or being planted in the chests of surprised men, or piercing cheeks or eyeballs. Other weapons crush, stun, or dismember. While these are injuries that one would expect to see in combat, Miura adds a certain inventiveness that outshines other works in the genre. It's not unusual for Guts to cleave people in two, or even for him to kill several at once, waves of blood following the warrior's sword. In addition to wounds of war, *Berserk* shows us terrible torture. Once again, Miura has not tried to paper over the horrors inflicted on the body throughout history. Boiling oil down the esophagus, back pierced with metal spikes, various forms of quartering, etc. The tortures are as numerous as they are hard to describe. A torture chamber is a diabolical, inhumane temple where body horror reigns supreme. It's interesting to note that torture was used to get victims to confess, whatever they might say. Above all, though, it was meant to break a person. Griffith illustrates this last point: after the horrors he endures in the Tower of Rebirth (skinned alive, tendons and tongue cut out, etc.), the Falcon is but a shadow of his former self, stripped forever of his power to fascinate others. By destroying his body, they broke his soul. He no longer evokes anything but the extreme pity that you feel when you see a person to whom life has not been kind. This shows how the body is the ultimate sanctuary, the intimate space that we must protect above all else. That's why body horror is so "effective"... and so hard to look at. It allows us to identify with the victim and imagine how we would feel if someone violated our most prized and most fragile of possessions. Miura also does not skimp on bodies ravaged by life: There's Vargas and his disfigured face, Mozgus' underlings and their congenital deformities, Shisu's suppurating buboes, and more. There are also mutilations, like Guts and his severed arm. However, the Oscar for body horror goes to the apostles. An apostle is a mutated human capable of transforming into an extremely powerful, unspeakable abomination. Body horror masterpieces like David Cronenberg's *The Fly* (1986) or John Carpenter's *The Thing* (1982) explored these themes of transformation with huge success. In general, this mutation into a monster, while it can give the person new powers, inevitably leads to a social and physical decline. The condition of the apostles adds an interesting twist because they are capable of hiding their true nature and choosing when to transform. They can also return to their human form at will, making them formidable, undetectable enemies. The Guardian Angels also present certain aspects of body horror. Among these, Void takes the cake, with his skinless face topped by an enormous, exposed brain. His nose is cut off, his gums are exposed, the skin on his cheeks seems to be pulled back toward his ears, as if he abandoned the operating table in the middle of some bizarre face-lift. A detail that perfects the tableau of horror: Void's eyelids are sewn shut. Finally, although I must again underscore the fact that Miura withdrew this aspect from the final publication, the Idea of Evil, the "final boss," if you will, is nothing more than a giant human heart floating in a vortex. In *Berserk*, the body is constantly mistreated and tormented.

While the most conspicuous aspect of body horror in the series is the bloodiness of combat, there is another form of body horror that is much more destructive and that recurs disturbingly often in the manga: rape. With this theme, we are entering into a quite sensitive part of our analysis because, to this day, rape is a scourge affecting every country and all levels of society. Rape victims suffer from psychological damage and often physical trauma too. A common consequence is that victims wall themselves off and stay silent about the traumatic event and their psychological state. Indeed, society does not always make it easy for victims to get help and be heard. Victims can even be blamed and held responsible for what happened to them rather than going after the aggressors, thus skirting the real causes of the problem. Thus, it is not a "neutral" subject and Miura certainly does not tackle it as such. What's more, the fact that it is such a recurring and central act in the series makes it hard to ignore. It is even one of the most "controversial" aspects of the manga. It's a subject of division among readers and a hot topic in discussion forums. To make a long story short, some people reproach Miura for having too many rape scenes in his story, to the point that some are concerned about a sort of cavalier attitude toward such a serious subject. People are certainly entitled to that opinion, and it's healthy to be uncomfortable with reading passages depicting these acts. I must admit that I read these pages faster than normal because their subject is so revolting and gut-wrenching. The question is, can we rule out the—disturbing—idea that Miura is engaging in "fan service"? Basically, is Miura gratifying readers who want to see rape scenes? Japan, the birthplace of *hentai*, has long blown past all reasonable limits when it comes to such transgressions, particularly of a sexual nature, so it's a question worth asking. Whether we like it or not, and no matter what we may think, Japanese culture permits certain things that we would find deviant, or even illegal, here in the West. So, it's a matter of culture and approach to fiction, but also probably the politics surrounding the issue of rape and the place of women in society. That's not where the debate lies, but it is to say that Miura comes from a culture where these issues are not seen in the same way that they are in the West. However, if you look at the issue more broadly based on the manga itself, it appears too simplistic to accuse Miura of being cavalier. It even seems likely that the author's message is actually more critical and political than many think. Firstly, is the *mangaka* close to the historical reality of the Middle Ages? In the early medieval period, rape was not considered a crime in its own right. For a long time, it was considered part and parcel of kidnapping, with girls abducted from their families to be forced into marriage. It wasn't until the 16th century that kidnapping and rape were distinguished in law. It is said, however, that throughout the Middle Ages, rape was considered a serious crime, even if it was at times called things like "ravishment." Although there were stiff penalties for rapists, such as hanging, men convicted most often got away with a heavy fine, banishment, or mutilation of a member in the most severe cases. On top of the misogynistic mentalities of the time, according to which, basically, "the woman asked for it in some way," women had to contend with the difficulty of "proving" they were raped. A woman had to have been a virgin, with the rupture of the hymen considered the ultimate proof... There were rarely witnesses and aggressors invariably claimed that the woman had consented. In other words, given how difficult it was for a woman to speak up and be heard, it's hard to imagine today the full magnitude of the phenomenon in the Middle Ages. We must also bear in mind that in the medieval period, for a time, "reparational marriage," i.e. marrying a victim to her rapist if they were both single, was permitted... It was then seen as "just reparation for the crime." This is because the victim suffered a double injury: in addition to the rape, she lost her "honor," and would then be difficult to marry off as she was no longer a virgin. Thanks to letters of clemency issued by the King of France, we have been able to generate statistics on the profiles of aggressors and the nature of their misdeeds. Gang rape was very common among single men, while individual rape was more common among married men. All social classes were affected, from peasants to soldiers, from knights to nobles to clergy. Finally, men with higher social status could use their position to get less harsh punishment, or even just a fine. In this context, can we really blame Miura for this recurring representation of rape, when we already know he tries to push all of the darkness of his imagined Middle Ages to the extreme? What's more, at no point in the manga is rape "validated." It is always represented as a terrifying, toxic, inhumane, and vile act. Miura shows that aggressors come in all shapes and sizes: they are mostly men, of course, with Donovan here being the archetype, but also on rare occasions they are women (for example, when Slan assaults Guts in the Qliphoth) or former victims of rape. Guts, who is a rape survivor himself, reproduces rape-like behavior with Casca, notably because he relives his own trauma. In this way, Miura shows the fact that anyone can be a victim of this trauma and anyone can be guilty of committing it. By making rape commonplace and by showing us the extent to which women can fall victim to it in a world dominated by men, the *mangaka* delivers a fairly feminist message, trying to show us the hell that they endure. It is even said of Casca that she is "just the right victim for the starving men." Incidentally, it is fascinating to see how the author depicts the monsters hiding in Casca's unconscious mind. Schierke and Farnese come face to face with these creatures, whose arms, legs, and heads are giant, muscular, terrifying penises. From a depiction that could have been ridiculous and laughable, Miura managed to create figures that perfectly embody the toxic masculinity that has frightened Casca since her rape. The fact that he constantly shows men's sexual brutality as a monstrous threat is yet more proof that Miura is not complacent about the issue of rape. He was indeed intentional about placing this theme at the heart of his manga, and that's another matter of interest. First, rape has a central place in the twists and turns of the story because *Berserk* possesses many aspects of a film subgenre: "rape and revenge." The most famous film of this category is probably Wes Craven's *The Last House on the Left* (1972), but there are a number of other feature-length films in the subgenre. In these films, the structure is always the same: a young woman is left for dead after being savagely raped by criminals, but against the odds, she manages to survive. She heals herself and does physical training while plotting her revenge. In the third act of Wes Craven's film, revenge is exacted on the young woman's attackers in the most violent way imaginable. To a certain extent, *Berserk* falls into this category because of Griffith's rape of Casca. Furthermore, in a rape and revenge story, it is sometimes someone close to the victim who punishes the criminals for them. Again in *The Last House on the Left*, it's the girl's parents who exact vengeance for their daughter, just as Guts does for Casca. The audience for such a story goes from, first, absolute terror, witnessing a violent scene (one of rape), to then accepting the worst atrocities toward the aggressors out of great empathy for the victim. In *Berserk*, Miura uses the same psychological mechanisms to get us to understand the horrible tragedy of this violation. He of course shows this through Guts' childhood, with the abuse he suffers and the difficulty he has healing emotionally, but also, particularly, through the tragic events that Casca lives through. The young woman, who has Griffith to thank for escaping rape a first time, is raped by her onetime savior. In addition, she ends up losing her child (who, on top of that, is contaminated) and her psyche is temporarily destroyed because of the act. The rest of the story looks at the consequences of this tragedy for Casca, the repercussions for those close to her, and the solitude and suffering that she endures. The entire quest of the latest volumes is dedicated to "curing" Casca psychologically, giving her the strength to recover her memory so that she can be herself again and get her life back together. And when she snaps out of it, it's finally the Casca we know and love who reappears. All of the suspense rests on the way in which she will now handle her past, whatever desire she may have for revenge, the consequences for her relationship with Guts, etc. Instead of a vulgar apology for rape, we find in *Berserk* many signs that show us that Miura seems to be sensitive to the issue of rape and the scourge that it represents, for men and, above all, for women. While there are many of these rape scenes, they always have a meaning in the story or for the psychology of the characters. Rape is never glorified and each time, it evokes unspeakable terror and sadness. Always taking the side of the weakest, the *mangaka* certainly presents us with shocking scenes, but they are designed to get us to react, to give us a desire for revenge, or at least a desire to see the victims triumph. There is a final clue showing that Miura intends more to tell us about the damage caused by such an act rather than using rape just for fun: from the very beginning of the manga, even before we see any scenes of rape or Guts' childhood, the Black Swordsman hates being touched. As such, the rape of Guts is a sort of justified revelation in the plot as is explains why Guts is so angry and why the rape suffered by Casca is so traumatic, obviously for her, but also for Guts, who, through her experience, relives his worst nightmare. More broadly, the vision Miura presents of sex, including when it is not forced, shows a certain deviancy. The orgies of the Satanic cult look more like a Black Mass in honor of body horror than a happy bacchanal. Even the chaste Farnese uses Guts' sword to sexually pleasure herself while she chokes him with a rope, showing that the young girl, who we believed to be virtuous, has an almost borderline approach to sexual relations. In the end, there is no vanilla sexuality in *Berserk*. The darkness pervades even the most intimate aspects of the protagonists' lives.

ALL THE FACES OF EVIL

In the Kingdom of Midland, there is an invisible energy in the air and in people's minds: Evil. It is a vast concept with many facets that Miura has worked to explore in all its forms. To define Evil, we could say that it is the opposite of Good and that it is associated "with events, accidental or otherwise, behaviors, or states of affairs considered harmful, destructive, or immoral and that cause mental or physical suffering." In *Berserk*, Evil is absolutely everywhere and, first and foremost, takes on a classic form: criminal evil. It applies to any person or being that harms in any way the physical well-being of another person. The series is full of criminal evil: highway bandits who rob and assault women, conniving rapists, groups of assassins, murderers, bloodthirsty mercenaries, sadistic despots, ardent devil worshipers, the list goes on. It's the evil of the faithless and lawless, a creeping evil that totally eats away at any society. As soon as there are laws, there are outlaws and, statistically, you will always find people who scorn society's rules, whether out of necessity, out of covetousness, or out of perverse pleasure. As usual, Miura does not hold back with the degree of danger on the roads of Midland, making the country an open-air slaughterhouse where the weakest are crushed and those who "play by the rules" are not rewarded. Ultimately, it's a quite ordinary evil because it is so widespread and such a part of human society. Moreover, our protagonists are not exempt from this criminal evil, participating to varying degrees: Isidro is a thief, Farnese tortured animals as a little girl, Griffith locks his enemies in a room and sets it on fire, Guts kills a child... Evil can sometime be found among the good guys. As the saying goes, the road to hell is paved with good intentions: sometimes people may do evil things while thinking that they're doing good. This is an involuntary, accidental evil, but an evil nonetheless. That's exactly what happens with the Skull Knight who, wanting to save the world, instead plunges it into a new age of darkness... Similarly, the Princess Charlotte and the Pope lend their love and support, respectively, to Griffith, unaware of his true evil nature. Without realizing it, they allow Evil to carry out its plan, playing the role of innocent but wicked vessels. Given that it's possible to "do evil" without knowing it, Miura also shows us that it can come from those closest to us. Sometimes it's out of opportunism, as we see with the scheming of Magnifico Vandimion, who, as a guest in Skellig, tries to play an evil trick on its inhabitants. The King of Midland is the most tragic example, as he poses a threat to his own daughter, thus showing that evil can interfere in even a parent-child relationship. However, the most extensive and most emblematic example is that of the apostles: the dark magic that transforms them into monsters requires a sacrifice made to Evil itself. The person you most trust, the person you love more than anyone else may in fact have a killer inside of them. Behind this offering is a crime that was long considered the

"ultimate" transgression: betrayal. Griffith is the epitome of this, as he sacrifices all of his friends to become a servant of Evil. In sum, in Miura's series, there is no shield from Evil. It is capable of spawning itself; all it needs is a heart, a brain, a bit of misfortune, and some desires to exist and spread. Evil can also gain strength in numbers, for example, through the power of a group: several times throughout the manga, we see the vengeful masses attending executions and throwing stones at convicts. There's also the case of the Satanic orgies, in which dozens of bodies writhe against each other and their owners become obsessed, fanatical, when in another context, each person on their own, they would undoubtedly be totally ordinary people. It's when they mass together like microbes and think as a single unit, abandoning, in a way, their own ability to think, that these people show a frightening side of themselves. This is also true even in smaller groups. For example, when they are together, Mozgus' torturing minions are absolutely terrifying, but once the crow-headed torturer is alone and tells his story, we are almost moved by his experiences. This shows that an amorphous mass of individuals can take on an evil that would not have existed otherwise. This is also shown by the dozens of armies and bands all across Midland. Serving in wars in which they have no choice, the soldiers are transformed into blind killers. For example, when the King of Midland goes mad, certain men do question his orders, but they still end up carrying them out. Finally, religion essentially falls into the same traps: once you give more credence to absurd texts than to your own humanity, then you allow a particularly vicious and destructive evil to spread, an evil that believes itself to be on the side of Good. As soon as common sense and reason disappear, evil acts are free to spread. We see this in the story's "brutes," those ultra-violent warriors who aren't the brightest crayons in the box; instead, they let their primal, savage instincts do all the talking. Adon Coborlwitz, Boscogn, Samson, Grunbeld, and even Zondark are perfect examples. They are the personification of brutality, but suffer more from an absence of goodness and wisdom than from an actual evil essence. They demonstrate a crude, factual evil. Although he comes close to this category, Wyald embodies an even higher level of evil: he seems to be profoundly nasty and vile, as he has no morals (he kills women and children, pillaging and destroying everything in his path). Where he seems to be more evil than the others is in the unconcealed pleasure he appears to take from the suffering he causes. To this list of unequivocal Sadists, we can of course add Ganishka, who perfectly represents the demented, murderous invader archetype. And then there's the apostles, who are no amateurs when it comes to committing atrocities. Finally, Femto, for his actions during the Eclipse, takes the grand prize for evildoing: massacre, betrayal, rape, and torture, all in the same night. Oh, and let's not forget about the deleted chapter, because the dark God of *Berserk* is actually called the Idea of Evil. It is the very essence of this concept, a gigantic heart created by the sum of all the bad thoughts of humans. It is Evil in its purest form, the quintessence of the force that guides our wicked actions. The fact that Miura made Evil the God of his story shows the importance of the concept in his universe. All in all, it's quite logical: the entire manga revolves around the philosophical questions about the darkness that eats away at humanity. *Berserk* may be a work of fiction, but it is essentially political and comments on the world and human nature. Miura aims to understand what moves us as individuals and why we sometimes end up acting "inhumanely." This exploration of evil is at the source of it all, going hand in hand with our free will, which allows us to do whatever we want, including the worst. While *Berserk* is filled with fantastic and horrific monsters, it's humans who are the real evildoers. Let's not forget that the apostles and Guardian Angels were originally humans. They are not monsters from the imagination; they are men and women who chose to become monsters. They made that choice as a way out of the frustrating condition of being imperfect and powerless human beings. It's in human nature that we find the seed of their monstrousness. "Do what thou wilt, that's the only commandment for us apostles!" They made a pact with the devil, a contract with Evil. A particularly interesting monster in Berserk is the "blob," that black, shapeless mass that covers everything during the rebirth of Griffith. Puck says that it is made up of "the malice of those who've died of plague or torture in this place! It's absorbin' the feelin's of the people it's swallowed and steadily expandin'! It's fulla' their bitterness and desire for salvation!" Here, Miura brings up the idea that Evil can be born of suffering and despair. Once again, it's not a concept coming from some outside force: the Idea of Evil comes from the hearts of people. It would have been easy for Miura to stick with a simplistic duality of values. Instead, some of the "good guys" can be quite mean... and vice versa, at least so it appears. In the new Band of the Falcon that Griffith creates after the Eclipse, the knight Locus is very odd. Even though he's joined up with the Falcon, and is thus considered a bad guy because we know the horrible things that Griffith has done, Locus seems to be a fairly decent, proud, and valorous person. Before joining the Band of the Falcon, the "Moonlight Knight" was considered to be a legendary figure. Children would grow up hearing stories of his exploits. He teams up with Griffith after receiving a prediction from an oracle and he seems to believe that the Falcon will bring peace and stability to Midland. Locus sees all knights as equals, including his enemies. Even though he too is an apostle, it's hard for us to associate him with the ranks of demons. Indeed, even his transformation into an apostle is unusual. While most of his fellow apostles take on monstrous or grotesque characteristics, Locus transforms into a steel centaur reminiscent of the sensual metal figures of Hajime Sorayama's androids (*Sexy Robot*, 1983). He is proof that one can be on the side of Evil while maintaining certain values. This idea is even more pronounced with the mysterious archer Irvine, who also joins

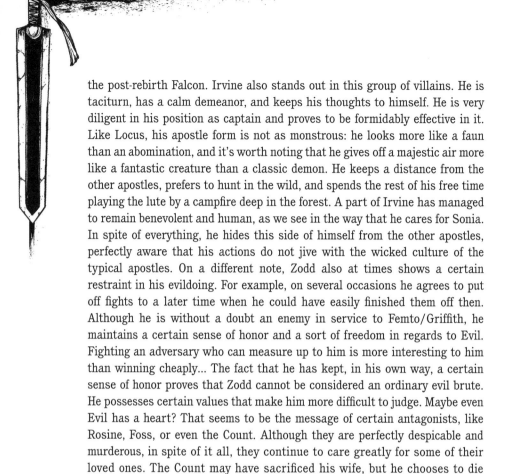

the post-rebirth Falcon. Irvine also stands out in this group of villains. He is taciturn, has a calm demeanor, and keeps his thoughts to himself. He is very diligent in his position as captain and proves to be formidably effective in it. Like Locus, his apostle form is not as monstrous: he looks more like a faun than an abomination, and it's worth noting that he gives off a majestic air more like a fantastic creature than a classic demon. He keeps a distance from the other apostles, prefers to hunt in the wild, and spends the rest of his free time playing the lute by a campfire deep in the forest. A part of Irvine has managed to remain benevolent and human, as we see in the way that he cares for Sonia. In spite of everything, he hides this side of himself from the other apostles, perfectly aware that his actions do not jive with the wicked culture of the typical apostles. On a different note, Zodd also at times shows a certain restraint in his evildoing. For example, on several occasions he agrees to put off fights to a later time when he could have easily finished them off then. Although he is without a doubt an enemy in service to Femto/Griffith, he maintains a certain sense of honor and a sort of freedom in regards to Evil. Fighting an adversary who can measure up to him is more interesting to him than winning cheaply... The fact that he has kept, in his own way, a certain sense of honor proves that Zodd cannot be considered an ordinary evil brute. He possesses certain values that make him more difficult to judge. Maybe even Evil has a heart? That seems to be the message of certain antagonists, like Rosine, Foss, or even the Count. Although they are perfectly despicable and murderous, in spite of it all, they continue to care greatly for some of their loved ones. The Count may have sacrificed his wife, but he chooses to die rather than burn Theresia to be saved a second time. It's actually quite beautiful and tragic. The killers sometimes have a soft spot that keeps them connected to Good and, in some cases like the Count's, that can lead to their demise.

Thus, Evil is everywhere in this series; even the story's God is made up of it. Still, *Berserk* is a manga that people devour and even end up cherishing. How is it that we can become so obsessed with such a sad story that prominently features individuals corrupted by the dark side? In other words, why is Evil so fascinating? First, it's a question of contrast. A character who's bad is, by nature, richer in personality than a good hero. The bad guy has flaws, a motivation, a plan, not to mention their appearance, which is often terrifying, to go with the darkness of their psyche. However, the viewer/reader is a strange beast: they want to explore their fears through archetypal figures that embody them. A person can be terrified of spiders, but love a movie with an invasion of tarantulas from outer space. A person can worry about the slightest illness, but still love zombie movies. There are certainly people who get no pleasure from feeling fear and who avoid any frightening images, but let's be honest, most people want to be surprised, shocked, and terrified.

There is something in the concept of evil that automatically fascinates the audience: it shows us what we shouldn't and can't be. It allows us to imagine and exorcise our fears within the safe boundaries of fiction. You can be nice and warm under the covers with a volume of *Berserk*, ready to face the worst atrocities. This is how humans are: they need a way to learn other than from experience. Art and fiction allow us to reflect on subjects, fears and dilemmas that we would never tackle otherwise. When we see a character do evil, we automatically question our own relationship to that act. What would I do or say in the victim's situation? If I were the killer, what choices would I have made? What's more, our love for monsters and demons also comes from their cachet, their often colorful personalities. They usually have a special kind of humor, a striking piece of equipment, terrifying and memorable powers, etc. On some level, there's nothing more boring than a good guy, because his values are our own and we already know that he's going to win in the end so that those values win out. Good is not as attractive as Evil, that's just how it is. Finally, there's a sort of catharsis we get from the actions of a bad guy. We spend all of our time in society remaining civilized and obeying the law. The bad guy, totally free to break all the rules, does for us all the things that we forbid ourselves from doing. The servants of Evil are also bringers of death and, on that point, they touch on one of the great questions of our humanity. To try to understand what drives a monster or a killer is, in a way, to make peace with the absurdity of the world and the evil that at times runs through it. In the same way that talking over a problem with a friend lifts a little of that weight off your shoulders, experiencing evil through a fictional story allows you to keep it at a distance, analyze it, and thus take away from it that unknown and incomprehensible nature that sparks so much fear. As we can see, Miura was smart not to play the card of being simplistic, making everything black and white, that we've seen a thousand times before. All of his characters are troubled and have Evil looming over them, just waiting to seize control. In the end, when we see Griffith's fate, we are left not really knowing what to think about these notions of good and evil. Griffith takes responsibility for what he did, seemingly telling us that sacrificing his friends was a necessary bump in the road on his way to achieving his dreams of greatness. If the Falcon saves Midland, what moral are we supposed to take away from that? Ganishka was a monster and he was vanquished only to be replaced by another, less destructive monster. It's like the only way to escape supreme Evil is... a lesser evil.

A BEASTLY BESTIARY

If you spend some time taking stock of all the creatures that make an appearance in Miura's work, you might end up feeling a little dizzy from their great number and extraordinary diversity. The *Berserk* universe is so vast and rich that there's room for all of the imaginary creatures you can think of. In this chapter, we'll set aside those that are purely from the realm of fantasy— and come back to them later—to focus on those that belong to the manga's mythology. Once again, Miura impresses us with his depth and creativity, as exemplified by the complexity of his fantastical bestiary. We should first mention that there are many definitions of "monster." First, "monster" can describe a real person whose appearance is so different from what we're used to that they seem non-human. In *Berserk*, characters like Vargas or Mozgus' minions fall into this category. Whether they're congenital or caused by accidents, their deformities, seen as repulsive, result in them being marginalized by society. The word "monster" shares roots with the French verb "*montrer*," meaning to show. Thus, the old American tradition of "freak shows" fits perfectly into this etymological lineage. Today, the term "monster" can describe three different categories: a criminal monster (an assassin, for example), a monster of science, or a monster of fiction. This last category is of greatest interest to us; it's also the oldest of the three. Monsters hold a special place in the legends of mythology and religion. While today monsters are only found in certain types of fiction, at one time, they served a very important socio-cultural function, on top of carrying great symbolism and teaching lessons. It's this type of monster that seems to fascinate Miura: the kind that is capable of giving off an almost mythological aura. As we will see, the *mangaka* does not only take his inspirations from Antiquity; he also draws from much more modern works. Above all, we must take into account that Miura takes his monsters seriously, giving them an aura, describing their motivations, and giving them very human appearances so that we can connect with them. However, for an artist, especially a dark fantasy *mangaka*, monsters are a story device offering freedom: you can make up whatever you want. Forget anatomical limitations or demands for realism: the creature can take on any form with any face. The fact that a monster must typically cause a certain level of fright also means that you have to look deep within yourself, examine your own fears and sources of disgust, in order to magnify those aspects in a fascinating, iconic form. I'm sure you've already gotten the idea: Miura aims to bring together every single monster imaginable in a single story. He does this in his typical fashion by drawing inspiration from existing fantastic beasts and then delivering his own versions. As it turns out, there are not many monsters in the series that don't connect to an image from our collective imagination, such as from myths or pop culture. Once again, it's his virtuosic talent for drawing and his artistic choices that manage to make everything fluid and coherent, in spite of it being a dizzying patchwork. Above all, Miura knows how to take the necessary liberties to make a fictional figure his own. For him, the idea is to deliver his own vision and reinterpret the myth. A perfect example of this point in *Berserk* is the Sea God. Guts and his band are sailing by ship to Skellig. Out on the open seas, they come across a creature with toothed tentacles. With a death grip, the monster uses its appendages to try to drag the ship down to the bottom of the ocean. This image immediately calls to mind imaginary creatures like the kraken and other giant squids. The world's first sailors must have come across big octopuses or giant squids and their stories were eventually distorted to the point that krakens were used to decorate old sailing maps. Similarly, the legendary kraken is inspired by the Leviathan, the sea monster from the Bible who rises up against God and is thus slain by the Almighty. As such, it's fair to say that having a sea monster appear in a sailing scene of a fantasy story is, all in all, to be expected; however, the way in which Miura surprises us is how he connects this "kraken" to another legend, one created by H.P. Lovecraft. When Guts lands at Solitary Island, inhabited only by some gloomy sailors and a young girl all on her own, there are several details that allude to a novella by Lovecraft: *The Shadow over Innsmouth*, a text in which we find the figure of Dagon, a sea monster worshiped by the residents of the port of Innsmouth. In the novella, a young man named Robert Olmstead arrives in the coastal village of Innsmouth, a dreary little town with an unpleasant odor inhabited by seedy-looking fishermen with heads that seem to be a cross between that of a fish and that of a frog. Olmstead discovers that the townspeople belong to a cult called the Esoteric Order of Dagon, devoted to an ancient creature that lives under the sea and supposedly commands the "Deep Ones." In the story, there is even a "Devil's Reef," a rock formation near the village where the sea dwellers come to get their offerings from the villagers. Miura borrows this exact same set-up, with disfigured island dwellers who hide in their homes and cult statues dispersed across the island shaped like Lovecraft's sea creature Cthulhu. The similarities are clear; there's no mistaking it. And when the Sea God finally emerges from its cave and appears, it does right by its forefather: Miura presents us with a creature that's almost "unspeakable," a concept very dear to Lovecraft. It's the idea that something is so wonderfully horrible that there are no words to describe it. The Sea God is a sort of gigantic black dome with a wide, carnivorous mouth in the middle, from which flow thousands of long, thin tentacles with teeth on their ends... The very same tentacles that attacked Guts' ship. As such, what we previously took to be an entire kraken turns out to actually just be one of the tentacles of a colossal monster hidden deep below an island. In this way, Miura "physically" connects two myths in one. However, he does not stop there: to vanquish the Sea God, Guts enters the belly of the beast so that he can strike it from inside, at its weak spot. Entering the belly of a sea creature... Naturally, this makes us think of the biblical myth of Jonah, who, thrown overboard by the sailors on his boat, is swallowed by a giant fish, inside which he spends three days and three nights. Similarly, when Guts enters the belly of the Sea God, he

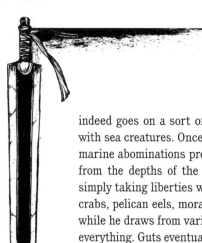

indeed goes on a sort of adventure there, as the beast's insides are infested with sea creatures. Once again, Miura did not go the easy route here: all of the marine abominations protecting the entrails of the Sea God are real monsters from the depths of the sea that the *mangaka* toiled to faithfully represent, simply taking liberties with their actual sizes. There are giant isopods, spider crabs, pelican eels, moray eels, and more. In this way, Miura shows that even while he draws from various myths, he works to establish a certain realism in everything. Guts eventually manages to escape from the Sea God, nearly losing his life in the process. This example of the Sea God reveals the way in which the *mangaka* works to produce his monsters: he creates chimeras, mixing together multiple monstrous characteristics. The creatures he creates never come out of nowhere, but they don't look like anything we know. That's one facet of Miura's genius. The Sea God is a humongous divine being, but not the only one to have such impressive dimensions. In the final stage of Ganishka's transformation—once again, very Lovecraftian in the way it's put together—we can see that the author is fond of unreasonably large creatures. For example, Grunbeld, when he transforms into the crystal dragon, also takes on enormous proportions. At these points in the story, it's hard not to think fondly of the *kaiju*, gargantuan monsters, like Godzilla, that fight each other, destroying entire cities in the process. They are authentically Japanese monsters that Miura could not possibly have ignored. However, these supersized creatures are far from the majority. The apostles, generally smaller in size, nonetheless remain the most terrifying beings in the manga. There are hundreds of them. Their shapes and sizes are so varied that it would be impossible to describe them all. However, in spite of this, we can see that Miura has quite a similar way of creating them. The author does a sort of vivisection of the imaginary, having his apostles transform into half-human, half-animal monstrosities. Sometimes, the blend is simple: Rosine is a woman-butterfly, the Count is a sort of snail, the Egg of the Perfect World is frog-like, etc. Wyald is even nicknamed "the Ape." However, the inter-species blends are quite often more complex. Miura fuses together the traits of up to eight different animals in a single apostle. What's more, he is not content to mindlessly copy animal forms; instead, he draws inspiration from their morphology to extract the monstrous characteristics. And there are real-life monsters in the animal kingdom; if you're not convinced, just look at an acarid under a microscope. For example, during the Eclipse, Casca is surrounded by three creatures; one of them holds her captive in its tentacles. This tentacled monster has buffalo horns, another horn on its forehead like a rhinoceros, and tiny arms reminiscent of chicken wings or the arms of a *Tyrannosaurus rex*. Perfecting this creature, its overall form makes you think of sexual organs, like an open vulva exposing a set of teeth and a sort of head covering that evokes the foreskin. This kind of monstrous construction is seen in many of the apostles and, while the sexual dimension is often present in their design in one way or another, it is the borrowings from the animal kingdom and the blends derived therefrom that are the most impressive: we find bits of creatures from the deep ocean, but also many attributes that are specific to insects or mammals. That said, the mixtures of different animals are built into shapeless piles of flesh, to the point that it's impossible to nail them down as any particular animal. It takes longer observation of an apostle to decipher what forms inspired it. What makes these beings so monstrous is the placement, size, and number of their characteristics: they have several dozen eyes, mouths with hundreds of teeth, more than two arms, multiple heads, etc. Miura explores every possibility. Here we must pay tribute to the artist who inspired the *mangaka* in this choice to create chimerical monsters: Go Nagai, more specifically his 1972 manga *Devilman*, which Miura has always admired and which he recognizes as one of his inspirations for *Berserk*. In fact, when you flip through *Devilman*, there's an uncanny resemblance between some of its monsters and those in *Berserk*, for example, between Rosine and the winged demon Sirene. Nagai's demons have that creepy, savage, abominable, hellish quality that we find in Miura's work. However, when we look at the Eclipse, we can see that Miura wanted to venture further than his hero into the vision of monstrosity. Each of the monsters in *Berserk* is unique and the author's creativity appears infinite when it comes to abominations.

As we've seen, the apostles are not the only monstrous beings in the manga, not by a long shot. Miura keeps churning out new creatures and tributes to other creators, to the point where he seems unstoppable. For example, when Guts faces an army of skeleton soldiers in a forest, the *mangaka* pays homage to an incredible scene in *Jason and the Argonauts* (Don Chaffey, 1963) in which the hero and his band combat exactly the same creatures as the Black Swordsman. The special effects in the scene in question are amazing for a film from 1963, thanks to the genius of Ray Harryhausen, a giant among animators. This scene is such a classic and the skeletons are so iconic that the homage is unmistakable. Miura tries to incorporate all of the monsters that have sparked his imagination over the years. For example, the Snake Lord of Koka's Castle is based off of the reptilian monster in the 1984 Joseph Ruben film *Dreamscape*. Even clearer among his tributes, Miura includes a giant straw man on fire, which takes its name and inspiration from the Robin Hardy film *The Wicker Man* (1973), in which such an "idol" is worshiped by a pagan cult. The *mangaka* chooses to give it life, even though in the film it's just a wooden statue. Griffith's mask, as we know, is borrowed from the Brian de Palma film *Phantom of the Paradise* (1974). Ubik's glasses are an homage to Butterball the Cenobite from *Hellraiser*. You can even find a reference to the 1988 film *The Blob* (Chuck Russell): during Griffith's rebirth, a sort of black, viscous "blob" covers everything around it, exactly as in the movie, which is about a substance that swallows everything in its path, including humans. Sometimes, the inspirations for monsters are more subtle, but present nonetheless: the first monster in the manga—the female apostle who tries to devour Guts during sexual intercourse—is strongly inspired by the work of the great visual artist Hans Ruedi Giger. Miura goes even further with his homage to the Swiss artist, as the Guardian Angel Conrad is directly inspired by one of the faces in Giger's painting *Landscape XVIII*. It's often hard to not be reminded of David Cronenberg, an essential filmmaker for anyone fascinated by the monstrous side of the human body and its sexual dimension. For example, there's the scene in which the Count pulls a parasite out of his mouth to "inseminate" Zondark, a tableau of pure, Cronenberg-style body horror. Miura's influences are so varied that one could spend an eternity listing them all: a many-headed hydra, incubi, bloodthirsty trolls, a rapist horse, a pack of human-headed dogs, pumpkin-headed monsters and scarecrows, zombies attached to wooden wheels, etc. That's not to mention the millions of indescribable creatures that cover the Qliphoth or the "flooring" of the Eclipse, composed of a mass of many faces. Then there's the specters that are capable of taking possession of a living being and turning them into a monster. However, the greatest horror of all probably has to be Ganishka's abominable uterus, a factory for monsters that is described by Rakshas as follows: "They're using apostles to birth demons. Of course. Those apostle body interiors are linked to the beyond. They're patched together, still alive and filled with amniotic fluid. When pregnant women are submerged, the offspring are infused with evil and demon children are born." Other than the way in which trolls reproduce, there are few things that reach such a height of monstrous infamy in the manga. While in the Fantasia arc Miura seems to focus more on fantasy creatures, he nonetheless continues to freely explore every facet of monstrosity.

WRITTEN IN DARKNESS

PART THREE
The Builder of the Universe

MULTIDIMENSIONAL MAPS

"The world doesn't extend in merely two dimensions.
There exist profound depths within itself."

It's with these words that the witch Flora reveals to us the nature of the *Berserk* universe: the manga of course possesses a "horizontal," terrestrial realm, but it is stacked in several layers of reality, several "vertical" dimensions, that plunge to great depths or rise up to the heavens. Miura has created an incredibly rich and complex universe that still has some unknown regions to this day and that is unveiled bit by bit as the manga progresses. Certain places are realistic and are situated in the physical world; others are located on planes of existence that are harder to define, offering fantastical and terrifying visions and never-before-seen landscapes. Let's start with what we know best: Midland. In *Berserk*, the physical plane is the "human world," an imaginary yet credible version of medieval Europe. The action mainly takes place in the Kingdom of Midland, i.e. "the land in the middle." While Midland is surrounded by other nations, including Tudor, Balden, Randel, and Paneria, the manga principally takes us through several Midland cities, particularly Wyndham, the country's capital. Although Miura doesn't name all of the towns and castles that his characters visit, he succeeds in fleshing out an enormous kingdom with real geographical and geopolitical substance. There's Doldrey Castle on the border with Tudor, Albion and its abbey, and Lumias, in the south of Midland, which finds itself under the yoke of the Kushan invaders. Tracking a traveling band of characters allows the author to continually change up the story's settings and thus spatially expand his universe and gradually add detail to its maps. In Miura's way of creating his landscapes and towns, we can tell that he has done extensive research through documents and iconography to be consistent with medieval Europe, to the point that some readers believe that he based his world off of the actual geography of our European countries. Indeed, there are a few examples that lend credence to this theory. When Ganishka is slain, a humongous dome of light (reminiscent of a nuclear explosion) stretches over a portion of the globe. To render this, Miura draws a "satellite" view of the planet, as it might be seen from a space station, and gives glimpses of certain parts of *Berserk*'s world. Although the dome and clouds hide most of the map, a few dedicated observers think that they've detected the coasts of France, Great

Britain, Sardinia, and even a bit of Italy's boot. There are several competing theories: some have Midland centered on France (particularly because of the manga's Hundred Years' War), others say Denmark. According to meticulous estimations based off of the ground zero of Ganishka's explosion and the countries that people think they recognize, Denmark could indeed be the epicenter of the kingdom. It doesn't much matter if it's true and who's right, the fact that a story generates this kind of debate shows its impact. We identify with the world in the story. At the same time, we know that it's not really our own: this allows Miura to not have to comply with any sort of historical accuracy, while offering us strong points of reference. For that matter, *Berserk*'s universe is filled with historical references that lead to inferences about geography. For example, although the lands of the Kushan Empire are never drawn, its very existence implies that other peoples exist in *Berserk* besides those of the protagonists. Miura could have just focused solely on Midland, but he chose to have the entire world play a role on his paper stage. Although the *mangaka* only takes very loose inspiration from it, a Kushan Empire really did exist. Founded in the first century CE, one of the greatest rulers of the Kushan dynasty was... Kanishka I. Although at its height the Kushan Empire did cover territory stretching from Tajikistan to the Caspian Sea and from Afghanistan to the Ganges river valley to the south, Miura's illustrations again seem to blend together several cultures. This further accentuates one of the author's key choices: to draw inspiration from the real world, then contort it and muddy the waters. As such, there's no use in hoping to one day receive a definitive answer about the manga's true geography.

While Miura succeeds in creating a tangible and realistic "human" universe, it's in his approach to creating parallel realities that the artist shows true originality. *Berserk* hides a mille-feuille of dimensions stacked on the physical reality. Moreover, these dimensions are not visible to all people or at all times. The universe operates more or less on a trinity of parallel dimensions: the Physical World, the Astral World, and the Ideal World. The Astral World, also called the "Netherworld" or the "World of Spirits," is a realm between the Physical World and the Ideal World. On the border that separates the Physical and Astral Worlds is a particular space-time: the Interstice, also called the "Threshold." This zone is the junction that allows certain creatures to pass between the worlds. Theoretically, humans are not supposed to be capable of seeing this shallow layer of the Astral World, as this ability is supposed to be reserved for a few "chosen ones." The Interstice is home to, for example, the ghosts of dead people who haven't accepted their death, wandering the edges of life as souls of the damned. Those who practice magic can also access the Astral plane using spells. What's more, certain places or objects can generate temporary junctions between the Physical and Astral Worlds. This is the case for Flora's Mansion of the Spirit Tree, but also the island of Skellig, home to

Elfhelm. Finally, the deepest layer of the Interstice is the Qliphoth, the infernal realm where Slan materializes before Guts. However, this thin opening between two realities, above all, affects bearers of the Brand of Sacrifice, who are condemned to constantly live in this zone that only they can see. This invisible portal is a perpetual threat for those who are branded, as the Skull Knight explains to Guts: "This is the reality that you must walk through from here on. A world invisible to eyes of the flesh. You must stand in the interval between two worlds that, while mutually significant, do not make contact with each other." This Interstice–scientifically defined as "a narrow empty space between two parts of a whole"–allows Miura to incorporate monsters into his story and open a temporary hole in the realism of his story, without sacrificing its credibility. On this Threshold, the *mangaka* also places "living astral beings," i.e. legendary creatures: unicorns, trolls, elves, fairies, and goblins. In the artist's cosmology, a child can, for example, come across a troll in a forest if the monster has managed to slip into the Physical World through the Interstice. When she receives Guts and his friends, Flora explains what takes place in the Astral World. After explaining what's found in the Interstice, she reveals that in deeper layers there are immense "astral entities," what we humans might call gods and demons in our religions. Even further down is a "Nexus" where the Occultation ceremonies take place. The Guardian Angels materialize in this space, with a giant vortex swirling above them, from which occasionally emerge colossal clusters of bodies forming titanic tentacles that latch onto the apostles when they die. Flora implies that this is where we would find what we call "Heaven and Hell." In the eye of the cyclone is a portal to the Abyss, a mysterious place that makes up the deepest level of the Astral World. It's said that a strange divine being lives there, commanding the Guardian Angels of the God Hand: the Idea of Evil. The Abyss is supposed to constitute a perfect mirror image of a third and final plane of existence, in addition to the Physical and Astral Worlds: the Ideal World. We know very little about this place, which is briefly mentioned by Schierke. She simply defines it as "the soul of the origin of all existence, the world of Idea," thus wholly maintaining the mystery of this dimension.

The names that Miura uses for these various planes of reality are not chosen randomly: Qliphoth, the Abyss, the Astral World... These are references to different concepts tied to religions and the occult. In Jewish Kabbalistic mysticism, the Qliphoth are representations of evil, impure spiritual forces, in opposition to the angelic Sephiroth that represent good. Similarly, the word "Abyss" has additional meaning: in Greek mythology, the abyss is the deepest region of Tartarus, the prison of the underworld. In Catholicism, abyss has this same meaning of "underground" and "infernal," but also describes the state of darkness preceding the creation of the universe. Choosing such a term to be home to a deity is no innocent act by the author. Once again, he aims to give

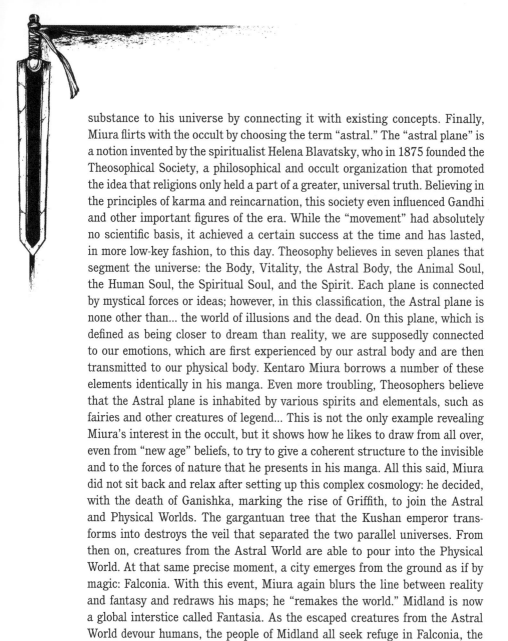

substance to his universe by connecting it with existing concepts. Finally, Miura flirts with the occult by choosing the term "astral." The "astral plane" is a notion invented by the spiritualist Helena Blavatsky, who in 1875 founded the Theosophical Society, a philosophical and occult organization that promoted the idea that religions only held a part of a greater, universal truth. Believing in the principles of karma and reincarnation, this society even influenced Gandhi and other important figures of the era. While the "movement" had absolutely no scientific basis, it achieved a certain success at the time and has lasted, in more low-key fashion, to this day. Theosophy believes in seven planes that segment the universe: the Body, Vitality, the Astral Body, the Animal Soul, the Human Soul, the Spiritual Soul, and the Spirit. Each plane is connected by mystical forces or ideas; however, in this classification, the Astral plane is none other than... the world of illusions and the dead. On this plane, which is defined as being closer to dream than reality, we are supposedly connected to our emotions, which are first experienced by our astral body and are then transmitted to our physical body. Kentaro Miura borrows a number of these elements identically in his manga. Even more troubling, Theosophers believe that the Astral plane is inhabited by various spirits and elementals, such as fairies and other creatures of legend... This is not the only example revealing Miura's interest in the occult, but it shows how he likes to draw from all over, even from "new age" beliefs, to try to give a coherent structure to the invisible and to the forces of nature that he presents in his manga. All this said, Miura did not sit back and relax after setting up this complex cosmology: he decided, with the death of Ganishka, marking the rise of Griffith, to join the Astral and Physical Worlds. The gargantuan tree that the Kushan emperor transforms into destroys the veil that separated the two parallel universes. From then on, creatures from the Astral World are able to pour into the Physical World. At that same precise moment, a city emerges from the ground as if by magic: Falconia. With this event, Miura again blurs the line between reality and fantasy and redraws his maps; he "remakes the world." Midland is now a global interstice called Fantasia. As the escaped creatures from the Astral World devour humans, the people of Midland all seek refuge in Falconia, the only safe place, which allows the author to make it a central location for the future plot... To be totally thorough, there are two other ways for "uninitiated" people to visit the Astral plane: the "road of elves," which leads to the superficial layers of the Netherworld, and, notably, the "road of dragons," which is a path to the deepest layers of the Astral World. This is the type of road that a beherit opens up, allowing the Guardian Angels to appear through the hole torn in the veil of the Physical World, notably during the Eclipse. As such, the *mangaka* did not simply invent a vague imaginary world in which his story would take place; instead, he established a whole universe, both physical and supernatural. This construction fits into Miura's ultimate plans, which we will discuss later, i.e. to build a fictional universe capable of containing all concepts of the imagination.

HISTORY AS A PLAYING FIELD

In volume 10, when Guts and his band descend into the bowels of the Tower of Rebirth in Wyndham, Casca drops a torch, which disappears deep in the void. As it falls, the torch's light reveals the ruins hiding in this pit. We see Greek and Etruscan remains, destroyed temples and giant statues, as well as a mass grave in which all of the bodies bear the Brand of Sacrifice on their foreheads. Ruins and dead people: that's exactly what you find when you start looking into history. This scene is the perfect introduction for this chapter because we too are going to throw a torch down into the depths of the manga to try to identify how Miura plays on history. It's as Judeau says as they penetrate deeper and deeper below the tower, "So that was our unknown history tour." Miura chose to situate *Berserk* in a medieval universe when he realized that Vlad Tepes, Lord of Wallachia, who inspired the figure of Dracula, was briefly a contemporary of Joan of Arc. This gave him the idea to have his characters traverse a fantasy medieval Europe. History itself delivered a world of imagination and an aesthetic that Miura found to be distinct and that he could easily blend together. Vlad Tepes was even the name of a character in the pilot version of *Berserk*. So, history is indeed the foundation for the *mangaka*'s central inspirations. That said, the manga is far from a "historical" work, if only because of the heavy dose of fantasy:

"I've collected quite a lot of material, like images. When I first started my work, I actually racked my brain to decide on whether to go for a historical manga, faithfully following History, or to do a fantasy manga. [...] I thought the range of my imagination might become narrow if I already depended on history while I was still young[1]."

From the very first pages of the manga, which opens with Guts having sexual relations with a woman who turns into a demon, we understand that we're going to be reading an "unrealistic" fantasy story. Thanks to this, Miura is totally free to pepper his manga with historical references without having to be concerned about any factual accuracy. Moreover, he makes greater use of the Middle Ages as imagined in our collective unconscious rather than as proven by experts via texts and archeology. However, to make the magic happen and

1. Interview given in December 1996 in Kentaro Miura's studio, published in *Berserk: Illustrations File*. See Bibliography.

for his work to enter into our collective imagination, the author has to prove himself. Readers have to feel that he knows his subject well and that he's done everything possible to make it believable. In my opinion, it's an excellent choice on the part of Miura because he took a position that gives him the greatest freedom with his art and the story, while still being able to play around with our history. We see this freedom, in particular, in the anachronisms that the author subtly incorporates:

"There are rough things in the very early Middle Ages, but brilliant things like the Palace of Versailles are far after that. In the end, I created one age that looked like it spanned from the early Middle Ages to the end of the Middle Ages in Europe. For example, the ball in Midland is, I think, close to the end of it. But the story of the Lords comes long before that time. The same is true for the Inquisition[2]."

Drawing inspiration from the real world is such a natural process for any story writer that it seems absurd to talk about it here. However, it's essential that we examine certain mechanisms because the *mangaka* uses them all with remarkable verve. These mechanisms allow us to understand how the artist perceives the world and reproduces it in his work once it's gone through the filters of his personal vision and affect. It's also a way for him to exorcise or analyze the horrors of history:

"I think I've said this in an interview before, but when I learned about Tutsi and Hutu, it did influence *Berserk*. I was writing *Berserk* watching the incident on the news. And a little while later I wrote about mob psychology in *Berserk*. I believe that incident made me want to write about it so I would understand it myself[3]."

From any historical fact, no matter how specific it may be, an author can extract a lesson, a system, a protocol, or even just memorable anecdotes that they can inject into their own story. It's by this means that Miura makes use of history in his manga, inserting little touches here and there, at varying levels of salience, and also incorporating elements gleaned from his research. Sometimes, he borrows directly: for example, he calls one of the conflicts in Midland the "Hundred Years' War." In doing so, the author is most probably trying to evoke the idea of an endless war and give a historic flavor to the victory by the Band of the Falcon. Borrowing an actual, well-known name

---

2. Interview given for the American release of the *Berserk* anime series, as an audio supplement for the zone-3 DVDs. See Bibliography.
3. *Ibid.*

in a fictional story allows him to add a sort of credibility: it allows us to connect the story to our vision of the world and history. The example of real-life Kushans and Kanishka I, mentioned previously, shows that Miura has little care for historical consistency. Without worrying about what historians will say, he shops around through human history. A culture that fascinates him? The name of a leader that sounds good and has cachet? That's all Miura needs to slip it into *Berserk*. Emperor Gaiseric, a bit like Ganishka, also has an infamous forebear: Gaiseric, King of the Vandals, who reigned over Europe in the fifth century. Once you know that the *mangaka* uses this writing trick, you can have some fun looking for all of the master's borrowings, which can also come from real-life places. At times, he simply pays homage to a piece of architecture that he really likes, as when he reproduces the column-filled room of the Mosque-Cathedral of Córdoba in the lower levels of the Vandimion manor. When he receives the band in this space, Serpico even says that it was long ago built by the Kushans, as if to underscore this nod to history. Blending references with total freedom, Miura copies the ballroom in the same house off of none other than the Hall of Mirrors in the Palace of Versailles.

Architecture is undeniably a vector for history and culture. To make reference to it in an artistic work is to evoke a piece of humanity's past, as if invoking a spirit. And the *mangaka* did not shy away from this pleasure, as we can see from the architectural marvels found throughout the series. The castle in Griffith's dream, for example, is inspired by the Alcazar of Segovia, a splendid Spanish fortress; the Fortress of Doldrey is modeled off of the Castle of Coca, also located in the Spanish province of Segovia. Spain is a major inspiration for Miura, who also recreates San Martin church in Frómista as the church in his Enoch Village. Not to worry, though, Spain leaves some opportunities for its European neighbors: the cathedral in Wyndham copies the cathedral in Reims, France. From there, the author takes us to Italy, incorporating into *Berserk* monuments reminiscent of the Pantheon in Rome, Villa La Rotonda near Venice, and the Palazzo Vecchio in Florence. The fact that the author chose to include all of these distinct places in a single kingdom explains why there's so much debate about the "real" country that inspired Midland. The *mangaka* enjoys mixing all of these periods and architectural influences, but does so in a way that doesn't distract the reader from the story. Actually, if taken out of context, Miura's various choices could give an impression of inconsistency in his work, but as soon as you start racing through the volumes, the author's drawings and plot manage to perfectly unite all of these references, in spite of their heterogeneity. Each time, he makes necessary modifications so that these cultural tidbits fit right into his own creation. Given that he was artistically inspired by these many places, it's only natural that he wanted to use some of them for his "ideal story."

However, the manga's locations are far from the only conveyors of history: the *mangaka*'s meticulous attention to the various outfits is stunning. With styles ranging from the 14th to the 18th centuries, he adeptly reproduces the attire that would have been found in European courts in these various periods. It's so evident that you end up not noticing it, and there's never a point where a costume pops out at us because of a lack of credibility. His obsession with detail is the glue that holds it all together. Miura's attention to armor, as well as arms, is even more astounding. He appears irreproachable in the way in which they were designed, produced, decorated, and maintained. Several pieces of armor presented by Miura are inspired by real-life examples that can be found today in museums. While Miura may be a master when it comes to inventing totally original forms, we can also see that when he comes across something from real life that fascinates him, he leaves it "as is," as if the reality was so crazy that there was no need to add anything to it. Other, more discreet, historical references can be found in the realism of the events and actions that appear in the series. The sword and combat techniques are inspired by actual practices like, for example, the celebrated *kenjutsu*, the samurai art of swords-manship. Miura also displays techniques specific to fighting with a longsword, known only to serious fans of medieval arms and armor, for example, the idea of using the sword as a lever. More generally, the fighting shows a genuine concern for realism (once you set aside the fantasy aspect) and each blow dealt has a sense to it so that the dynamic of combat is fluid and understandable for the reader. But that's not all: certain military strategies in the story perfectly illustrate the theories of Sun Tzu in his illustrious treatise *The Art of War*. On two occasions, Griffith uses techniques from this age-old manual of strategy. During the siege of Doldrey, Griffith and his troops end up backed up against the river, unable to retreat, and he gives them this speech: "No way! Even if we run, were would we go? The river's behind us. If we're gonna drown anyway, I'd rather die fighting!" By leaving victory as the only option for survival, Griffith is applying Sun Tzu's "burn your boats" strategy to a T. The Chinese master called for, in extreme cases, burning your own troops' boats so that they wouldn't have the option of fleeing in them. That way they would have no other choice but to give it their all in an ultimate battle, which could, in a way, turn their fear into a weapon. Another technique from *The Art of War* is Griffith's strategy of sparing the lives of enemies who choose to flee or lay down their arms, thus giving enemy soldiers in retreat who don't want to die a chance to save their skin: "Commence hunting down the enemy remnants! If they flee this place, well enough!" By this decision alone, Griffith accelerates the downfall of the opposing army. Miura illustrates this scene with soldiers who begin to doubt: "It's no use. At this... At this rate, we'll be killed." As the entire army retreats, its leader, Lord Gennon, falls miserably from his horse, as if to symbolize his power evaporating.

So, the *mangaka* manages to scatter elements taken from history throughout his story without the references necessarily being clear. Above all, they're there for people in the know. The author also quite credibly reproduces the power structures of the medieval period: for example, there's the way in which a monarch used the services of mercenaries and then rewarded them with titles of nobility or social favors. We see the same realism in the court intrigue, the plotting to interfere in the royal line of succession, the economic and political power of religious authorities, the complexity of alliances in war, etc. In certain bits of dialog, we occasionally catch words that are closely tied to history: "peasant revolt," "crusade," "mercenary," "colonies," "independence," etc. All of these terms we use solely to reference historical "moments." By using a single word, Miura evokes an entire system. In a free and understated fashion, he places his fantasy story in a quite naturalistic setting that shows a real love for history's treasures. We also see this in the faithfulness and minute detail that Miura strives for in reproducing objects: his work on the various ships that appear in the series is incredible. Once again, he doesn't just perfectly reproduce the physical aspects of the ships; the realism carries over into how they're used in the story, associated with actual tactical movements used historically in naval battles.

Kentaro Miura doesn't stop at laying out a thousand references gathered from his meticulous research; he also allows himself to play around with history and explore the creative potential of the fantasies it inspires. For example, it's hard not to see in Godot and his successor, Rickert, the spirit of Leonardo da Vinci. Their ability to come up with ingenious devices, ahead of their time, from arms and armor—how about that precursor to the rocket launcher?—to fire extinguishers to prosthetics, makes it irresistible to compare them to this immortally famous historical figure, whose works and inventions continue to surprise and intrigue people to this day. The inspiration is so evident that there's no need to overtly call out this Italian genius to create the association with Godot and Rickert; however, Miura also amuses himself by hiding more subtle references. For example, the young witch Schierke gets her name from a little German village that you would only recognize if you've read Goethe's *Faust*. The German author sets his Walpurgis Night[4] scene in the "District of Schierke and Elend"... Farnese gets her name from an illustrious, wealthy Italian family that existed in real life and was very much like the Vandimion family. Along the same lines, Mozgus' habit of striking his face against the floor is inspired by Ivan the Terrible, the first Tsar of Russia, who is said to have had the same practice. While at times the references follow a tortuous

---

4. Walpurgis Night is a pagan celebration that takes place on the night of April 30 to May 1. Although it is meant to celebrate the end of winter, it has been identified as a Witches' Sabbath for having been banned by the Church.

path or are difficult to decipher, they are still thrilling to ferret out. By doing so, we discover how Miura plays with ideas and what historical sources he draws from to fashion his own story. While Falconia certainly evokes ancient Rome at the height of the empire, it is also reminiscent of more recent "architecture of power," like the imposing buildings of 20th century dictatorships and their inhuman urban "utopias." While Falconia is without a doubt magnificent, it nonetheless has martial, menacing proportions. Falconia is not a human-scale city; it is one of divine scale. Moreover, as if to support this totalitarian aspect, Falconia appears after a blast, a sort of explosion of light, evoking all our apocalyptic imaginings of nuclear explosions. I don't need to remind you that Japan is the only country in history to have experienced the horrible reality of a nuclear bomb. One of Miura's final techniques is to have two very distinct representations collide. When the door to Mozgus' torture chamber is closed, it has a decoration on it in the form of an immense face with a gaping mouth, seemingly inspired by a strange stone sculpture in the Gardens of Bomarzo in Italy. Also called the "Park of the Monsters," these gardens, which date back to the Renaissance, are home to some unusual, monumental sculptures. Besides its appearance, it's the name and meaning of this statue that call to mind *Berserk*'s hall of horrors. This piece by Simone Moschino, entitled *Orcus Mouth*, is meant to symbolize the entry into Hell... This reference perfectly foreshadows the atrocities that take place in the manga behind this very door. The victims who pass through it will end up being devoured by a blind god.

Miura's ultimate technique for playing with history is to rewrite it, imagining a secret, alternative history hiding behind the official version. It's a way of filling in the gaps in human knowledge, offering a fanciful and fantastical interpretation. For an example of this, take a look at the stunning passage in which the megaliths of Stonehenge appear in the manga. This is probably the most extreme example of how Miura "plays" with history. Although these stones do indeed exist and have long sparked people's imagination about their purpose and how they were erected, they most certainly were not used for teleportation, as Miura suggests. Put simply, Miura uses the mystery that has long surrounded Stonehenge as a prop in his story: in this way, we get the feeling that Griffith was actually part of history and that his actions in the past are responsible for some of our world's mysteries. In spite of the total improbability of this explanation of Stonehenge, we can tell that it's meant to be an homage to the incredible influence these stones have had on our imagination. Miura's love for making references and filling his story with nods to history ultimately serves to solidify the fantastic nature of *Berserk*. A literary, visual, or cinematic work of art is considered "fantasy" if it "transgresses reality" by incorporating dreams, the supernatural, magic, horror, or science fiction. Basically, without "reality," we can't show what is not real... In other words, for Miura to get us to believe in trolls and dragons, it was essential for him to add a certain realism to his vision of the Middle Ages. Without this impression of a quasi-historical and "credible" story, the fantastic elements in *Berserk* would have less of an impact.

THE DEVIL'S ARCHANGELS

What separates a work that people like from one that becomes a cult classic? Without going out on a limb, we can say that the latter has that extra something that "immerses" us in the story, to the point where it sticks with us for years and we harbor an indescribable love for it. The scene that got me "hooked" on *Berserk*, the one that made me realize that I would love this series much more than most others, was the first appearance of the God Hand... and, more generally, the way in which they were designed. I must confess, at the risk of sounding crazy, and as I've already explained, monsters are much more fascinating than heroes. As just one example, we see this in the success of horror films: everyone goes to see a new installment in the *Nightmare on Elm Street* franchise (the first film in the series, directed by Wes Craven, came out in 1984) to see what mischief Freddy Krueger is getting into now; in *Ring* (Hideo Nakata, 1998), we find ourselves hoping for Sadako to finally crawl out of the screen; and in *The Thing* (John Carpenter, 1982), we remember the creature more than its victims... Monstrosity is the lifeblood of a work of horror. Of course, most often, the "bad guys" are there for the good guys to beat, but we can't deny that the evildoers fascinate us. They embody our most vile impulses. They enjoy a form of total freedom that the heroes do not because their role is to preserve the established order. Demons are more creative than angels. They have greater freedom when it comes to sexuality, impulses, and desire. And even beyond their moral values, we see a particularly fascinating aesthetic differentiation play out in their appearances: a monster can take on any appearance imaginable. Moreover, a monster is not always a bad guy. From Sloth in *The Goonies* (Richard Donner, 1985) to *Elephant Man* (David Lynch, 1980), they can even take on the role of hero. All in all, the figure of the monster, of the enemy, of "evil," is much more fun to work with for a creator than the inflexible, virtuous hero; the monster is the skeleton key that opens up all possibilities. We can say that evil adds depth to a fictional story and, what's more, contemplating a monster relieves, in a way, one of the audience's frustrations: it allows us to "face" that which we will never come across in reality. It gives a face to our unnamed fears. But beyond all of the philosophical and symbolic functions of the evil figure, it's often their "look," their characteristics, and their *modus operandi* that make them iconic. To that point, Miura has succeeded in creating, with his God Hand, perfectly legendary and "cult" enemies, both in terms of their appearance and the mythology that surrounds them. But again, these figures do not come purely from the author's imagination. Indeed, the Guardian Angels of the God Hand seem to bear relation to a family of monsters created not long before the first issue of the manga: the Cenobites. The years 1987 and 1988 saw the successive releases of *Hellraiser* and *Hellbound: Hellraiser II*, two films from the tortured mind of Clive Barker, a rising star at the time in the world of horror literature who made the jump to behind the camera. The films, which Miura says served as inspiration for his God Hand, present a mythology that is both rich and terrifying: it features a mysterious artifact–Lemarchand's box–that supposedly allows its holder to invoke monstrous beings from a diabolical dimension called the Cenobites. Their appearance is ghastly: dressed in black leather suits, the Cenobites look like clergymen who've just come out of a BDSM dungeon maintained by a butcher. While this simile sounds ridiculous, it's actually consistent with Barker's original idea, and when you see the Cenobites on screen, the comparison ceases to be laughable and becomes terrifying. These totally unforgettable and fascinating monsters are different in that they're calm, almost cheerful, and they stand out from all other horror figures of their time thanks to the sensuality and cold cynicism that they project. When the Cenobites pay you a visit, it's to assess your intentions: depending on whether you violate or comply with their deviant moral code, you will either be skinned alive and condemned to Hell or you will join their order of demon lords. We should add a final major element of mythology found in *Hellraiser*: the Hell imagined by Barker does not match classical representations. Indeed, for him, Hell is a giant, cold, blue-tinged labyrinth, as wide as it is deep, with its structures stretching out as far as the eye can see. There's no Satan reigning over this Hell; instead, a huge, floating octahedron serves as its deity. Its name is Leviathan, in tribute to the sea monster from the Bible, as Barker too is a fan of borrowed, intertextual references. The complex architecture of Barker's labyrinth, where the Cenobites lurk, is inspired by two artists. The first is Giovanni Battista Piranesi, an Italian architect and etching artist from the 18th century who produced a series of etchings called *Carceri d'invenzione*, "imaginary prisons," that are absolutely horrifying and which have influenced many an artist. Piranesi sketched immense, stifling jails, filled with chains and hanging cages. The etchings give the feeling of being... in Hell. So, it's no surprise that Barker paid homage to Piranesi in designing his labyrinth. The second artist who served as inspiration for Barker's hellish vision was Maurits Cornelis Escher, a Dutch genius of art, optical illusions, and impossible architecture. Having been a big fan of *Hellraiser* before ever reading *Berserk*, my first encounter with the manga's Guardian Angels gave me an immediate shock: I had finally found a story universe that got close to *Hellraiser*. In *Berserk*, the beherit replaces Lemarchand's box, but it serves the same function: a key used to summon the demon lords. Escher's labyrinth is found in both works, as the

God Hand appear in this same type of architecture, composed of stairways crisscrossing each other in different directions and with impossible trajectories. Finally, the Guardian Angels' looks are astoundingly similar to Barker's work. The God Hand is so inspired by the Cenobites that one of them, Ubik, even has the same glasses as Butterball, the repugnant Cenobite imagined by Barker. Finally, the Idea of Evil, like Barker's Leviathan, is a mass floating in the air and filling Hell with its dark energy. It's as if Miura is delivering his own version of the *Hellraiser* mythology and does so openly. When you ask him if he had direct inspirations, the *mangaka* doesn't hide it:

> "There are many things. Movies like *Hellraiser* and *The Name of the Rose*. I've liked Escher for a very long time. Well, I think Berserk readers would already know this kind of thing from 'behind the scenes' features...[5]"

This is no accident; Miura understood Barker's lesson: what makes a monster successful is the degree of fascination that it can spark. While the *mangaka* also chooses to create entities that give off a macabre, sexual aura, he adds in his own concepts so as not to deliver a simple copy of his model. The main strength of the God Hand is the mystery that shrouds them. Even Flora, knowledgeable though she may be about so many subjects, admits that she doesn't know much about them: "That is one of the great mysteries for those of us who explore the Astral World. What I do know is that they were once human. And that as reincarnations, they are the executors of the will of something lurking in the distant Abyss of the Astral World. Perhaps in that domain, it is unattainable for one to arrive as a person, clad in the ethereal body called ego." The most original thing about this band of demons is their elusive nature: they hide in a parallel dimension and, although they were once humans, no longer have any "tangible" existence in the Physical World. The Skull Knight explains this clearly: "They exist everywhere in this world. Any place negative human thoughts swirl in a large concentration. But at the same time, it can be said that as huge body of thought, they cannot take flesh in this world, thus they exist nowhere." So, how can you kill something that exists nowhere? Moreover, hiding monsters in a different reality gives them an almost extraterrestrial, otherworldly aspect. This "science fiction" aspect is discreetly cultivated by Miura who, as a big fan of the genre, chose to give four of his Guardian Angels names taken from futurist literary works. Void's name is a reference to a book by Frank Herbert, the author of *Dune*, called *Destination: Void*. Slan gets her name from the A.E. van Vogt novel simply entitled: *Slan*. The

---

5. Interview given in December 1996 in Kentaro Miura's studio, published in *Berserk: Illustrations File*. See Bibliography.

novel ... *And Call Me Conrad* (also called *This Immortal* in English) by Roger Zelazny inspired the Guardian Angel of the same name. While these references are more obscure, Ubik probably has the most famous name, getting it from the well-known novel *Ubik* by Philip K. Dick. In the end, it's Miura's way of subliminally giving them names from another space-time, the science-fictional future, that is.

With their Astral nature, these beings are distinguished from monstrous antagonists of a more familiar flavor, like a giant shark or a serial killer, for example, enemies that can be tracked down and killed. The Guardian Angels are beings from another world, one to which we don't have access, beyond our human reach. This gives them an almost divine aspect. Indeed, when he sees them appear, Guts cries out: "Gods... No, are they demons?" He feels torn in the presence of their aura, which is at once terrifying and fascinating. To shroud a bad guy in mystery, it's best to tell the reader as little as possible about them and let the reader's imagination run wild. As the mind is terrified of the unknown, when there's a dark spot in a story, our imagination tries to fill in the "blanks." This is the case with the Guardian Angels. Indeed, given that their human past is unknown—except for Femto/Griffith, who we see transformed and reincarnated—the God Hand is naturally a source of darkness that titillates the morbid side of our imagination: what could these people have done to merit being elevated to the ranks of the evil deities? What did they do with their Crimson Beherit? When we see the crimes Griffith committed with it in order to become a Guardian Angel, we can only imagine the worst. Void is the only one about whom a few snippets of biography are revealed, as he is apparently the oldest and highest ranking of the Guardian Angels. It's implied that he had some sort of conflict with Emperor Gaiseric, who, as we will discuss later on, seemingly became the Skull Knight. It's thought that Void might be the first-ever Guardian Angel, which would explain his ability to generate and administer the Brand of Sacrifice. He also put together an army of apostles as he waited for the other future Guardian Angels to find the Crimson Beherit. However, these are just assumptions as Miura has continued to obscure the origins of the God Hand and the reasons for their transformations. The backstories of Ubik, Slan, and Conrad are a total mystery to us. Since we don't know their biographies, we don't know how they came to be and what motivates them. All we can do is marvel at the extent of their evil powers. Even their way of materializing is hard to comprehend because the God Hand seems to simply need a bit of matter to take form: for example, Conrad uses rats and other vermin to materialize; Slan assumes a body in the bowels of trolls in the depths of the Qliphoth. As such, they have no place of residence or permanent physical existence and they seem to only materialize when they are invoked. The fact that they are part of the ether of the universe only adds to their mystery given that, we assume, this form makes them invincible. During the Eclipse, they emerge from the infinite carpet of tortured faces; during the Incarnation Ceremony, they come out of the black blob that covers Mozgus' lair. This generation from amorphous matter is truly original in the pantheon of horror as few monsters share this special characteristic. The genius of Miura is that he created these demons in the context of a very structured mythology, with, for example, the Angels being called by beherits, their influence over fate, their 216-year and 1,000-year cycles, etc. The God Hand comes in the form of a cosmogonic legend, giving them a mythical aura with touches of grandeur and terror. Giving them a "rank" in a demonic hierarchy, mirroring that of the Church, is a great touch. The hierarchy of Evil in *Berserk* is actually reminiscent of *Star Wars*. The Guardian Angles are, in a way, five monsters on par with Darth Vader; the apostles are analogous to the army of the Galactic Empire; which makes the Idea of Evil equivalent to the Emperor. Since the Idea of Evil was eliminated from the final version of the manga, the reader might be inclined to think that the God Hand is at the top of the hierarchy and that they simply answer to a mysterious entity that no human has ever seen. What is the God Hand's goal? One might be tempted to say that their aim is to spread woe throughout the world. Thus, the advent of Griffith is just another opportunity to torture humanity. With his rebirth, the Physical and Astral planes are united and the God Hand can now manifest in the real world... Slan's tirade during the reincarnation of Griffith gives several clues about their plans: "The time of darkness descends. Wickedness, sacredness. Illusion, reality. Hostility, hope. Hatred, love. The dead, the living. An age when every darkness shall eclipse light. Yes... As when the moon covers the light of the sun. I suppose that's what people will call it afterwards. The age of darkness." They want to put the "dark" in Dark Ages. It's humanity's fall into the most shadowy of possible futures. That said, their plan, which brings about Femto's rebirth as Griffith, seems to bring a sort of peace at first. So, what do they have in store? One of the terrifying elements of the Guardian Angels' toxic aura is their knowledge of human weaknesses. A bit like Freddy Krueger hunting young patients sleeping in a psychiatric hospital, the God Hand waits for the moment when you're most desperate to manifest. Many religions suggest that we find God in life's difficult moments. The Guardian Angels appear in exactly the same context, but instead of providing relief and "forgiving" you, they merrily push you over the edge into the precipice of Evil. They are monsters who will transform you into a monster. This fact makes the God Hand similar to a sort of cult, a secret society of absolute evil, using an arcane ritual that offers you a new identity and new powers, provided that you give up something dear to you as a sacrifice. The God Hand leads a sect in which each new member, in order to join, must abandon their humanity. Like mentors with ill intentions, it manipulates people and Griffith, in particular, bears the brunt of this power just before making his sacrifice during the Eclipse, when the Guardian Angel

Ubik creates a projection of Griffith's mind as a child and, in so doing, takes him on a trip through his past in order to convince him to come to the dark side. One aspect in particular seems to suggest that Ubik is mentally manipulating Griffith: in the dream sequence, Griffith speaks with an old weaver woman. At the end of the dream, we see Ubik wearing a mask of the old woman, suggesting that it was actually him playing a part in order to deceive the young Falcon. The same thing happened to Rosine, an abused child who left home to become an elf, seeking a better life, but who realized much too late that the God Hand had tricked her, transforming her into a demon instead of the elf she had hoped to be... Dishonest, vile, and manipulative, as repugnant as they are seductive, the God Hand forms an apocalyptic sect that worships the very idea of Evil. Finally, the Guardian Angels have a role as military leaders, as they command the legions of apostles that they themselves created. Incidentally, the Eclipse is presented as a feast to reward the apostles, an offering from the God Hand to its faithful servants. Now that we've examined the little that we know about the Guardian Angels, an important question remains: are these infinite, corruptive beings invincible? It seems that only the Dragon Slayer is capable of doing them harm, as this blade has drawn more apostle blood than any other and, during their face-off in the Qliphoth, Guts even manages to stab Slan with the giant sword. The Guardian Angels of the God Hand are memorable enemies, of the kind that one never forgets once they've seen them at work, and I must confess that I religiously await their next appearance...

THE CEREMONIES OF THE GOD HAND

The sinister Guardian Angels, the manga's antagonists, appear first and foremost during "ceremonies." There are multiple types of ceremonies, following different cycles. The first type is "normal" ceremonies, those that bring about the transformation of a human into an apostle. For this to happen, the human needs an ordinary beherit, some blood (or tears), and the blessing of "causality" for the Guardian Angels to grant them an audience and carry out their deepest desire. The price to be paid is always the same: offer the life of a loved one in exchange. Given the astronomical number of apostles that appear in the series, we can assume that this type of ceremony happens quite frequently. As such, it's only logical that they do not follow a specific cycle. On the contrary, another type of ceremony, the Eclipse, occurs at a regular interval: every 216 years. It is highly unlikely that Kentaro Miura chose this number at random. That would be too great of a coincidence, as 216 subtly hides a satanic symbol ($6 \times 6 \times 6 = 216$). So, this cycle conceals the number of the Beast; if it was chosen at random, then I would have to believe that the *mangaka* is unknowingly guided by a demon. It is totally consistent for the author to want to give his cycle a hidden dimension, a masked arithmetic. While researching cycles used in history or in beliefs, I stumbled upon a stunning bit of information, but it's one that, in my opinion, may not have influenced Miura, though I wouldn't put it past him. In Antiquity, when a person wanted to invoke spirits, they had two opposing practices they could rely on: theurgy, the magical art of communicating with the gods to carry out a noble purpose, or goetia, the art of conjuring demons. The very definition of ancient theurgy is reminiscent of the Guardian Angels' ceremony in a quite eerie way: theurgy is defined as the set of mystical rituals and practices enabling the soul to fuse mystically with higher beings: heroes, gods, demons, angels... or guardian angels, for example. By offering sacrifices or invocations, a person could achieve "unity with the divine" via mystical ecstasy. That is the exact nature of the ceremonies imagined by Miura. However, the most uncanny similarity relates to the ideas of the Neoplatonic philosopher Proclus (born circa 412 CE), who practiced theurgy. Proclus firmly believed that he was the reincarnation of Nicomachus of Gerasa (who died in 196 CE) and he also believed that the period of time between two incarnations of a soul was... 216 years. This was a belief in transmigration of the soul: the idea that a soul passes from one body to another, or more generally, certain elements of the soul pass from the body to new forms of existence. We see this at work in the transformation of the apostles, but it is even more representative of the Eclipse, taking place every 216 years. Coincidence? All of the apostles are summoned to this grand banquet, as the sacrifices will be served up to them. "The time has come... The time of the great nocturnal festival! The feast that happens once every 216 years. The Eclipse!" More specifically, this gathering marks the birth of a new Guardian Angel and requires a special beherit called the Crimson Beherit or the Egg of the King. The one that we see in the manga consecrates Femto as the fifth member of the God Hand, which "receives" Griffith's soul after he sacrifices his entire band. This is the price exacted to make sure that any last traces of humanity left in the person who wants to join the forces of Evil are wiped away. It is a way of signing their pact, showing that you are truly ready to give everything up. During this ceremony, the sacrificed victims are marked with the Brand of Sacrifice. Their despair is used as fuel for the transmigration of the demon's soul. These ceremonies are always the site of Shakespearean tragedies in which the disoriented victims are faced with all of the treachery of which the person they trusted is capable. The metaphor of the solar eclipse is very well chosen, as the way in which the moon eclipses the sun is the perfect symbol of the triumph of darkness over light, of vice over virtue. When an Eclipse takes place, reality is plunged into darkness, as if time itself has stopped. The phenomenon of heavenly bodies aligning is rare and gives off a mystical aura in which certain cultures have seen an apocalyptic omen. Moreover, although Puck says it with a joking tone, his remark is quite frightening and ultimately fits well with the reality of the manga: "I'll bet some big god or devil or somethin' is peekin' through that hole." Finally, there is a third type of ceremony that occurs every 1,000 years: the Incarnation Ceremony. During this event, a Guardian Angel takes on human form, which is exactly what Femto does, being reborn as Griffith with all of his physical and mental abilities recovered. The first time the reader encounters a ceremony in the series is in volume 3, the second time that the Count invokes the Guardian Angels. When the beherit is activated, the palace in which Guts finds himself is transformed into a surreal setting. Stairways overlap each other infinitely in what looks like a three-dimensional labyrinth. Guts, Puck, and Theresia are dumbfounded by this magnificent yet terrifying environment. The Count, on the other hand, knows exactly what's happening because he's already been through a ceremony: this impossible architecture heralds the coming of the Guardian Angels. They stand on platforms that seem to have different centers of gravity, further accentuating the nightmarish nature of the scene. In the real world, during the ceremony, a giant vortex hangs over the city where the palace is located, seemingly a portal allowing the demons to pass through. As such, we know that these ceremonies are not dreams or hallucinations; they are events that take place in reality. The apostle ceremony appears to create a pathway between the Astral World and the Physical World, forming a direct passage to Hell. The Eclipse, on the other hand, follows slightly different rules, with apparently another protocol at work. While, similar to the apostle ceremony, you need to "awaken" the beherit with blood, what follows is quite distinct. In this case, the humans are not transported to a gravity-defying labyrinth; instead, reality itself is transformed before our eyes. What was previously an expanse of water turns into a lake of blood. From the ground emerge faces that grow, like dunes of flesh, until they reach the size of mountains. The sky undergoes the same transformation, a tapestry of deathly faces covering the heavens. After just a few moments, we feel like we've been transported to the depths of Hell. Unlike during an ordinary ceremony, during the Eclipse, all of the apostles are summoned. It is a gathering that closes with a beastly feast in which the main dish is made of poor souls trapped in this "portable" hell. What's more, the Guardian Angels do not make their entry in the same way they would during a normal ceremony. While during a run-of-the-mill ceremony they simply appear in the labyrinth, during the Eclipse, they take form from the setting itself, materializing from the matter there. For example, one of the "face-dunes" is actually Slan's head, which emerges bit by bit from the infinite quilt of faces; Ubik, meanwhile, falls from the sky like a huge, viscous raindrop; Conrad also emerges from the ground, his body composed of an agglomeration of faces; finally, Void's head materializes from the black hole of the Eclipse, with the demon's body taking shape around it. As such, this event offers a much more organic and tormented backdrop than the cold architecture in which the apostle ceremonies take place. The fact that there are thousands of apostles gives the Eclipse scene an even more Dantean and demonic aura. Just after the apparition of the Guardian Angels, an enormous right hand suddenly emerges from the ocean of tormented faces to serve as the Angels' throne, overlooking the apocalyptic scene from a dizzying height. This is the God Hand. Seen from the outside, from reality, the Eclipse resembles a gargantuan tornado, one slightly different from the one seen during the Count's second ceremony. The Eclipse tornado, which assumes the shape of two bells stacked on top of each other, looks much bigger and its summit disappears into the heavens. Even the clouds are sucked into the powerful movement of the cyclone, the eye of which holds the ceremony, allowing it to remain hidden from the outside world. The power of the insane visions and of the dramatic deaths that occur during the Occultation is such that volumes 12 and 13 have become *Berserk* classics. In fact, for fans, it's not unusual when you meet a new reader to ask them if they've already gotten past these volumes so that you can find out what they thought of these dark, indelible events. It's a bit like *Berserk* really starts at the moment of the Eclipse.

TEARS OF THE BEHERIT

One of the central points in the saga has to do with mysterious artifacts: the beherits. They have an ovular shape; one of them is even called the "Egg of the King." These strange objects have designs on them that look like the parts of a human face: eyes, nose, mouth, etc., all placed randomly across the egg. The beherits have two phases: active or inactive. Most of the time, they're harmless, as if they're "sleeping," and they just look like carved stones. Puck even says: "It's really well made. It's Art... yeah, Art!" The beherit's other phase is when it's activated: when that happens, the scattered designs begin to move across the surface of the egg to come together as a face. From the wide-open eyes flow rivers of thick blood; the mouth opens in a grimace of suffering. These are the signs that the ceremony is set to begin. The very nature of the beherit is hard to nail down, as it fluctuates between inert material and living organ, as Guts explains: "Well, it may be alive, but it's no danger in its current state! Let's say it's a kind of a tool." It's not an artifact that one can trigger at will. There's no known "instruction manual" for it, as no sacred text, even among the most ancient, makes reference to it. There's no mechanism to get it working or invocation to be used. The beherit will awake at a precise moment and for a designated person as causality decides. Besides working in mysterious ways, we also don't know the origins of the beherits. Their dual nature as both object and creature raises questions about their "conception." Are they produced by some strange artisan who brings objects to life with a magical incantation? Or could they be macabre eggs laid by a creature that we have yet to see? Maybe they're generated by the universe itself in other dimensions? Vargas, the scientist who stole the Count's beherit, admits that he has been unable to discover its origins: "Since then, seven years have passed. During that time, I've tirelessly researched every aspect of religion and the occult. But I could never uncover a single clue about the nature of this thing." So, even after diving into the occult, this eminent researcher hasn't gotten anywhere. And yet, discovering the origins of the beherits would likely give us a more comprehensive view of the Machiavellian plan in which they take part and of how they fit into that scheme. We learn a little more about the nature of beherits from Flora when she describes them as keys that connect the Physical World with the deepest (and thus darkest) layer of the Astral World, thus enabling contact with the five infamous Guardian Angels. More interesting still, Flora describes the beherits as ultimate spiritual beings that control the fate of humans. By leaving these objects shrouded in mystery, Kentaro Miura demonstrates a perfect balancing act in the way in which he incorporates them into his plot: these objects are so powerful, so central to the story, and at the same time so enigmatic that they make our imaginations run wild. Each time the author delivers new information about the nature of the beherits, it brings with it new mysteries and a new batch of questions. The beherits are like the magic lamp from the story *Aladdin and the Wonderful Lamp* from *One Thousand and One Nights*, which allows the holder to call on a genie to grant a wish. Except that, in this case, you can't simply rub the beherit; you have to spill a little blood on it and have reached a certain level of frustration or despair for the egg to come to life, offering you a sinister way forward ("The wailing of your soul, which could never be eased by the gods of this world, opened up a portal to another dimension"). Just as there are different types of ceremonies, there are several different "keys" for opening this dimensional portal. The "classic" beherits are given to all humans destined to become apostles. As Ubik says: "After all, all the apostles gathered here used Beherits to obtain their proper form." They come in colors that range from gray-blue to green, depending on the depiction, and are apparently reusable, as the Count proves. However, the Count refuses to sacrifice his daughter Theresia during his second ceremony. As a punishment, he is swallowed up by the Vortex of Souls... So, the beherit's demands are not to be taken lightly. While at times the rules governing the usage of these evil "toys" may seem vague, they are actually a quite specific set of instructions. The egg that proves to have the most elaborate way of working is the "Crimson Beherit," intended for the "conquering king." Indeed, it comes to life after a certain period of time and only for a specific individual chosen by causality, the *Berserk* term for fate. Once all the conditions are met, this egg opens a portal to the Abyss of the Astral World, allowing the Eclipse to begin.

As such, it is a very special key held by Griffith, as the Guardian Angels confirm: "Furthermore, the Beherit you hold is no ordinary Beherit. Only one who can be reborn as one of us, the Guardian Angels of the God Hand, receives it. The Crimson Beherit. The Egg of the King." We should note that the beherit works to protect its bearer, as it saves Griffith from death by preventing a poisoned arrow from piercing his chest. Nothing is to interfere with fate and the beherit makes sure of this.

One of the plot challenges in regards to beherits was to find a credible way for them to make it into the hands of the chosen ones because these artifacts must be obtained naturally, or at the very least incorporated into the story coherently. First, we should note that a beherit cannot be used "universally"; it is person-specific. An egg is destined for a particular person and anyone else who wants to use it will not gain access to its powers. Griffith tells us that he bought his in his youth from an old fortune-teller just passing through town, without knowing its true nature. Similarly, the Kushan Emperor Ganishka received his as a gift from a "sadhu," an ascetic who remains anonymous. A commonality between the future Guardian Angel and apostle: both despots obtained their beherits from occult sources tied to forms of divination. Did the "magi" who passed on the beherits to these two characters know what they were doing or was it purely chance? Later in the manga, the creature referred to as the "Egg of the Perfect World" discovers its beherit in a castle's garbage heap while searching for something to eat. The Count, on the other hand, buys his from a merchant in a traveling caravan who says that he found it in an antique store in a town in the East. So, beherits can travel around and use "chance" as a channel to reach their intended owners. However, the natural mode of transport most often used by these stones is simply water, like Rosine's beherit, which she finds "by the river." Even more striking, we witness the aquatic "journey" of a beherit. When Griffith is arrested and is being tortured, his torturer notices the pendant that he wears. Intrigued by the beherit, the torturer holds it in his hands, but as this egg is not intended for him, it escapes him and falls in the sewer. We see it float away into the darkness, thinking that the artifact is lost forever. In the next volume, we discover that the pendant is lying in the bed of a river that the sewers must have drained into. A year later, when Griffith is going to trigger the Eclipse, he falls precisely in the spot of shallow water where the beherit was waiting, as if by magic. This lucky find in the "guiding" water gives the impression that an invisible force guides the destiny of these cursed eggs and that same force seems to use nature to discretely convey these objects of misfortune. Once the beherit finds its predestined host, it waits for the right moment to transform. The beherit most likely has an effect on its carrier even before it comes to life, but it's once the key is activated and has opened a portal to Hell that it forever changes the carrier's nature and fate. There are rare occasions where

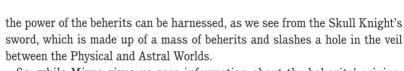

the power of the beherits can be harnessed, as we see from the Skull Knight's sword, which is made up of a mass of beherits and slashes a hole in the veil between the Physical and Astral Worlds.

So, while Miura gives us zero information about the beherits' origins, certain references offer some interesting clues. Following the trend of references to Satanism, the word "beherit" comes from the ancient Syriac language and translates to "devil"... Given what we know about the evil god Miura revealed in his deleted chapter, we can imagine that the author wanted to create these artifacts to be a sort of virus, a distillation of pure evil, a vector for causality. Diabolical or not, the beherit is the kind of thing you'd find "in the storeroom of the Museum of Horrors," as Puck puts it (in the French version), on the shelf next to other famous evil artifacts from fiction, like the VHS tape from *Ring* that causes the death of anyone who watches it, or the ring that contains the power of Sauron and corrupts Middle-earth in Tolkien's famous series. Comics and mangas are brimming with this type of dangerous magical object. However, Kentaro Miura's greatest influence can likely be found in the Lemarchand's boxes from the mind of Clive Barker, as mentioned previously. To explain this point, I must take a moment to stress the uncanny resemblance between the beherits and the Lemarchand's boxes. Indeed, the boxes, most often cubic in shape, are keys that, once activated, open a portal to another dimension, allowing evil entities to enter the real world. In *Hellraiser*, there is a very rich and complex backstory to where these objects came from and how they work, but in both authors we see careful attention paid to the design of these story devices. The boxes, like the beherits, are incredible tools for storytelling, triggering action that is at once harrowing and fascinating. In both sagas, the artifacts are intended for chosen ones, humans selected by a terrifying, unseen force. While the *Hellraiser* films are Barker's best-known works, there are numerous comic books in his extended universe. In these comics, the reader discovers that the Lemarchand's boxes have been passed down through the ages and have found themselves in many different pairs of hands. For example, one of those pairs belonged to a knight returning from the Crusades who brought back one of these boxes, allowing him to call on the Cenobites. This episode could have fit in perfectly in the *Berserk* universe as they share so many concepts. However, instead of creating a mechanism crafted by an artisan, Miura chose to focus on the symbolism of the egg. On that point, I can't help but think of the age-old conundrum: which came first, the chicken or the egg? The Guardian Angel Ubik, without saying it outright, makes reference to this dilemma while speaking to Griffith during the Eclipse: "From the moment you took possession of that Crimson Beherit, you had the qualities to become a demon. No. Perhaps I should say that because you had those qualities, it fell into your hands. That you used the beherit to summon us is evidence that you are qualified to be our kinsman." Is the bearer of the beherit under the influence of an all-powerful extrinsic evil or are they personally the source of that evil? The symbolism attached to eggs in general is quite rich in meaning, making it a perfect choice for the beherits. As the first stage of life, the egg symbolizes fertility, rebirth, and protection, and in many myths, it is associated with the birth of the world. Given the "dimensional" effects of the Crimson Beherit, it's interesting to compare it to this snippet from Chinese mythology, as told by Xu Zheng in his *Story of Three Sovereigns and Five Emperors*: "The sky and the earth were mixed, like a chicken egg; Pangu was in the middle. After 18,000 years, the sky and earth separated: the pure yang became the sky and the troubled yin became the earth. Pangu, in the middle, transformed nine times every day, the divine joining the sky and the demonic joining the earth." While it has been the subject of numerous beliefs, magical rituals, and superstitions, the egg can also symbolize the renewal of nature; in particular, that's what we celebrate with the tradition of Easter eggs. However, the symbolism of eggs most relevant to *Berserk* has to be gestation and rebirth. Any person who owns a beherit is a demon in the making, a disaster waiting to hatch. Once the ceremony begins, that person must break the shell of their humanity by sacrificing their loved ones in order to be reborn with a new form. This idea of an evil egg hatching is even more fitting in the case of Griffith, as he transforms into Femto and his wings form an egg-shaped shield around him. Covered in blood, he cries out like a chick that's just hatched. Along different lines, the very principle of an egg can be found in Casca's pregnancy when, during the Eclipse, Femto rapes the young woman and thus "inseminates" the fetus with evil, transforming it into a future demon. Clearly, the egg motif was not chosen randomly by the author when designing his beherit.

CAUSALITY ACCORDING TO MIURA

"On that day, something beyond human comprehension
was set in motion."

The obscure notion of "causality" is the philosophical "backbone" of *Berserk*. Throughout his manga, Miura asks these essential questions: Do we have a destiny already written for us? If so, are events all tied together to lead us to a predestined moment? Is it possible to veer away from this destiny? And, above all, who (or what) decides what will happen, and for what purpose? In philosophy as in science, causality refers to the relationship of cause and effect. In the manga, causality is a "force" that influences a person's fate and decisions throughout their life. Causality is hidden in the smallest of details. As if writing an essay on philosophy, Miura clearly lays out the central question of Berserk on a particular page of volume 5, introducing the chapter "The

Wind of Swords": "In this world, is the destiny of mankind controlled by some transcendental entity or law? Is it like the hand of god hovering above? Can men free themselves by their own will?" These sentences are illustrated in an absolutely iconic fashion: a giant, demonic hand seems to emerge from a strange fog; we don't know if it consists of heavenly clouds or smoke from hell. Held by the claw-like, skeletal demon fingers: a beherit, the bloody cog in the machinery of destiny. The author peppers his story with clues leading us to this observation: we are all–as far as we can tell–puppets of causality. However, as the story progresses, we discover that this notion is complex and that not everyone receives equal treatment under this force: some serve causality while others suffer it. To untangle the threads of causality and attempt to understand it more clearly, you have to gather the fragments of information scattered throughout the series. Several of these tell us that Guts is one of the key pieces in an immense puzzle, of which he knows neither the exact size nor the image it forms. The Black Swordsman often comes across characters–both friends and foes–who seem to know more about his destiny than he does. Of course, nothing is ever said very clearly, but beings like Zodd the Immortal and the Skull Knight are constantly dropping cryptic phrases on Guts about his impending death or the future misdeeds of the God Hand. Moreover, Guts seems to end up convinced of this himself, believing he is the armed toy of destiny: "No... Actually, compared to what my hand's touched, my sword's touched a thousand times more." Many other elements back up this idea that there is no free will, that each individual story is already written out. What's sure is that this infamous force seems to be neither benevolent nor positive. When Guts says, "Unfortunately, there's no way for man to change the course of this festival. We already subsist within the current of causality," he's speaking about destiny as if it were a mighty river in which humans are swept away, soon to be pulled under. We never get the slightest hint of hope in the foreshadowing of what's to come. Additionally, it seems that "negotiating" with this force is not an option, as the Count tells us, associating it with a higher power: "Divine providence cannot be thwarted by man's effort." It's during the Eclipse that many events begin to make sense. It's at that point that we understand that myriad little invisible bricks have long been stacking up to form the bloody wall that is the Eclipse. It's Void who reveals the truth and confirms our fears of powerlessness against destiny: "All lies within the currents of causality! Everything has been determined. All of your lives have been spun into this sacred point in time, the Eclipse." Incidentally, this surprise is not for lack of forewarning: prophecies are legion in *Berserk* and many future events are announced in advance, as we see with the Egg of the Perfect World when he tells Luca: "All are omens pointing to that time." The time he's referring to is the Eclipse, and the Skull Knight straight-out describes it for us in volume 9, four volumes before it occurs: "So, the gears have indeed begun turning. You struggler, take heed. One year hence shall be the time of the Eclipse. You and your friends! Those yet unseen of the fleshless flesh! And that unkingly half of yours shall all be gathered in that place. A torrent of madness. A tempest of death for which the human body could never atone shall sweep over you!" With these prophetic words, we can clearly see that the story has been written in advance. Other more subtle signs are hidden throughout the manga, like when the Band of the Falcon is renamed the White Phoenix Knights. As the phoenix is a mythical bird capable of being reborn from its own ashes, how could we not interpret this name as a sign of what will happen to Griffith? His physical and mystical rebirth, which takes him from the bowels of a dungeon where he endures a thousand tortures to the pinnacle of power in the great Falconia, is that not phoenix-like? While specific actions lead to others and eventually wind up at a particular fate, choices that are not the result of an individual's will also count. For example, if Guts had stayed by Casca's side after the Eclipse, maybe he could have prevented her from closing herself off in an injured, infantile, solitary mutism. Similarly, the King of Midland could have made a more strategic choice when he discovered that Griffith and his daughter had slept together. The Falcon was already his preferred successor and he could have demanded a marriage to seal the union and "wash away the insult"; however, the King's anger—or is it causality?—causes him to act irrationally. It's out of a dumb decision by the King that Griffith begins his transformation into a demonic god and destiny takes its course. Even worse, our actions sometimes have the opposite effect of what was intended. This is the case for the Skull Knight, who, intending to use his sword to save the world, ultimately pushes it in the enemy's direction by unintentionally creating the great tree and Falconia. This demonstrates the power of causality: even a character as omniscient as the Skull Knight is a slave to it. Incidentally, he recognizes as much in coded language while speaking to Zodd: "Void would say that this too lies within causality's current." Even if we could change the course of events, it wouldn't necessarily be desirable. That's what's implied in a dialog between Puck and a fortune-teller when the elf asks the old woman why she didn't stop Rickert, even though she had just seen in the future "a terrible omen" regarding him. By warning him, she could have saved him from a cruel fate. However, her response suggests that causality is a force that's much harder to control than Puck imagines: "No, we mustn't. The boy has a large effect on this gathering. That he was here now is itself evidence of that. It's his fate. To interfere recklessly in one's fate is against my principles. No, it's impossible to do such things in the first place. Everyone is how they are, how they must be." From this, we can deduce that the *Berserk* universe is the realm of synchronicity: in the analytical psychology of Carl Jung, synchronicity is the "simultaneous occurrence of at least two events that do not show any link of causality, but whose association has meaning for the person perceiving them." If you believe in synchronicity, it means that there is no randomness, that everything happens for a reason, and that each person must be in a specific place at a specific time for destiny to unfold as planned. Finally, the fortune-teller implies that people have absolutely no power to influence such a force because it is much greater than them. "After all, what determines a good omen or bad omen is human reason. None are able to measure the ways of God." It appears that causality is not as easy to understand as one might think. What's clear is that people/beings do not all receive equal treatment from causality: it has its victims... and its chosen ones. These "chosen ones" include, notably, those who are given an audience with the Guardian Angels. The most common of such cases is that of the apostles, who, by activating their beherits, trigger a ceremony. For example, Void tells the count that he was "chosen by causality" because he was ripe for the picking, desperate enough, fate seemingly relying on people's unspoken desires and weaknesses in order to carry out a secret, grand plan. Another example, during the Eclipse, Void tells Griffith: "Thee, honorable child consecrated by the laws of causality. The Falcon. Thou art the chosen one. At this time, in this place, the one chosen by the hand of the great God." These people are "chosen" by a force because that force has an objective. That means that destiny has, in a way, a political aim. I'm sure we'll have to wait for the end of the manga to find out what the ultimate plan is. Maybe we'll even be surprised and causality will turn out to have been leading to a positive goal, in spite of the horrors needed to reach that destiny. What we can say for sure is that characters' actions are not isolated or without consequence: all of the story's humans are connected to each other by the invisible ties of an ancient force. Puck appears to confirm this: "All lies within the causal current or somethin' like that? [...] I guess it's like we're all tied together by a red thread of destiny."

While everything seems to converge on the idea of an inevitable destiny of which no one can change the course, Miura implies with other clues that, perhaps, certain unforeseen "anomalies" can disturb this flow of events... First and foremost, there's the infamous Eclipse, which was supposed to kill Guts, but partly failed. "Destiny. Destiny. Destiny. Shut the hell up! [...] Tell 'em leavin' me half-eaten is gonna be the end of you!" He and Casca managed to escape this deadly ambush, making them the wrench in a machine that was supposed to be well-oiled. The Skull Knight concedes that causality is not an exact science: "Though minute singular details certainly can occur at the time junction point that even they can't predict." It would even seem that escaping fate offers you a special status. Indeed, while Guts is condemned to suffer constant threats from the Interstice, this rift between the worlds may actually give him special powers: "Furthermore, that brand carved into you. It may be of unanticipated aid. [...] It's merely half a step, but you are outside the reason of the world." So, does that mean that causality has a sort of sphere of influence that a lucky few people manage to escape from? It's fascinating to see how this question is a subject of debate, including among the Guardian Angels, the very "administrators" of causality. When the Skull Knight and his mount break the circle of darkness that covers the sun, he interrupts the Eclipse and manages to save Guts and Casca at the last second. The Guardian Angels, surprised by this unforeseen turn of events, argue about the fallibility of causality. Ubik wonders aloud: "Astounding! Fascinating! How unforeseen! An unpredictable thing happens at the temporal junction point. Albeit an extremely minute thing... It's impossible to anticipate everything. We ourselves are not gods, after all." Thus, the future is not set in stone and has surprises in store, even for those who believe to be masters of it. Slan tries to downplay those surprises by calling them "trivial," believing they are of no consequence. She compares Guts' escape to a fish jumping out of the river: while the fish can fly free for a few seconds, ultimately it will come back down to be swept by the current. In the overall context of the manga, this is both true and false. If you consider *Berserk* to be the story of Griffith's ascension from being a nobody to being a demigod, then Guts is the only person to have interfered in that perfect rise. Moreover, Griffith admits this himself: "You're the only one who made me forget my dream." The Black Swordsman is the only person to have made the Falcon deviate from the fate that seemed to have been laid out for him in his "channel" of causality. One can even wonder if Guts might have defied fate from the moment of his birth, having been born from a woman who had just died. As if some force–perhaps another, more positive side of causality–had ensured that he entered the world, in spite of it all, for him to foil the plans of Griffith and the Guardian Angels. In this way, Guts is, in a manner of speaking, an affront to destiny. From another perspective, the Black Swordsman proves Slan right in her theory of the powerless fish because, in spite of his efforts, he did not succeed in stopping the transformation of his friend into a demon, nor his resurrection to become the despot of Midland. Truly, only the manga's ending will tell us whether or not it is possible to change the course of the destinies laid out since the beginning of time. Until then, Miura's concept of causality is fascinating in the way that it creates a sort of "invisible mechanism." Philosopher David Hume explained this idea quite elegantly. He used the analogy of billiard balls: we see the movement of one ball, then the movement of a second ball struck by the first, but we do not see the active energy, the effective power, the cause that produces the movement: "All events seem entirely loose and separate. One event follows another; but we never can observe any tie between them." In the manga, we get the strong impression that causality according to Miura also follows secret laws and plans of which we will never see anything, other than the consequences. That's the real strength and drama of this concept: it is almighty and imperceptible. If someone were to tell you that an invisible force governs your actions and decisions, you would have a thousand questions: Who pulls the strings of causality? For what purpose? To believe in causality often requires faith, which is the basis for all religions. Most believers might say that God is invisible, but he watches over them and has a "plan." That's probably why Miura decided to delete chapter 83, which revealed the source of causality, so that its mechanism would remain invisible. As soon as you reveal something, it loses its mystery; people stop having "faith." So that we as readers could keep developing theories, the *mangaka* made sure that the ways of the Lord would remain mysterious. Hidetaka Miyazaki would agree: the more fascinating gray areas a story has, the more room there is for readers to use their imaginations. However, above all, it could be that Miura does not want to answer the age-old question that comes with the issue of "freedom of choice." This question, which is at the heart of Christianity, has to do with "free will." Does it really exist? Do we, as human beings, have control over our own destiny? When Adam and Eve were expelled from paradise, they found themselves left to their own devices with the burden of freedom: they had to make their own choices. "God bestows upon us fate. But it is the children of men who choose it." In this quotation, Flora makes reference to the Christian view, unheard of for a witch. However, she says something that's even more interesting and almost upends the principle of causality: "People may appear to repeat the same mistakes, but karma is by no means a circle. Indeed, it is a spiral." Perhaps the story is cyclical and, in spite of the repetitions and the yoke of destiny, new choices will be possible?

We've seen how causality forces numerous micro-events to all converge on the same, predetermined end point. Coupled with this idea, Miura brings up another pattern later in the series: the butterfly effect. According to this law, the beating of a butterfly's wings can cause a hurricane on the other side of the world, suggesting that a minuscule event can have huge consequences. It's Puck who puts this idea out there: "A small whirlwind blown from this island, would sweep up many fates before returning as a raging tempest. [...] 'tis I, someone who swallows up everyone around them in a great maelstrom of destiny." Two paradoxical worldviews seem to clash here. Is it that, no matter what you do, everything converges on a single, unalterable point, or can an isolated action change the course of events in unforeseeable ways? Perhaps the manga's conclusion will provide an answer, but it's very unlikely that Miura will be able to resolve an unsolvable philosophical dilemma that goes back to the beginning of time.

LIVING WITH THE BRAND OF SACRIFICE

"Those branded with that become an offering to
those of the darkness until their dying breath."

In the first few volumes of the manga, we see that Guts bears a strange "tattoo," a singular mark that begins to bleed when demons approach. While a few mysterious hints are delivered early on, we have to wait until the Eclipse to learn the nature and origins of the mark. Let's go back to the context of a ceremony: using their beherit, a human invokes the Guardian Angels and asks them to make their dream come true. In exchange, the Angels ask the human for a sacrifice: the people they cherish more than anything in the world. Once the victims have been designated, the ritual can begin, and that's where the brand comes in. It seems that Void is the only one who can carve it into the bodies of the future sacrifices, doing so by conjuring in his skeletal hands a sort of shining hologram in the shape of the brand. Once a certain dose of energy has built up, the shape rises up above the Angel. Then, in a sort of fireworks display, Void announces that the thread of causality has just been spun. Suddenly, a multitude of undulating rays emanate from the brand to shoot off, like shooting stars, to seek their target. Each ray, like an evil spermatozoid, heads off to brand a mark on each of the victims designated for the ritual. While Guts' mark is branded on his neck, that's not the case for everyone: Judeau gets it on his hand, Pippin on his forearm, Corkus on his forehead, and Casca... over her heart. With this brand, the deal made by the apostle is sealed. Then, a process of dark magic begins: the branding catalyzes a power that will enable the advent of a new Guardian Angel ("They become food for the new child of darkness") or the transformation of a human into an apostle. Once this energy has been collected during the ritual, the millions of monsters in attendance at the ceremony jump on the poor condemned souls bearing the mark of death, finally allowed to feast on the flesh of these chosen victims. The metaphor of branded cattle fits perfectly here: this practice used by ranchers involves marking the animals in a herd using a white-hot brand; each ranch has its own symbol so that the livestock don't get mixed up. When he is branded, we see on Guts a smoking burn mark, exactly as if he had been marked with a cattle brand. And, just like cows on a ranch, the bearers of the Brand of Sacrifice are also destined for slaughter. In the way that the blood of a fish in the water drives a shark into a frenzy, the apostles watching the ritual go after the brands so that they can devour the people bearing them. Once branded, a person becomes an "offering," a macabre gift ready to be engulfed in terrible suffering. This is how most of the Band of the Falcon is decimated during the Occultation, and at that point we finally know how Guts and Casca, the only two survivors, got this characteristic mark. Although they escaped from this monstrous feast, our two heroes' nightmare was just beginning, as the brand then works as a curse: monsters constantly hunt Guts and Casca, attracted by their tattoos, which act like GPS beacons. Any monster nearby detects the brand and its bearer will never again live in peace, as the Skull Knight explains to Guts shortly after the Eclipse: "The brand of sacrifice. It has drawn those of darkness. [...] After all, to them you are a torch tossed into the darkness. No doubt you shine through brilliantly for them. This is the reality that you must walk through from here on. A world invisible to eyes of the flesh. You must stand in the interval between two worlds that, while mutually significant, do not make contact with each other. That is the destiny of those who receive the brand of sacrifice. Your body, your every last drop of blood in it, has been given as an offering to those of the darkness." No one is supposed to survive this ritual; thus, it's an extremely unusual case to see two humans wandering the real world after being branded. It's even so surprising that they are admired by the apostles. The Count tells Guts, during a fight, that he would never have expected to come across a living creature bearing this mark. In fact, surviving this branding makes you different from all other humans: if you are branded, you live in the "Interstice," where the creatures of the Astral World can come and try to eat you. The brand has an infectious dimension to it: the mark is like an incurable disease, with no hope of getting better or finding relief from its symptoms, because living in the Interstice means that you have to fight monstrous, spectral visions that only you can see, pushing you away from society as you flirt with insanity. As Guts often says, being a companion to a bearer of the mark exposes you to a violent and certain death. As we've seen, the brand itself produces a sort of allergic reaction when apostles are near, with the scar beginning to ooze blood as they approach.

The brand's tragic dimension is quite convenient for Miura in terms of story-telling and visuals. *Berserk* is not the only work to explore the advantages of such a device; another example is the video game *Silent Hill*, in which the radio you carry begins to crackle and produce a stress-inducing white noise whenever a monster is in the vicinity. So, the only advantage for Guts is that the scar allows him to "sense" an enemy; he can even tell how dangerous the threat is based on the pain he feels or how much he bleeds ("for lesser demons, you might feel little more than a needle pick," but it's implied that the brand can kill its bearer if the approaching evil is too strong). As the mark serves as a lure for the apostles, Miura doesn't need to justify their sudden appearances: by nature, they are attracted to the branded person. If Guts just sits around a campfire or walks through a forest, a multitude of ravenous abominations will show up for no other reason. This injury that serves as a detector is a motif found in many other story universes. For example, young Harry Potter, the hero of the saga by the same name written by J. K. Rowling, feels pain in the scar on his forehead when Voldemort is nearby; there's Captain Ahab from

Herman Melville's *Moby Dick* (1851), who gets sensations in his wooden leg when the whale Moby Dick approaches his ship. The brands on Guts and Casca build a certain tension: if the brand bleeds, the reader knows that something horrible is about to happen. As such, it's an ideal tool for preparing readers for a violent scene and for building terrifying suspense without really showing anything. Even the design of the Brand of Sacrifice is not without meaning: its shape seems to be related to Futhark, the oldest form of runic alphabet. It appears that Miura superimposed several runic characters to create his own symbol. This choice of alphabet is not random: runes are commonly used in magical folklore for the purposes of divination. As such, using a "magical" alphabet is a great way for Miura to serve his purpose: the Brand is a curse placed on a person that will stick with them until their death. We can't finish with this topic without highlighting the fact that the Brand of Sacrifice is also a superb "logo," the *mangaka* creating an emblematic symbol to be associated with his series. How many T-shirts do you think have been sold with this runic symbol on them? How many fans have gotten themselves tattooed with one on their arms or even their necks, as a tribute to the Black Swordsman? It's hard to say if the author took this sort of thing into consideration ahead of time, but what's clear is that the Brand of Sacrifice is an essential piece of the series' mythology and that it is seared in people's minds thanks to its immediately iconic aura.

THE LOST CHAPTER

Before we begin, I'd like to give a little warning for anyone who is not aware of the story of "episode 83." Although we have already mentioned the concept of the Idea of Evil, revealed in this infamous chapter, several times, Miura eliminated it from the series' final publication because he felt that it exposed too much of his mythology. All websites analyzing the series treat the Idea of Evil as part of canon since, as far as we know, it is indeed valid. In volume 13, while Griffith is having a mystical revelation, he encounters the Idea of Evil. However, apart from an enigmatic close-up that doesn't reveal much, we don't learn anything more about this "God of the Abyss." Episode 83 explains what this entity is and presents the dialog between the Idea and Griffith. As it can be found on the internet in just a few clicks, it's not much of a secret. Still, out of respect for the author's choice, and to spare readers who want to remain unspoiled by more specific revelations, I invite anyone who wants to to skip ahead to the next chapter, on page 144.

For an author, especially a *mangaka*, deleting a chapter is no trivial thing. Most *Berserk* fans are aware, but many still don't know: there is a mysterious part of the story that is now excluded from official publications: the legendary episode 83. It was by a request from Miura himself that this episode was withdrawn and, to be precise, only Japanese readers of *Young Animal*, the magazine in which the manga is first published, had laid eyes on it. Indeed, that was the only publication of this episode and the author regretted it so much that he had it eliminated from the story and asked for it not to appear in the final collected volume. As such, the issue of *Young Animal* containing the lost chapter has become a true collector's item, selling for a pretty penny on auction websites. But what could those 17 pages hold that made Miura so want to reverse course? The "official" episode 82 stops when Griffith is about to meet the supreme being that gives orders to the Guardian Angels. At that moment, we can't even really make out the appearance of the Idea of Evil; the deleted chapter, on the other hand, begins by revealing what this evil god looks like. When we see it, the first thing we think of is a giant human heart, but with many more blood vessels connected to it. This insane-looking heart is floating in a gigantic maelstrom made up of all of humanity's negative thoughts: "An endless swirl of consciousness, endless and evil, as if all the evil in the world were gathered here." From the bottom of the heart, two blood vessels extend out and form a double helix, seeming to plunge downward to infinity. This floating organ does not pump blood, but rather the toxic flows of energy that swirl around it, as if this fluid of woe gives it life. The heart's fleshy walls are covered in thousands of eyes spaced out at regular intervals. The being then reveals its true nature to Griffith: "I am this world. The darkness that dwells in every human heart. The Idea of Evil. This is God." In sum, the Idea of Evil is a creature that took form in response to the desire of humans to have a cause for their misfortune, in order to give meaning to such a difficult life. "Reasons for pain. Reasons for sadness. Reasons for life. Reasons for death. Why were their lives filled with suffering? Why were their deaths absurd? They wanted reasons for the destiny that kept transcending their knowledge. And that was God. And I produce those. As it is what I've been brought to existence for. I control destiny." In this way, Miura flips the script, since it's the Idea of Evil that controls humans, in spite of the fact that it was created by them. Basically, humans gave the keys to their destiny to a virtual entity that they themselves created out of their own weakness. As if they were incapable of handling free will. "Obeying the will of the essence of human kind, I weave every man's destiny." This god is in fact the sum of human unconscious minds, humanity's "ego," in psychoanalytical terms. As if all humans had a hidden part of their brains, all connected to each other in a different space-time... It's in this abstract place that a divine being came into existence to control them in spite of themselves. Finally, the Idea of Evil explains to a stunned Griffith that all that has happened in his life has been orchestrated behind the scenes by the Idea, which implies that this deity has a specific plan, whose objective is hard to make out: "It was established that you would be here in the distant past.

By influencing the lower levels of human consciousness, and merging blood with blood, I created the lineage that would give birth to the man you are." The Idea of Evil even seems to have taken great pains to make sure that Griffith would reach this point: "To pave the way for the times you would be born in, I manipulated history and created an appropriate context for you. All the encounters you have had so far were a part of the destiny that led you here." We can now better understand why Miura wanted to delete this episode because, while its concepts and revelations are certainly of interest, they expose far too much of the enigmas that run through *Berserk*. Once we know the face of "God," it loses its mystery. Indeed, faith relies on believing in something that you can't see or prove. If Miura shows his God of Evil, then his story loses some of its mystical depth. That said, episode 83 is put together superbly and I think that Miura wouldn't disavow these concepts; it's just that he realized that delivering them so early in the story undercut much of its strength. The less you show, the more powerful it is. To draw a parallel, this "less is more" philosophy is clearly what makes the *Dark Souls* video games so intriguing. It seems that Hidetaka Miyazaki learned Master Miura's lesson: the games' key pieces of information are so murky and hidden that the player must be totally invested to uncover the story. In *Berserk*, with episode 83 withdrawn, we don't know what Griffith and "God" said to each other during the Eclipse and thus the Falcon's choice is that much more surprising. What could have happened for him to make such a horrendous decision? What did he see at the heart of that "ocean of feelings" to get to this point? Any good fiction story must maintain a gray area, a gateway for our fantasies, and as Miura has said, by revealing so early on the "behind-the-scenes" of the plot, he was likely backing himself into a corner with storytelling choices he might regret. We can certainly see in this a narrative relation to Lovecraft's concept of the "unspeakable." H.P. Lovecraft often used this same device: the abominations seen by the narrators in his stories were said to be so terrible... that they couldn't be described. The use of the "unspeakable" is much more effective than a precise description of a monster because the reader is forced to use their imagination to project the monster's appearance based on snippets of description provided by the author. And the human mind is such that it will automatically go to its greatest fear: it will search in the darkest corners of the unconscious. If I were to tell you: "Imagine a creature so horrible that people would be scared to death upon seeing it," your imagination would go searching through your own catalog of phobias to come up with the worst possible vision. This act of getting inside the reader's imagination is a power specific to literature: the page just provides words and it's up to us to create the images, and from the time we're very young, this exercise comes to us quite naturally. On the other hand, once the text comes with an image, as is the case with a manga, things work differently, given that showing something necessarily means "fixing" the reader's imagination. As such, by showing what the Idea of Evil looks like, Miura deprived millions of readers from imagining their own personal and terrifying vision. He also deprived all fans who love developing theories by delivering the "answer" too soon. There is also, in my opinion, a certain beauty and great humility in this gesture from the author given that, by deciding to go back on his previous choice, he shows that, for the good of his story, it's OK to admit a mistake. It takes a sort of courage to resolve in this way to erase a vision, something that comes from the bottom of the creator's heart and required hours of work and reflection. We get the impression that when Miura saw episode 83 printed, he must have realized that something was breaking down in the overall machinery of his story. Maybe he even felt the need to keep a little mystery for himself because if readers know the end of the story, then they'll just slog through to get to the finish line and the road to get there will be devoid of surprises. The *mangaka* must have wanted to push back for as long as possible the moment when he would hand over to the audience the final keys to his story.

Finally, there's one last point worth discussing: in the end, was episode 83 too "political" or too philosophically brutal? Religion and faith are, unfortunately, subjects that are hard to tackle, as the views between believers and non-believers differ so strongly, not to mention the competing dogmas between different groups of believers. In episode 83, Miura provides a version of God that is so original and, when it comes down to it, so unsettlingly true to life that the episode is naturally divisive. It poses real philosophical question and provides fatalistic answers, raising more questions about our own history and religions. The first shock, which we've already discussed, is showing a god driven and preoccupied by evil, going completely against all monotheistic religions. Next, this god is not a divine being at the source of all creation; rather, it is humans that created this god. And in fact, without passing judgment on whether or not a god exists, our religions were indeed invented... by people. Certain psychoanalytical theories suggest that we created the image of a god to play the role of a "father," someone who can guide us, even when we're adults. That's exactly what the Idea of Evil says: it was created by humans to show them the way. Miura also tells us that, as in our world, religions have gotten away from us to become a form of submission rather than liberation, and he goes even further by adding a psychoanalytical dimension to his god. Indeed, the being says that it is humanity's "ego." It's a way of signifying that the only god that exists is in our heads and that it is the sum of our primal instincts, of our collective unconscious. If we keep going with this idea, the fate of the world depends solely on our intentions and our degree of empathy; except that the message that Miura delivers here is much darker: we are so fearful and selfish that the god we have created is an evil god whose only goal is to cause our misfortune... This adds a political and extremely fatalistic dimension to the artist's message. Before the internet existed, one could have hoped to make such a chapter "disappear," but with such a dense network out there, all that was needed was a scanner and a team of volunteer translators for this secret part of the story to be made available to readers all over the world. Although I'm not in much of a position to talk about it, this raises questions about the control an author has over their own story, over what they consider to be canon, and about respecting the author's choices. We can justifiably say that if Miura had it removed, then this episode no longer exists and we should completely ignore it. However, this book aims to analyze *Berserk* while trying to understand the relationship the artist has with his creation, and, given this subject, deleting this chapter is such an inordinately strong action that I felt it was essential that we discuss it. By doing so, we understand the plot choices that Miura had in mind before reversing course, but above all, we see the "sculptor" side of the *mangaka* come out. When you write an epic more than 9,000 pages long, you find yourself facing a story that is so enormous and so dense that sometimes you need to sculpt that hulking mass with some careful chiseling to maintain that monolith. If you add an element that unbalances it, then the edifice can crumble. For example, when Miura kills the entire Band of the Falcon during the Eclipse, he lops off a huge piece of his sculpture so that he can completely revamp it. Similarly, when he withdrew episode 83, it was as if he had sculpted a face on his statue... then realized that it took all of the mystery out of his work. Moreover, episode 83 is not the author's only "regret," as we see with the first few pages of *Berserk* showing Guts having sex with a monstrous apostle. Yet, on the one hand, at that point in the story, the Black Swordsman is supposed to be in a relationship with Casca and, on the other hand, given his personality, this scene is not like him. The error is forgivable given that Miura had not yet come up with Casca when he produced those first frames, but nonetheless, he would come to regret that scene. What's funny is the subliminal way the author goes about getting us to forget that little inconsistency: during the Eclipse, Corkus comes face to face with the very same apostle, reproduced identically, in the same position, so that we will then associate this creature with the traumatic death of Corkus instead of Guts' sex life. While we can't be certain of this interpretation, how else can we explain the fact that Miura identically reproduced a creature that Guts had left for dead the first time we saw her? It must be terribly frustrating for an author to have a small piece of their story that doesn't fit into the framework they chose later on and I personally find it very touching and humble that Miura is able to question himself and have doubts, that he is willing to go to any lengths to deliver the best possible story, whether that means killing half of his characters in one fell swoop or deleting an entire episode.

This "disappearance" of part of the series also kind of makes this episode legendary. As another example, if we found out tomorrow that Stan Lee had withdrawn an issue of *Spider-Man* and hidden it in a safe, thousands of fans would be willing to do anything to find out what was in it. Everyone would be fantasizing about what could be in that issue and why it was kept secret... When you love a story, you often want to know all there is to know about it, as well as about the author. You want to know the smallest details and anecdotes about its creation. So, if someone were to tell you that there was an ill-fated chapter, a Holy Grail of the story revealing a huge plot point, you would of course be foaming at the mouth. I don't think that Miura disavows the mythology of the Idea of Evil revealed in episode 83; he simply wanted to keep it to himself. He has admitted that he doesn't know if he will reincorporate the Idea of Evil into the manga. All we can say for now is that, to this point, nothing has either contradicted or nullified the revelations in this mysterious episode...

THE BIBLE OF DARKNESS

In the immense patchwork quilt of references that is *Berserk*, the number of symbols and facts that connect directly to Catholicism is impressive. Of course, pop culture of the 20th century is full of nods to the Bible and the hundreds of stories that it has established in our Judeo-Christian collective unconscious, and although *Berserk* is of Japanese origin, it is no exception to this rule. That said, the series focuses in particular on delivering a critical, pointed, and only barely fantastical understanding of religious obscurantism when it was at its peak. There's no mistaking the signs: Miura includes in his series a religion led by a "Holy See" (direct reference to the Vatican), a monotheistic religion analogous to the Catholic church. The Holy See in the series has a pope, priests, bishops, and even a "holy" Inquisition. The vestments worn by the clergymen and the rituals performed are taken directly from Catholic traditions. Even the political positioning of the Church in the manga is reminiscent of the ultra-wealthy, inflexible, power-hungry popes of old who were close to the powerful figures of their time. While the Bible is never mentioned by name, there is indeed a holy book that echoes it, which Miura calls the "Canon." This term, which is now also used for fiction universes, connects directly to a religious principle: indeed, a text is considered "canon" if it is officially recognized by Church authorities, which means that the Church alone establishes what's right and what's wrong. Because of this, the "Canon" is more of an instrument of oppression than a text of love. This idea reaches its ultra-violent height when Mozgus literally crushes someone's head using the sacred text. Other references are scattered throughout the series, notably the use of emblematic phrases like "may the Lord be with you," a classic phrase derived from the Catholic Mass, or "this is my body," a phrase pronounced during the Mass for the blessing of the Eucharist before Communion. Other words from the religious lexical field can be found, like Guardian Angel, faith, etc. Void even speaks of "ye lambs of the ungodly god born of a man," a direct reference to the classic metaphor of believers being sheep guided by Christ, their shepherd. Miura uses religion here in the same way that he does his other borrowings: we can clearly see that he's talking about Catholicism, and yet he never uses this word, nor the words Christ or Jesus. Moreover, it's likely Miura's way of saying that he has nothing against the Christian message or the humanistic values of religion; instead, he saves all of his criticism for the crazy dogma and its derivatives, as well as for the way in which Church leaders have strayed from Christly benevolence to become toxic, violent figures. Miura hides many, more visual, nods to religion throughout the series. The first volume of *Berserk* opens with an image of Guts, his eyes closed and his arms stretched out, reminiscent of Christ's position on the cross. Similarly, the religion of the manga's Holy See uses a bird with its wings opened wide as its symbol, a shape subtly reminiscent of the Christian cross. Another subtle example, in volume 10: just after Guts and Casca have made love, they lounge around, naked, in a peaceful, solitary forest. If you didn't know better, you would say it was a scene of the everyday life of Adam and Eve in the Garden of Eden, with the sun shining through the leaves and the water whispering from the waterfall nearby. While their private parts may not be covered with fig leaves, Miura carefully chooses angles that show them as little as possible, as if to preserve the purity of this Eden. To finish with this comparison, this passage concludes with a frame showing Griffith's beherit in the river: it can be seen as the apple that will later get them expelled from paradise. Miura knows how to perfectly use Christian symbols to give his manga a certain aura, as we see with the famous cover of volume 13, showing Guts on an apocalyptic background, holding Casca in his arms in a position strongly reminiscent of Michelangelo's *Pietà*, a famous statue of the *Mater dolorosa*, or "Our Lady of Sorrows," showing the mother of Christ holding her dead son on her lap. He has just been taken down from the cross. The sculptor chose to depict this heart-wrenching moment just before Jesus was laid in his tomb. Invoking this symbol when we know the metaphorical crucifixion that Casca experiences in this volume is not just appropriate, but doubly powerful. While Miura doesn't hold back from roundly criticizing religion, he also doesn't hide the fascination it inspires in him, as the *mangaka* seems to have deep knowledge of the Church's dogma and even its most unusual bodies. The Order of the Holy See, led by Farnese, has the objective of investigating the veracity of any miracle reported to the Holy See and of deciding between what's divine fact and what's heresy. This order is a direct reference to a religious body that actually existed called the Congregation of the Holy Office, which itself was the successor of the Inquisition. Its mission was to "promote and safeguard the doctrine of the faith

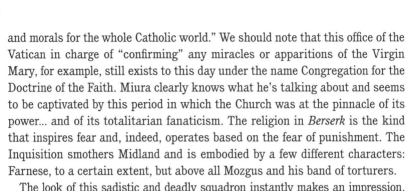

and morals for the whole Catholic world." We should note that this office of the Vatican in charge of "confirming" any miracles or apparitions of the Virgin Mary, for example, still exists to this day under the name Congregation for the Doctrine of the Faith. Miura clearly knows what he's talking about and seems to be captivated by this period in which the Church was at the pinnacle of its power... and of its totalitarian fanaticism. The religion in *Berserk* is the kind that inspires fear and, indeed, operates based on the fear of punishment. The Inquisition smothers Midland and is embodied by a few different characters: Farnese, to a certain extent, but above all Mozgus and his band of torturers.

The look of this sadistic and deadly squadron instantly makes an impression. Their first appearance shows Mozgus getting out of his armored carriage, giving off a troubling, authoritarian vibe, surrounded by his henchmen, who, even without really doing anything, immediately spark terror thanks to their get-ups, their "tools," and the way they hold themselves. They're not a homogeneous group; each one seems to have a different story and their own morbid specialty: the smallest of the bunch, a muscular, toned guy whose face is covered by a mask with two horns, making him look like a little demon, holds in his hands a pair of tongs almost as big as he is. Beside him is a pair of muscular and yet paunchy twins holding giant saws on their shoulders, saws that are so big that it's not quite clear how they could use them; to heighten their terrifying air, their hoods give us a glimpse at an interesting fact: their faces seem to be extremely deformed, given the placement of the mouth and eye holes in their hoods. The group also includes a mountain of muscles with a tiny head on top covered with a hood that comes down to the base of his neck; his favorite weapon is a giant wheel studded with metal rivets that, although fictional, is inspired by the "breaking wheel," a device once used by executioners to crush the bones of criminals. The tallest man in this sinister crew, wearing an apron that looks like one a butcher would wear, looms over the group of torturers with an ominous air. His deformed head and protruding jaw give him a creepy look and he is armed with chains that have some sort of tongs hanging from the end; we don't even want to image the torture they might inflict. Although it's just a historical legend popularized by literature and films, putting hoods on all of these characters indicates to us that they are torturers, such people supposedly wanting to remain anonymous to avoid any reprisals. Finally, there's one last distinguished member of the crew: the "Crow." Dressed in a baggy tunic that hides all of his body and sporting a plague doctor mask, shaped like a bird's head, the Crow wields a lance that ends in a garrote that looks like a wolf trap, allowing him to seize his victims by the neck. Incidentally, it's via this character that we learn more about the nature of this tight-knit band: as we learn about his past, we understand what led these men to serve the insane principles of their leader, demonstrating once more Miura's talent for "humanizing" the worst characters. Once again, he uses a subtle historical reference to "circus freaks" to recount the past of these torturers. The Crow explains the situation very well himself: "They are good-natured. We have been each cruelly persecuted because of our appearance. We have been chased from villages and towns, sold to circuses, and some among us have lived secretly in forests, loathed as monsters." By mentioning "circuses," Miura conjures up our imaginings of "freak shows," inhumane exhibitions in the 19th century exploiting humans with deformities in circuses or traveling carnivals. In exchange for the money of gawkers eager to see something sensational, these shows would exhibit people who were abnormally large or small, suffering from congenital conditions, such as bearded women or conjoined twins, etc. The film world latched onto these tragic figures in two absolute masterpieces: Tod Browning's *Freaks* (1932) and David Lynch's *Elephant Man* (1980). These highly stigmatized individuals, subjected to the baseness and cupidity of humanity, generally delivered a message of tolerance and evoked empathy in spectators. Miura inverts this theme in *Berserk* by transforming these victims of chance into atrocious torturers thanks to the intervention of Mozgus, who is the only person to consider the fate of these poor souls. By swooping into the lives of these outcasts like a savior and by feeding them mystical ideas, he manages to turn them into fanatics, convincing them that their suffering has meaning, that God has chosen this fate for them and he needs them. Miura demonstrates here one of a religion's mechanisms for getting buy-in: people are sometimes so desperate that they'll believe anything, as long as it offers them a wild hope. In this case, the hope that Mozgus provides is the hope of acceptance, of feeling important, and of serving a great cause, of which they are the armed wing. In addition to humanizing these characters, Miura makes them credible: we can easily imagine these deformed people, rejected by society, slaking their thirst for vengeance by torturing those who previously scorned them, in the name of a religion that has been the only part of society to understand them. The last shall be the first... to get revenge. While this band commits horrendous torture on numerous innocent people, it's without a doubt Mozgus the Inquisitor who takes the blue ribbon for fanaticism in the manga. This man, nicknamed "Bloody Scripture Mozgus," is an absolutely iconic character. As Chief Inquisitor of the Holy See, he has been directed by the Pope to hunt down heretics and get them back on the straight and narrow path, using terrible corporal punishment if necessary. As such, his role is to put the fear of God in the hearts of believers. In creating Mozgus, Miura again relies on historical facts and on a moral and philosophical debate between the founding fathers of the Christian church. Does God offer universal salvation (everyone will be saved, no matter what they've done, because God is love) or are certain people bound for eternal damnation (if you sin too much, you're headed for suffering in Hell)? The Church came to a decision: salvation for all does not exist and it became "anathema," i.e. forbidden, to even mention universal forgiveness. This then led to the establishment of the idea of mortal sins and Hell to solidify the Church's power over believers. This Church that chose fear over love reached its apex with the Inquisition, whose abuses went on for centuries, and it's these excesses that Miura, drawing inspiration from them, tries to shine a light on. The words that Mozgus speaks to Farnese as she turns her gaze away from a torture session prove this: "Thou shalt not avert thine eyes. This hellish spectacle is one aspect of the Holy See to which you belong. God does not rain benevolence alone upon his earth. He is also a strict arbiter." Mozgus spends his time applying this principle and hunting all those who commit heresy, as when he lists off sinners who surround the monastery in Albion, giving them in ascending order of the gravity of their sins: thieves, rapists, killers, and... heretics. Moreover, heresy can be defined as any act or thought that goes against the religion. This is very convenient because it's that same religion that gets to decide what fits with its dogma and what doesn't, in an arbitrary and totalitarian fashion. For a man of the Church, Mozgus demonstrates very little empathy, as he tortures a young mother he's just separated from her child without batting an eye after making her believe in divine salvation. The Inquisitor is the archetype of the religious zealot, cold and calculating, never questioning his principles, as he applies them to himself. His face, so smashed that it has sharp angles, shows his extreme fanaticism as it is the result of the prayer that Mozgus offers up to God each day. Indeed, a thousand times each morning and a thousand times each evening, he slams his face against the ground, smashing his face on stone to show God his devotion and to feel in turn the pain that he inflicts on God's flock throughout the day. I'm sure this sort of exercise must drive a person completely mad as the brain must end up being damaged by the repetition of such a ritual. It's this sort of detail that gives you chills: Mozgus is so totally convinced of what he preaches that he applies it to himself, making him devoid of all pity. While we know that Miura drew inspiration from the film based on Umberto Eco's *The Name of the Rose* (Jean-Jacques Annaud, 1986) in creating Mozgus, it's also worth mentioning here the excellent but lesser-known Ken Russell film *The Devils* (1971), which explores many of the themes found in the Conviction arc. I would not be surprised if Miura knows the film because Mozgus shares many similarities with the character of Father Barre who, in the film, is a crazed, sadistic inquisitor who sees heretics everywhere. This is a great film not just for its very critical view of the Inquisition, which I'm sure the *mangaka* would approve of, but also for its incredible scenes of "ungodly" orgies and torture, which are strongly reminiscent of similar scenes in the manga.

The final chapter in Miura's Bible of Darkness is devoted to torture. In this regard, the author did not necessarily aim for originality, as most of the scenes and instruments of torture that he shows in the manga are borrowed from historical facts. When Mozgus brings Farnese into his torture chamber, as the doors open, we see an absolutely nightmarish two-page spread. We see Mozgus' band of torturers inflicting terrible punishments that, sadly, we know have been employed in the course of history. In chambers where "the question" (as torture used to be called in France) was carried out, poor souls really were forced to sit on "iron chairs," which were chairs covered in spikes, or had boiling oil poured down their throats. People were hung by their feet, dismembered, attached to wheels intended to break their bones, and had the soles of their feet burned with red-hot brands. Miura shows all of these tortures on this same two-page spread. When it came to torture in the Middle Ages, the sophistication in terms of sadism and inhumanity knew no bounds, as we see from things like the "iron maiden," a sort of sarcophagus filled with spikes in which a victim was locked (Casca is placed in such a device later on in the story). We get the impression that the *mangaka* did meticulous research on the horrors of medieval torture. Further proof of his concern for realism: the manga's Tower of Conviction is most likely inspired by the "Alcázar de los Reyes Cristianos" in Cordoba, Spain, whose main tower was called the Tower of the Inquisition and served as the headquarters for the Spanish Inquisition starting in the late 15th century. Inside, the tower hid many prisons and torture chambers. When an author wants to explore the dark side of the human soul, describing what goes on in a torture chamber is the surest way to dive right in there.

Coming from a Japanese perspective, Miura must view our dark history of the Inquisition with a certain fascination, as he devoted an entire story arc in his series to it, and he makes sure to point out this immense contradiction: certain men of the Church acted in a truly "demonic" way. Catholicism is based in particular on the teachings of Jesus and the acts of love he is supposed to have carried out, acts so inspiring that people follow him to this day. Christ certainly preached a religion of peace and called for kindness to our neighbors: "Love one another" is no call for hatred. And the Bible also tells us that he died on the cross to absolve us of our sins, out of pure love for humanity. Could it be that Miura is trying to understand what could have caused this clearly humanistic discourse to devolve into a fanatical, totalitarian doctrine that crushed the weak? To a certain extent, it's strange that a religion that claims to follow a deceased prophet who was crucified, and thus tortured, would in turn commit this sort of atrocity on women and men who could have been the Jesus of their time. This inconsistency between words and actions is perfectly illustrated in Mozgus, as his words, though wise and loving, are totally contradicted by his absolutely horrific actions. Miura shows how a discourse of love, when twisted, can bring about catastrophic consequences... This hijacking of religion, with a message of love becoming one of fear, is expressed perfectly by Nina as she contemplates the Tower of Conviction: "Here, we're in the shadow of that tower almost all day. Even though God is here, why does it seem so grave and terrible? [...] I'm scared... so scared. I can't stand it Luca.

Of dying, of living, of this world, of God!" Finally, the *mangaka* also excoriates the clergymen who put on airs of hypocritical virtue and feel entitled to dictate to others what is right, even though they themselves partake in the sinning for which they punish others. Farnese really embodies this idea. She seems to take almost sexual pleasure while whipping herself out of atonement in the privacy of her tent; the same goes for when she excitedly watches heretics being burned at the stake. In sum, being religious doesn't make you immune from "perversion." Farnese's perversion, in this case, is taking pleasure from suffering, an idea expressed openly in a scene in which the young woman falls victim to a schizophrenic internal dialog after being taken by Guts. "Even plugging your ears is futile. Because this is your inner voice. Then. You felt it then. While you trashed that man's steel physique. You know you felt it. It swells within you. This morbid lust. [...] When you lashed yourself, feigning introspection, you were constantly discovering pleasure, even within that pain. You simply lie to your own soul behind your religion and devote your body to shameful pleasure. That is you." In these examples, we can clearly see that the author caricatures Catholicism and uses its excesses to write his story. However, while Miura offers criticism of dogma and of perverted religious figures, at the same time, he infuses *Berserk* with a biblical dimension, particularly via the story's messianic and apocalyptic aspects. The figure of Griffith is totally based off of that of Christ, but in a reverse, evil "mirror image." Like Jesus, Griffith was condemned and tortured because of his influence, and both were reborn, resurrected. However, while Christ sacrificed himself for his faithful, Griffith sacrificed his friends to achieve his goal, thus playing a Judas role. Other such hints are peppered throughout the manga and connect back to this inversion of values. The most notable example is the fact that the story's monsters are called "apostles." Like a prophet, the Skull Knight speaks in parables and constantly predicts mysterious and apocalyptic events. All of *Berserk* exudes these references to religious narrative themes, thus giving the story an epic, Dantean air and endowing it with moral and philosophical depth, all while delivering a critical view of religion. It's a way of paying homage to the most-read imaginary and fantastical story of all time: the Bible. Even if you're not a Christian, you have to be able to recognize the exceptional narrative model offered by the Bible because, when it comes down to it, there are few modern mythological works of fiction that don't make reference to it.

THE SHADOW OF BAPHOMET

While there are many biblical and Christian references in the manga, they are outnumbered by references to the Devil and, through him, the concept of evil. In this case again, the fact that the story is set in the medieval period is no coincidence. While the Devil appears in the Bible, it was essentially in the Middle Ages that this figure became popular and was actually incorporated into our folklore. Along with the threat of Hell, the Devil was one of the tools used by the Church to spread fear of sin among believers; this historical context was also the source for "modern" notions of witchcraft, as well as the first treatises on demonology. As such, it is a key period for demonic figures. Thus, it's totally logical that the story is blanketed with diabolical motifs. However, Miura does not limit himself to this time period: he also draws from much more recent sources of Satanic and occult symbolism. Speaking of "the Devil" in the singular is actually, in itself, a mistake and that's one of the essential things to know when examining this subject: the Devil is not a single, fixed entity; rather, there exist multiple "visions" and descriptions of the Devil, presenting different symbolism and sometimes different origins. The four main sources that have shaped the faces of the Devil are religion, literature, folklore, and the occult. Certain depictions borrow from different mythologies and some contradict each other at times. They have all ended up totally blended together in our collective unconscious. These four sources then had their depictions incorporated into pop culture and the Devil became a very fluid being, difficult to define universally. Miura plays into this to a certain extent in that he subtly mixes together in his series the many different ways in which the Devil has manifested in our imagination. Using specific references, whether overt or hidden, the *mangaka* shows that he has done his research on this captivating topic so that he can play with its fascinating protocols, but also so that he can question the concepts of evil conveyed by diabolical figures in the history of mythology. The first type of Satanism represented is theistic Satanism, also known as traditional Satanism or spiritual Satanism. It is an anti-Christian religious movement that worships the fallen angels and their supreme leader, Satan. As such, it's a form of Satanism that recognizes the existence of God, but which hates God and adores the Devil, precisely because he is the adversary of the Almighty. Satanists also perform religious rituals, mimicking Christian dogma with a blasphemous spin on it. In *Berserk*, the cult of worshipers of the Great Goat partially meets this definition, since they show their hostility toward the religion of the Holy See, as we hear from the preacher who leads them: "As all of you know, the stone pillar deified in the Tower of Conviction is no longer potent nor significant! It has no power to manifest even a single mystery. The tower has instead been reduced to a vile lodge of swine who use sophistry in an attempt to oppress and control us. But we are aware! Aware of the one truly deserving of reverence!" The message is clear. And I might add that this cult also performs rituals used in Satanic Masses. This concept of the "Black Mass" is similar to Witches' Sabbaths, nocturnal gatherings of witches which included pagan ceremonies and even orgies. Moreover, in the Middle Ages, the word "Sabbath" began to be associated with Satanism and, under the

Inquisition, judges would often link the two phenomena together, claiming that these women worshiped the Devil. In Jean-Michel Sallmann's book *Les Sorcières, fiancées de Satan* ("Witches, the Betrothed of Satan," 1989), here's how the stereotype of the Sabbath is described around the year 1430: "There are wizards and witches. They cover their bodies in an ointment made from the flesh of ritually sacrificed children. They fly fast and far through the air astride animals or brooms. They gather in a remote place. There, they participate in a ceremony presided over by the Devil, who is represented by a goat. They worship the Devil and kiss his anus (*osculum infame*). They reject the Christian faith. They trample the insignias of Christianity. The ceremony ends with an orgy for all in which the wizards copulate with succubi and the witches with incubi. This is followed by a great feast during which the children previously ritually slaughtered are devoured." It almost seems like Miura simply illustrated this text, as it so perfectly matches certain scenes depicted in the manga, proving yet again that he really does his research. When Nina brings Joachim to his first orgy, she says this to her leader: "Oh Great Goat. I have brought this one to have him convert." Then to Joachim: "You recite these words to defile god. Next kiss his heart and his member." Conversion, blasphemy, a mystical-sexual ritual: it's all there. Note that, next, Miura adds a hint of human sacrifice to perfect the tableau, as Joachim must drink a sinister mixture... that contains pieces of human flesh. However, the *mangaka* doesn't stop when he's on a roll. He continues to add other references to the Devil taken from various sources. Where things get more complicated is with the figure of the Great Goat... We have to go back through the history of myths and cults to understand why this particular animal is associated with the Devil. The origin of this association of evil with goats in Christianity is found in the New Testament, in the Gospel of Saint Matthew, chapter 25: "All the nations will be gathered before Him, and He will separate the people one from another, as a shepherd separates the sheep from the goats. He will place the sheep on His right and the goats on His left. [...] Then He will say to those on his left, 'Depart from me, you who are cursed, into the eternal fire prepared for the devil and his angels.'" So, it was in contrast to the Lord's "sheep" that the poor goat had this unfortunate symbolism attached to it. However, it's not just this metaphor in the New Testament that created the persistent and powerful association in our minds between goats and demons. In the Middle Ages, the clergy looked for ways to frighten its flock so that they would turn to the Church and its "solutions." To achieve this, they let certain pagan myths persist. While the Church had already established the concept of mortal sins and Hell appeared in sacred texts, they wanted to give the Devil a face so that he would become a source of fear. The first textual illuminations and other pictorial representations drew from Greek mythology, using the god Pan as a model. Pan was considered the protector of shepherds, a symbol of fertility and madness, an allegory for our uncontrollable, animal, lunar, and nocturnal sides. He was depicted as a chimera, a man-goat hybrid, similar to the satyrs who often surrounded him. Pan even appears in statue form in volume 7, page 191, in Gennon's castle. It's incredible to see the extent to which the medieval image of the Devil was inspired by the physical attributes of this ancient (non-Christian) deity. Pan looks like a goat that walks on its hind legs. Over time, Pan even came to be depicted with little horns poking up from his head. His feet became hooves. He was depicted with a long, horse-like tail coming from his lower back and with pointy ears. So, we can see that his physical attributes are exactly the same as those used for medieval representations of the Devil. However, Pan was not an evil deity for the Greeks... So, why did medieval Devil imagery borrow the looks of poor Pan, who never asked for such treatment? Simply because of one last characteristic of the god not yet mentioned: his giant penis, most often shown erect. Like his companions, the satyrs (a term that can still be used today to describe a sex-obsessed man), Pan was a frisky young playboy, symbolizing the erotic brutality of youth. Since the Church in the Middle Ages abhorred lust, the "sin of the flesh" mentioned by Miura, Pan's sexual dimension made him the perfect inspiration for the medieval image of the Devil. Of course, Devils in illuminated manuscripts were depicted as being much more ugly and monstrous than Pan. Over time, the Devil made his way into folklore and popular beliefs, to the point that the association with Pan was forgotten. The god of nature thus got to return to the peaceful green pastures of Greek mythology. Under the Inquisition, dealing with the devil became one of the top charges made against people in courts and supposed "Witches' Sabbaths" came into the Church's crosshairs. The clergy did not like the idea of cults worshiping someone other than the Lord and partaking in forbidden sexual pleasures. Incidentally, according to Miura's story, the Church was right to worry: in caves far from the prying eyes of the city, totally wild, and frankly troubling, orgies take place. The author could have chosen to present scenes of sexual liberation with a "new age" vibe, but when we see the orgy from the point of view of Joachim, who discovers these practices at the same time the reader does, we are disturbed and troubled by what we witness. Tribal-style percussion music barely covers the cries of pleasure from the dozens of naked, oiled-up people, as some sort of viscous liquid oozes and drips from their bodies. Joachim suspects that this is from the effects of a drug because he begins to have disturbing hallucinations. At one point, Joachim tries to grab Nina's breasts, but his hands go straight into the young woman's chest, in a way that's reminiscent of the insane, filthy end of the 1989 Brian Yuzna film *Society*. We can tell that Joachim is having a very bad acid trip. And that's when the Great Goat appears. Once again, Miura shows us his "patchwork of influences" with a goat-headed god who looks like... Baphomet, a legendary occult figure. Retracing the trail of images and symbols is fascinating, a little bit like diving into a police investigation. And luck, apparently, led me to "investigate" Baphomet just before I began writing this book. As it happens, I have recently taken a great interest in musical album covers, particularly those of metal groups, any of them really. The thing that drew me to album covers is that they are the only visual that a musical group can use to represent the universe of their music. To give the group a strong, recognizable identity, the album art must stand out from the crowd and stick in people's minds. I archived literally hundreds of different album covers by style of metal, organized in sub-folders on my computer. My interest in metal album art was stoked by the fact that, generally, they explore a dark, morbid aesthetic intended to allude to dark, occult symbolism. In my research, I tried to find commonalities between the various aesthetics and, indeed, there are certain motifs that recur quite often. But one detail really struck me: the ubiquity of the figure of Baphomet in the visual identity of many black metal, as well as death metal, groups. Most often, this imagery appears on the albums of groups that embrace the Satanic universe and its themes. Many horror films and comics also use this image of a goat with a pentacle, so it jumped out at me while reading *Berserk*. So, I researched the origins of Baphomet, and his history is both intriguing and complex. When I started collecting black metal album covers, I never thought that they would lead me back to the time of the Crusades, and yet, according to my sources, the first time the word "Baphomet" appeared was in a letter sent in 1098 by a Templar involved in the Siege of Antioch. This crusading Templar believed that the locals, who were Muslim, worshiped "Baphomet," which was really just a misspelling of the name Muhammad... Curiously, two centuries later, this mysterious name resurfaced in the reports of trials resulting in the conviction of the Knights Templar: Baphomet was the name given to an idol that the Templars supposedly worshiped in secret during the Crusades. Exiled in France, the Knights Templar were seen as a powerful financial and military force capable of rivaling the power of the monarchy, which had been weakened by debt. So, the King of France aimed to get rid of them, even willing to falsely accuse them of demonic practices... The story of the anti-Christian goat lord could have stopped there; instead, this figure was unexpectedly the subject of renewed interest much later, around the 19th century. In 1854, Baphomet came back into fashion in occultist circles and, in the two volumes of his *Dogma and Ritual of High Magic*, religious thinker and occultist Éliphas Lévi drew this famous image, which now serves as a reference for the appearance of Baphomet.

Éliphas Lévi – Baphomet

I'm sure you'll notice that this image appears in *Berserk*: when the Count catches his wife being unfaithful, it's in front of a statue of Baphomet. With this drawing, Éliphas Lévi aimed to symbolize much more than a reductive, evil dimension: for him, Baphomet represented the balance of the forces of nature. The winged, humanoid goat has enormous horns, the chest of a woman, a torso covered in scales, and a torch crowning his head. He also has a pentagram on his forehead, oriented with one point at the top, the symbol of light. His right hand is pointing to the white moon of *chesed*, while his left hand points to the black moon of *geburah*. This position of the arms, very representative of occultism, symbolizes the perfect harmony between mercy and justice. The flame of intelligence that shines between his horns represents the "magic of universal balance," embodying the concept of mind over matter. The goat head represents the horror of sin, connected to matter, which will suffer punishment while the soul stays safe. Finally, the phallic shaft coming from between his legs, with serpents twisted around it in a double helix, symbolizes eternal life; the scales symbolize water; and the semicircle around the stomach symbolizes the atmosphere. So, in this image we find much more than just a representation of the Devil. Lévi's Baphomet is much closer to a mystical and Luciferian approach that was a precursor to modern occultism. In *Berserk*, the worshipers of the Great Goat are a great representation of the fanaticism that we associate with occultism, which flourished in the first half of the 20th century with ritual orgies, drug usage, manipulative gurus, and the worship of pagan idols.

A PACT WITH THE OCCULT

One might think that Miura borrowed certain "classic" motifs of occultism just for their decorum, for the fascinating and exciting side of these images. However, this opinion is called into question by other references to the occult that the author incorporates: for example, we can compare the beherit to the renowned philosopher's stone. This artifact—which was recently revived by the *Harry Potter* series—is a hypothetical substance considered to be the "Great Work" in alchemy. Alchemists attributed various properties to this "stone": it was supposed to cure disease, change common metals into precious metals (such as lead into gold), and, above all, offer the user a lifespan much longer than that of common mortals. The beherit has these same powers, but in an evil version: it can transform a common mortal into a powerful monster or a demon lord, offering them superhuman capabilities and a divine (though evil) aura. The "material" sacrificed during this alchemical process is none other than the lives of their loved ones. I would propose that there is another reference here: the word "beherit" is not a name invented by Miura; rather, it's the Syriac name for Satan, as we've mentioned previously. However, while looking for sources to verify this origin, I did not find any that were consistent and solid. Indeed, the only "accessible" source where this name appears is in a strange, occult compilation: The Infernal Names, a list that comes from *The Satanic Bible*, written by occultist Anton LaVey, founder of the Church of Satan. This 1969 book comes from a colorful, controversial figure who, like most occultists, wavered between enlightenment and charlatanism. Still, when it was published, the book had a bit of success and drew outrage from the conservative moral authorities of the time. In it, LaVey laid out his "philosophy" and his Satanic commandments. However, the most interesting part, for me, is that this bible is a sort of ode to egotism, the idea that "I am God" (to very roughly summarize the book's discourse) and I'm certain that Griffith would embrace most of the commandments in this "self-help" book. Finally, to add a bit of folklore to his philosophical aims, LaVey incorporated this list of 76 "infernal names" that are to be recited during Satanic rituals in order to invoke their power. The occultist compiled all of the names connected to the Devil in all of the cultures he could find. Some are well known: Asmodeus, Ishtar, Lilith, Beelzebub, Loki, Marduk, and even Pan. However, most interestingly, this list includes three names that appear in *Berserk*: Shiva, Baphomet... and Beherit. Given Miura's knowledge of occult symbols and folklore, it would be no surprise to find out that the author got the name for his evil eggs from this list.

After Blavatsky's Astral World, Éliphas Lévi's Baphomet, and LaVey's list of infernal names, Miura references one of the final "stars" of scandalous occultism: Aleister Crowley. Crowley lived between the time of Lévi and the time of LaVey; as such, he was a link between these champions of an egocentric, individualist occultism.

Although most occultists have done unsavory things and, in their day, manipulated the ignorant masses with enticing mystical concepts, it would be a mistake to believe that occult Satanism actually matches the clichés we see in movies and rumors we hear on talk shows. Modern Satanism is seen more by its followers as a sort of atheist philosophy that aims to help us reach a form of supreme liberty and hermetic wisdom. This means that a Satanist is not so much a crazy person who sacrifices children to the Devil, but rather a human being wanting to assign a divine origin to their own desires. This worship of egotistical, ambitious individualism is at the heart of Satanism and, as I've already suggested, Griffith is an absolutely perfect example of this. Throughout the series, Miura leaves concrete proof of the importance of Aleister Crowley and his Satanism in the Falcon's character development. In episode 83, the "desired god" tells Griffith to be "as you will be," and it also drops this iconic phrase: "Do as you will do." Some English translations take this phrase a step further and reproduce Crowley's motto word-for-word: "Do what thou wilt shall be the whole of the Law," a powerfully striking reference that means much more than just an encouragement to follow our impulses. This proverb (itself stolen from François Rabelais' Abbey of Thelema) expresses a profound idea: you must identify within yourself what your true destiny is and then sacrifice everything to carry out that destiny. Basically, do what you "must" do, and do it however you want. Knowing Griffith's obsession with achieving his dream, the fact that the Idea of Evil tells him these words just before he resolves to sacrifice his friends is quite meaningful. While Miura shows us a more "positive" view of the Devil, one tied to occultism, he also doesn't hold back from exploring the more classic side, the "Evil One." As this name indicates, it's the version of the Devil that embodies evil for believers. This is just one of the many names for the Devil, but it perfectly represents the Christian adversary. "Lucifer," which means "bearer of light," comes from the Latin *lux* (light) and *ferre* (carry). From a theological point of view, Lucifer was an angel who revolted against God. Because of this, he fell from Heaven and was cast into Hell, i.e. on earth, symbolized in the Bible in the form of a serpent that uses deception to achieve his aims. The "Evil One" can be seen as the Devil who schemes and plots to interfere in the workings of the physical world. This concept fits perfectly with the Idea of Evil and its Guardian Angel Griffith. Causality is the instrument of the Evil One, pushing humans toward sin. Miura even speaks of "malignancy" to express the evil power of a demon, which can be measured, as I've mentioned before, by how much the Brand of Sacrifice bleeds. So, for Miura, evil is almost measurable; it's a form of energy, a sinister fuel. It's interesting to note that one acquires this evil after a deadly pact is made: "As a sacrificial offering for the invocation of doom, not just any lump of flesh and blood will do. It must be someone important to you, part of your soul... Someone so close to you that it's almost like giving up a part of you. By making such a sacrifice to demonkind, you'll be able to sever any last remnants of your own humanity, a fissure in your heart will open up into which evil will surge." In this quotation, Miura evokes a popular theme that is so dear to literature: the deal with the Devil. For their wish to be granted, a future apostle must give up their humanity, in other words their soul, for this malign essence that will give them power... Moreover, while giving one's soul to the Devil enables the transformation into a monstrous apostle, it also changes that person's "human" appearance. When Wyald dies, we discover that his ape-like, muscular appearance was in fact hiding a frail, little old man, symbolically suggesting that evil changes not only one's spirit, but also the human shell in which it resides. Of all the diabolical forms, pure, invisible evil is a smart and terrifying choice: it has no face. It prowls around, spreads, grows, but always remains imperceptible. As Miura very astutely highlights, evil is an idea... and that's what makes it so dangerous.

VISIONS OF HELL

Given the way in which Miura re-explores all of humanity's myths, it would have been very surprising if he had not examined the subject of Hell. While he never falls into the trap of delivering a classic Christian vision of Hell, he still plays around with different representations, which he expresses indirectly. If you want an analogy, the Qliphoth is probably closest to our stereotypical image of the underworld: a gloomy, underground place inhabited by corrupt lifeforms, filled with foul odors and mortal dangers. When Guts is at the entrance to the cursed cave, he comments on the deadly aura that the place gives off: "It's like descending into the depths of Hell." Once again, the *mangaka* shows us that he knows his classics by exploring the concept of "katabasis," a recurring motif in Greek epics. A katabasis is when a hero descends into the underworld. It's one of the most decisive ordeals in the initiation of an epic hero. Among the most famous katabases are those in Virgil's *Aeneid*, Dante's *Divine Comedy*, and *The Book of Enoch*. As an homage, Miura named a village in *Berserk* after the latter work, a legendary book that follows the adventures of Enoch, particularly his journey into Sheol, an ancient name for Hell in the Jewish tradition. The fact that the name Qliphoth—evil forces in opposition to the Sephiroth—is itself taken from Jewish Kabbalah is yet another sign of Miura's almost scientific rigor, his way of honoring the mythologies of Hell from which he drew inspiration. However, the Qliphoth is nothing in comparison to another vision of Hell that the author paints for us: the Eclipse. This event, which takes place "on top of reality," is a sort of Hell on earth, limited in time. When the Eclipse begins, the sun is covered and the landscape transforms. The ground becomes a carpet of faces lumped together, stretching out as far as the eye can see. Thousands of apostles are attracted by this ritual and, once the ceremony has started, they assume their monstrous forms, in the way one might don evening wear for a party. In this instance, we are in a more Dantean, classic vision of Hell, with thousands of demons ready to devour you in a morbid, infinite landscape. The God Hand that sprouts from this desert of woe looks like the throne of the Devil himself. With the Guardian Angels watching over the scene, we really get the impression that we've just been granted an audience in Hell. However, the references to Hell borrowed from great classics, some recent and some not, don't stop there. The two essential masterpieces that have shaped our contemporary vision of Hell are, of course, *The Divine Comedy* by Dante Alighieri and *Paradise Lost* by John Milton. While we can't say for sure that Kentaro Miura has read these two literary works, we do know with absolute certainty that he loves other works that make direct reference to them. The first part of *The Divine Comedy*, called *Inferno*, tells of Dante's journey through the nine circles of Hell, with each circle corresponding to specific vices and sins. In Dante's vision, this precipice, which plunges down to the center of the earth, was created by the impact of Lucifer's fall from Heaven. Incidentally, he is said to have fallen on the exact location of Jerusalem. At the very bottom of the ninth circle, Dante finds a passage to Purgatory, a sort of mountain whose shape is the mirror opposite of the tiered hole that is the circles of Hell. At the summit of that mountain is Paradise. To better visualize this shape, go open a volume of *Berserk* and take a look at the Tower of Conviction. As we've seen that Miura has created an inverted religion, we can speculate about the fact that this tower is an inversion of the circles of Hell. Instead of plunging down into the ground, in this case, Hell rises up to the sky in a tower where the same punishments you'd expect to find in the realm of the Devil are practiced. Whereas in Dante's *Inferno*, Lucifer sits on his throne in the deepest of the nine circles, the evil Guardian Angels appear at the top of the tower, which has collapsed into the form of a giant stone hand, the God Hand's classic throne. In the manga, many scenes and monsters evoke Dante's horrific visions of Hell. While I'm willing to bet that Miura has not necessarily read *The Divine Comedy*, there are two works that definitely would have introduced him to Dante's visions. First, he shows us that he is very familiar with the illustrations of Gustave Doré; second, he has closely read *Devilman*. Indeed, Go Nagai's cult manga series makes reference, in particular, to *The Divine Comedy* and draws inspiration from it in several aspects. Of these two works, for cultural reasons, it's likely that Nagai's manga had more influence on Miura. In 1972, Go Nagai was one of the first Japanese manga writers to create a manga with a universe centered on demons and the Devil, drawing inspiration from the Western, Christian tradition. Perhaps, without this precursor, Miura would not have settled on this type of demonic mythology. Nagai literally opened the doors to Hell in his manga: he included the frozen Hell in the deepest of Dante's nine circles, "the banks of the River Styx, which leads to Hell," and more. However, the number of elements from *Devilman* that were borrowed or expanded on by Miura is impressive: Nagai's manga tells the story of a friendship between two characters, Akira and Ryo, who are reminiscent of Guts and Griffith. Even Akira's transformation into Devilman makes you think of Guts when he "goes berserk." The relationship between *Devilman* and *Berserk* is even more clear when you look at the Witches' Sabbath scenes in *Berserk*, which echo the nightclub scenes in *Devilman*. In those frames, Nagai describes medieval Witches' Sabbaths in great detail, which seems to have strongly influenced Miura. It's as if Miura wanted to write a story in the mysterious past depicted by Nagai through his dialog. The similarities don't stop there: Devilman loses the same arm as Guts and Nagai's demons look so similar to *Berserk*'s apostles that they could be family. Other concepts in *Berserk* echo certain details from the 1972 manga, notably the fact that people have forgotten about the supernatural and no longer believe in monsters, putting them in mortal peril. As we can see, although Miura is not afraid to borrow ideas from works that are centuries old, he owes a lot to more contemporary creations, which in turn have also been inspired by the classics. But let's go back to the two main references mentioned at the beginning of this chapter and make a final leap back several centuries to talk about John Milton's *Paradise Lost*. This epic poem, written in 1667, tells a story that bears great resemblance to *Berserk*. At the beginning of the poem, Lucifer has just been defeated by God's armies, in spite of having been God's favorite angel. Falling victim to his immoderate pride, Lucifer believed that he was greater than God and started a war between God's obedient angels and his band of rebels. Lucifer is defeated and he falls from Heaven down into Hell with his troops. There, he takes control of Pandemonium, the palace of Hell's demons, and plots his revenge against his former master. Lucifer hears that God wants to create a new race—the human race—and, in retaliation, he goes to the Garden of Eden disguised as a serpent in order to trick Adam and Eve. He wants to have them expelled from paradise too and thus free them from God's guardianship. In addition, this would give humanity, to which we belong, free will. In *Berserk*, the first direct reference to Milton's poem is Pandemonium. This idea of a capital that's home to all of Hell's demons does not appear in the Bible: it's just a literary invention by Milton. Thus, to make reference to it is to expressly pay homage to the English poet's work. So, when the knight Locus brings Rickert behind the palace in Falconia, near a strange dome, he reveals to him that this "den of the war demons" bears the same name as Milton's mythical palace and he describes those demons as "the Falcon of Light's bodyguards." It's exactly as if *Berserk*'s Pandemonium is the barracks of demons described in the poem. Under this dome, monsters and apostles face off in a sort of vile gladiator arena. Upon seeing this macabre spectacle, Rickert comments in shock: "It's like a scene out of Hell!" Another clear homage to *Paradise Lost* is the scene of *Berserk* in which we see Zodd flying through moonlit clouds: it's almost an identical copy of the Gustave Doré engraving entitled *Satan Descends upon Earth*, which is actually an illustration of Milton's poem. However, the strongest reference has to be Griffith, who is a direct homage to Milton's Lucifer. First, there's the romantic vision that the 17th-century author delivers, which we could almost consider to be noble and poetic, but above all, Milton's Lucifer is a tragic antihero who constantly thinks about his paradise lost, much like Griffith, who pursues his dream with only a brief interruption. Just as Lucifer was cast out of Heaven by God for wanting to be greater than him, the King of Midland throws Griffith in a torture chamber for betraying him, stopping Griffith's dreams of domination and grandeur dead in their tracks. The wings that Femto acquires during the Eclipse are reminiscent of those of the fallen angel, a characteristic with which devils were long depicted. Just as Lucifer sneaks into the Garden of Eden disguised as a serpent, Femto infiltrates Falconia by passing himself off as Griffith the Liberator... In Milton's *Paradise Lost*, Satan's plan ultimately fails... Will the same be true for Griffith's dream?

SIGNS OF THE APOCALYPSE

Among all of the different literary forms represented in *Berserk*, there's one that gives the story a particular atmosphere: the apocalyptic tale. Our modern culture tends to give us an incomplete, biased image of the concept of "apocalypse." We tend to associate it with the end of the world and the extinction of humanity. At times, there's certainly a mystical dimension, but the meaning of apocalypse has been further misunderstood since the appearance of "post-apocalyptic" universes: from *Mad Max* to *I Am Legend*, we often see a devastated, wild, post-nuclear-holocaust world in which the few survivors return to a primal state. As such, the concept of apocalypse is often limited to the final disaster, to ruin and destruction, but while this "extraordinary" and catastrophic aspect does of course originate with the primary meaning of the term, restricting it to this definition means ignoring much greater complexity in its meaning. If we look at its etymology, the word "apocalypse" comes from a Greek word meaning "uncovering," or in its more religious sense, "revelation." In this sense, apocalypse does not refer so much to the end of the world as to the end of an era, which at the same time can mean the dawning of a new era. In this way, there's a positive dimension to apocalypse as it's a time of transition, a time in which that which has long been foretold is finally revealed. If we follow this line of thinking, there are many signs peppered throughout the manga that show that we are witnessing a veritable apocalyptic mythology in action. In the corpus of religious literature, there are many apocalyptic texts. However, the most famous of these has to be the Book of Revelation. It is the only source of this type to be recognized in the New Testament. In Revelation, the Apocalypse is described through a series of visions: the sky opens and reveals a "great sign in the sky." It's only then that the Judgment of the World takes place, demonstrating God's wrath. Then, seven seals appear, from which spring the Four Horsemen of the Apocalypse, as well as seven trumpets and seven angels. A series of disasters strikes the earth. They are only halted by "the 144,000 marked from every tribe of the Israelites." It's only after this that Revelation tells of the symbolic battle in which God, Christ, and their people face off against Satan and the powers that serve him. This is when we see the Dragon, "the ancient serpent, who is called the Devil and Satan," as well as the "false prophet," the Antichrist.

While Miura's apocalyptic tale does not follow that of John of Patmos exactly, it does incorporate several elements from it. First, there's the final battle against Ganishka, which is a condensed apocalypse. Thanks to its cataclysmic nature, Miura uses this passage to offer stunning visuals, of which he alone knows the secret. Indeed, volume 34 is filled with two-page spreads that expand the reader's field of vision and give larger views of the creatures depicted. The dimensions and scales of these monsters are dizzying, notably in the case of Ganishka's transformation, after which he looks more like one of H.P. Lovecraft's "Great Old Ones" than a traditional Japanese *kaiju*. The fighting makes the reader's head spin and shows the author's incredible mastery of visuals: he manages to bring together hundreds of creatures of very different sizes in a memorable, coherent, and epic battle. We can even see the Dantean sparring between apostles and amorphous abominations from the freshly opened Astral World. In this passage, Ganishka symbolizes the ultimate adversary, John the Revelator's infamous dragon: "I have obtained it. In the infernal abyss, I obtained it. The power!" He is the great Satan of the end of times. As they see him transform, some of the onlookers watching the scene, mesmerized, cry out: "What a sight... It's like... like witnessing the end of the world." To further underscore the idea, Miura defines Ganishka even more clearly with these words: "That's the Beast of the End. The one who brings to an end the reason of the world." But, curiously, evil seems to fail initially, as in the biblical text being referenced. Indeed, in the Book of Revelation, it's when Satan is defeated that a new world appears from the smoldering ruins of the old. The parallel with Falconia is striking: the city after the end of the world. John describes such a place clearly in his own apocalyptic vision as part of the coming of a new world and a new Heaven to replace the old ones that were destroyed. As part of this, a new Jerusalem comes down from Heaven... However, most importantly, *Berserk*'s "end of times" brings about a change in the junction between the Physical and Astral Worlds. This is precisely *Berserk*'s "revelation," the merging of the supernatural into the real world with the rise of Fantasia: "Amongst villages, cities, nations and peoples, for centuries–for millennia–stories have been told about them as if they really exist. People fear them, yearn for them, yet cannot catch or escape them. Thus have they gone on imagining this other half of the world and it now lies before their eyes." This apocalypse revealed a world which, up to that point, had been invisible to humans, a truth hidden behind reality. Finally, and above all, this apocalypse leads to the emergence of a false prophet masquerading as a "savior," a term used by the Pope himself to describe Griffith. He is the Antichrist with the face of an angel. This ambiguity is expressed by Laban: "A darkness that covers the world. I suppose that was a revelation. If it was, then... That Falcon... of Light..." Farnese, meanwhile, sees clearly through Griffith's duplicity: "The angel is the Falcon of Darkness. The master of the sinful black sheep, the king of the blind white sheep." As for Casca, she had already seen this prophetic dimension of the young Falcon very early on: "Back then I idolized Griffith. He was like some prophet or saint [...] A miracle. Yes, in my eyes, that's exactly what Griffith was."

Thus, Antichrist is among the many forms of the Devil embodied by Griffith and this side of him plays an important role in this apocalyptic drama. The concept of the Antichrist originated with the notion of "anti-messiah," which already existed in Judaism. The Antichrist is an evil, deceptive individual with a monstrous appearance or, on the contrary, a seductive one. The Antichrist's vile duplicity involves him playing the part of Jesus Christ over centuries. The coming of the Antichrist's reign, as part of the final ordeals before the end of the world, poses a risk to humanity. The figure of the Antichrist can be understood in different ways: it can be a group or an organization, a malign political system, or a false religion. However, most often, the Antichrist is interpreted as a single individual, who is supposed to usurp all of the love and adoration intended for the Christ alone, making him a false prophet. Over many volumes, *Berserk* foreshadows this apocalyptic process in which Griffith will play the role of Antichrist, with all of the prophecies throughout the manga predicting his coming. For example, while the Pope's Holy Iron Chain Knights are riding through the moors of Midland, they discover a strange lake whose waters seem to be of a deep red color. "Unmistakably, as prophesied, the red lake has appeared." As body parts float to the surface of the lake, Azan recites the passage from their holy book: "The revelations say that when the sun dies five times, a red lake will appear to the west of the city with a name both new and old. It is proof that the fifth angel will alight." The advent of Griffith is revealed in sacred texts and thus, the prophecies foretell volume 34, in which we see this apocalypse take place. Similarly, the dream that comes to all the inhabitants of Midland, including the Pope, also predicts the coming of Griffith. The way in which the Skull Knight speaks to Guts about the dream is quite revealing of this end of days: "Did you not see it too? The dream of the shining falcon? Likely every human in the world was witness to that same thing. It was a revelation. That someone who signifies the falcon is going to appear in this world. [...] The power of gods descended to earth... The concentration of that idea is called the Festival. And the Festival is essentially a divine work. It traces a phenomenon in the divine domain." It's yet another way in which Miura prepares us for this Final Judgment, this end of an era. As further proof of this analogy between Femto/Griffith and the Antichrist, these words appear during his transformation into a demon lord: "The fifth blessed king. The new demon king. Void. Slan. Ubik. Conrad. Thou art our extension. Our new kinsman to wear the mantle of evil. The wings of darkness Femto."

As is often the case, Miura muddies the waters, mixes together symbols, and turns value systems on their heads, which makes his influences and inspirations hard to untangle. His goal is not to be faithful to ancient texts, but rather simply to evoke, with subtle touches, the grandiose aspect of these apocalyptic tales.

DEUS EX MACHINA

The Skull Knight is peculiar in that his name is, well, just a physical description of him: he is an armor-clad skeleton riding a horse. While his moniker is not particularly original, everything else about him is actually quite unusual. First, there's his appearance: one of the only things that seems to physically differentiate him from an ordinary, inanimate skeleton is the pair of glowing orbs he has in place of eyeballs, giving this corpse a spark of humanity, an internal flame with immeasurable strength. While Miura sometimes modulates the intensity of the orbs' glow, the Skull Knight is, by nature, totally expressionless given that his face is just a skull with zero flesh remaining. This appearance is well chosen in that it gives him an archetypal human appearance—the skeleton—without giving him a face, thus connecting him to the human that he was before transforming into this enigmatic, spectral figure that comes out of nowhere in the night. The stoic air with which he proclaims his prophecies places him in the role of omniscient narrator who summarizes the story with the wisdom of the ancients. Furthermore, throughout the story, we also learn that the Skull Knight is not just a sage; he is actually one of the most powerful warriors in Midland history, with a legendary reputation. As proof, Nosferatu Zodd, the "battlefield god," says that the Skull Knight is the only adversary to have challenged him in 300 years. I have to say, the Skull Knight gives off an extraordinary aura, not to mention the fact that he looks like a horseman of the Apocalypse and he would fit perfectly into the role of a god of death. Moreover, that's exactly the impression that the young prostitute Luca gets when he saves her from a fatal fall. She takes him for the Grim Reaper himself. The skull is itself a symbol of death (largely popularized by the "Jolly Roger," the flag of pirate ships) and giving him this head is both simple and incredibly effective: he's a "good guy" who looks like a "bad guy." Even his armor is imposing and frightening: his torso is covered by a steel rib cage; sharp spikes cover his shoulders; metal barbs around his neck encircle and protect his sinister skull. He also has a classic shield ornamented with an emblem of a rose sitting on two interlinked circles of thorns. To add to the perfection of this undead warrior, Miura has him ride a powerful black stallion, who is also probably immortal, covered in pieces of armor in a similar style to that of his master; this horse also, unexpectedly, is capable of flying. What's more, it's likely that the Skull Knight cannot fly on his own; only his mount has this gift. The scene in which they emerge from the black circle covering the sun during the Eclipse is a memorable one and really illustrates the impressive appearance of this supernatural duo. The Skull Knight fights with a sword, which at first seems to be an ordinary weapon. Later on, we discover that he has the ability to "cover" his sword in all of the beherits he has previously swallowed. Indeed, each time he kills an apostle, the Skull Knight takes their beherit and swallows it whole. The process by which he is then able to cover his blade in the beherits, all clumped together, is not explained, but the resulting weapon has the strange ability to "shape" reality. Furthermore, this magical sword is neither innocent nor easy to wield. It gives off tremendous negative energy due to all of the suffering the beherits have caused. Moreover, on one of the rare occasions in which the Skull Knight uses the beherit sword, it produces an undesired effect: the Guardian Angels use its energy to carry out the merging of the Physical and Astral Worlds. One final physical characteristic that separates him from an ordinary skeleton: he has little bony horns around his skull, exactly as if he had a crown made of bone on his head. Could this be a clue of a royal past for this unique character?

Now that I've described everything we know for sure about the Skull Knight, everything that follows is at least somewhat speculative... Indeed, if you're one of those fans who likes to hypothesize about the secrets of *Berserk*, this character is probably one of your favorites. The Skull Knight is a veritable theory magnet. He is a conduit for knowledge of the story's hidden plot, as well as about the past and future of Midland. As such, one can't help but love this enigmatic figure and speculate about his nature. So, what is the story of this mysterious, shadowy character? How did he come to define himself as "the foe of the inhumans." Certain clues lead us to think that the Skull Knight is connected to the ancient Emperor Gaiseric, or even that he is Gaiseric's "ghost," his soul living on in a different incarnation. The fact that Gaiseric's armor was designed to look like a skeleton is just one of these clues. This would explain his involvement in the story and how he knows certain facts about the past that only people who lived at that time could know. Finally, his intense hatred of Void could go back to a time before the fall of the First Empire. Of course, Miura refuses to confirm this idea, but many fan theories point in this direction. There's another story that could explain the birth of the Guardian Angel Void: it's told that during the reign of Gaiseric, there was a sage that led a cult. The Emperor grew suspicious of its popularity. Jealous, he imprisoned the sage, who managed to invoke "an angel" to help him. While the story doesn't say much more than that, we learn from Charlotte that the fall, in a single night, of Gaiseric's empire was brought about by four or five angels... Without going further into theories, which remain speculative in spite of everything we know, we can ask ourselves this: if the Skull Knight is Gaiseric, could Void be the sage? This would explain their mutual hatred, or at least the Skull Knight's hatred for Void, since Void is the one who destroyed his empire... We also don't know how Gaiseric could have transformed from a human into a flying, skeletal ghost. Although it's very unlikely, the Skull Knight almost makes us think he could be a former apostle (or even Guardian Angel) who has changed sides. At the same time, after seeing the Skull Knight, Puck exclaims: "Maybe I imagined it, but that guy, he kinda felt like an elf..." Could he have gotten help from the elves to transform and become immortal? Also, what is the nature of his connection with the witch Flora? Clearly they have a past together because they seem to have known each other for a very long time and the Skull Knight seems to hold her in very high esteem. It's almost strange to see such a sinister and impressive character become so gentle and calm in the presence of the frail witch... Could Flora's magic be responsible for his immortality? Or, as he's said, was he "changed" from wearing the Berserker Armor? That would explain why he so often warns Guts about using it. Another thing about the Skull Knight that raises questions is his resemblance to the Black Swordsman in certain aspects. First, both are driven by vengeance against a common enemy; even if the Skull Knight wants Void's head while Guts wants

Femto's, they're both after the God Hand. They're both peerless warriors whose legendary battle prowess precedes them. When we see the Skull Knight fight, we get the impression that Guts is the only person who can match his mastery of the sword. Furthermore, the Skull Knight chooses the Black Swordsman to inherit the Berserker Armor because, although the gift is toxic, Flora and the Knight have confidence in him and believe that he is worthy of wearing it. At several points in the story, the Skull Knight gives Guts a warning, like a father or older brother would do, not to mention all of the times he saves Guts' life. The Skull Knight is also a sort of cautionary tale of what Guts could become if he ever lets himself be consumed by the armor: an empty shell, with his undying anger as his only companion.

If we assume that the Skull Knight is indeed Gaiseric, then it's important to note that this character has evolved significantly in terms of his values and actions. While the Emperor initially showed himself to be a strategic and gifted leader, having succeeded in building an empire by unifying the barbaric clans that inhabited the territories of Midland, he unfortunately ended up exploiting his own people. He came to be known as the "Demon King" or the "King of Galloping Death," and he was considered to be a merciless despot. Upon hearing his story, a member of the Band of the Falcon even says: "Sounds kind of like Griffith." In sum, supposing that Gaiseric and the Skull Knight are one and the same, then we can summarize his personal development as that of a repentant Griffith who becomes like Guts... Like Farnese, he is one of the characters who truly changes his values over time, transitioning from evil to good... Finally, the miraculous nature of the Skull Knight's appearances makes us wonder if perhaps he plays the role of a *deus ex machina*. Although this phrase is in Latin, the concept actually comes from the Greek theater world: in a tragedy, it was not unusual for a god to intervene on stage at a key point in the story. The idea was introduced by Aeschylus, a great Greek dramaturge, who most often used a *deus ex machina* to resolve conflicts and conclude the drama's plot. The actor playing the god was placed in a mechanism so that he would descend from above the stage, as if he were coming down from the heavens, hence the term "*deus ex machina*": god from a machine. Sometimes, the god would come out of a trap door or would come in from the side, but the principle remained the same. Over time, the phrase has taken on a slightly pejorative connotation: it refers to a sudden and improbable event that miraculously comes to get the protagonist out of a bad situation at the last second, much like the last-minute rescue by the Skull Knight during the Eclipse, when he saves Guts and Casca from a horrible and certain death. Along the same lines, the Skull Knight often comes to the rescue when Guts faces an adversary that is too strong for him, as when he fights Slan, Grunbeld, or the demonic crocodiles of the Kushan army. All of these examples support the idea that the Skull Knight is indeed a *deus ex machina*, watching over the story from behind the scenes, waiting for a situation requiring his intervention. He operates backstage; he sees what the audience does not. Miura manages this well because, in spite of everything, we hardly get the impression that the Skull Knight is used as an easy way out. Even though his interventions are often providential, they also often get the plot going again. The Skull Knight warns of a new danger while answering some of the reader's questions... and raising just as many new ones. In the end, thanks to his powers, his past, and his almost omniscient knowledge of the various plotlines, the Skull Knight gives us the impression that he is the true hero of a story much greater and much older than that of Guts. However, since his appearances are rare and his words are cryptic, he "feels like" a side character in *Berserk* who comes in at certain precise moments. However, the thing that pushes us to see him as an unsung hero is that he protects Guts and his friends, and that they share the same quest, just with different motives. Above all though, it's the Skull Knight's role as a *deus ex machina* that makes him such an important character. In *Berserk*'s world governed by causality, knowledge is power. In a way, the Skull Knight plays in a league higher than that of the common mortal. He is "above" the story and will probably have a central role in the manga's denouement. Thus, subtly pulling the strings enabled by this type of literary figure, Miura enshrouds the Skull Knight in a delectable narrative fog, giving us just enough to get our gears turning.

BERSERK

W R I T T E N   I N   D A R K N E S S

PART FOUR
The Labyrinth of the Imagination

RELIGION VERSUS IMAGINATION

Before we throw ourselves headlong into the imagination of artists, the subject of this final part of the book, we must take on one last battle. I'm talking about the fratricidal struggle between faith and imagination. This is one of the many themes that runs through the manga and Miura gives us many signs telling us that he is fascinated by this clash. In *Berserk*, this struggle mainly takes the form of a duel between a monotheistic religion—that of the Holy See—and pagan cults, presented as witches and witches' Sabbaths. While Miura's work does not in any way purport to be documentary, it's striking how the way in which he handles this subject echoes our own historical relationship with myths and religions. In this duel, while the author seems to be more critical of religion, the magical side takes quite a beating too. That's one of the *mangaka*'s subtleties: he does not give in to a simplistic, black-and-white worldview. First, he criticizes monotheism for trying to systematically discredit ancient beliefs and advance its own. For example, when a child throws a stone at Schierke, he yells: "The priest told us witches and trolls are the same!" When we see what horrendous creatures trolls are in the manga, we really understand the scorn that clergymen have for different religious practices. And they don't just try to discredit with words; they also do so with actions, for example, building a religious structure on a former pagan site. In a poignant monologue that's quite faithful to our reality, Schierke explains this takeover: "This hill upon which this church is built... It used to be a shrine to the spirits of this land. Many of the Holy See's churches are that way, literally crushing the sacred places of the spirit faith where they were built." When a site is destroyed, the witch's societal functions and ancient rites go with it: "Long ago, my mistress lived in a human habitation in this vicinity. She says she would go around the needy villages conveying the Spirits' voices to people, teaching about each season's weather and healing their sick. Who knows how many people were saved by my mistress' magic? But when the Holy See's sphere of influence spread through this region, they began building churches in villages. As if they had made a complete turnaround, people ostracized her and drove her into that forest." So, the Church works to crush the beliefs that preceded it by taking away land and smothering cultures and traditions. However, this aversion to pagan and magical cults is institutionalized to the point of totalitarianism as the Catholic Church invented a term—used identically by Mozgus—to

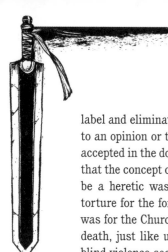

label and eliminate all that doesn't fit into its dogma: heresy. This word refers to an opinion or thought considered to be out of line with what's permitted or accepted in the domains of thought, knowledge, and religion. It was via religion that the concept of heresy took on its most sinister form. Anyone considered to be a heretic was tracked down, then punished or killed, most often using torture for the former and burning at the stake for the latter. All that it took was for the Church to decide that an act was impure for it to be punishable by death, just like under the worst dictatorships. This dogmatic absurdity and blind violence seems to both fascinate and revolt Miura, the result being that he focuses on the subject at length and in depth. He also bases his work off of real-life witch hunts and on the atrocities carried out after the publication of an evil religious text: the *Malleus Maleficarum*. I dare to use the term "evil" to describe this treatise, which was endorsed by the Church, because it led to the killing of thousands of "witches," or women arbitrarily labeled as such, in Germany, Switzerland, and France over several centuries. It's estimated that there were over 100,000 trials for witchcraft and researchers believe these resulted in somewhere between 40,000 and 60,000 executions. Thus, the *Malleus* brought about a veritable massacre aimed at stamping out the practice of witchcraft to leave only one possible belief, that is, in God. The *Malleus Maleficarum*, which means the "Hammer of Witches," as in the hammer to crush witches, is a treatise written in 1486 by two cold-blooded men: Henricus Institoris and Jacob Sprenger, both German Dominicans. Judge for yourself: the *Malleus* says that women, "because of their weakness and inferior intelligence, are, by nature, predisposed to give in more easily to Satan's temptations." These "witches" were supposedly responsible for storms, the destruction of crops, and orgies with demons. This book was intended for future judges overseeing witch trials, with the goal of helping them identify a witch thanks to certain signs and properly "investigate" the case. The second part of the text details how to capture, detain, and execute witches. You can read appalling accounts that show how these trials made a mockery of justice. For example, if a witch's lawyer put up too passionate of a defense? That meant she had bewitched him and so his defense was inadmissible. Conversely, judges, as representatives of God, were "immune" from any enchantments... The book lays out and illustrates the signs of witchcraft: clairvoyance, glossolalia (speaking in an incomprehensible language), and psychokinesis (acting on matter)... Finally, the *Malleus* shows the "marks of the Devil": abnormal spots on the skin or strange birthmarks, leanness, insensitive spots on the body, and even "toad's feet in the white of the eye." There was a custom of torturing the poor accused women to get them to confess to whatever (in *Berserk*, Nina denounces Casca under torture). In particular, the *Malleus* recommends using a red-hot iron to shave the entire body of the accused in order to find the supposed mark of the Devil. When you examine the contents of the *Malleus Maleficarum*, you find exactly the kind of text from which Mozgus draws his commandments. Indeed, the Inquisitor applies all of these atrocious precepts to a T. This is clearly shown in the way in which Mozgus' actions are described: "The wheel, impaling, stake burning, water torture... No less than five hundred people have been put to death under his judgment. And many times that number have lost their lives during torture. Those numbers are just like war. What's more, they say that once you're in his grasp, a single mole can make you a witch or heretic. He's the most famous and feared inquisitor the world over. For that alone, I'm sure he's the target of lots of spite and malice." As you might guess, this mention of "a single mole" is directly connected to the "mark of the Devil" in the *Malleus Maleficarum*. This insane, destructive fanaticism could at least do evil in service to a cause considered "just," but as Schierke explains, on top of everything else, those responsible ignore the truth and ruin what could have been their saving grace: "The current doctrine of the Holy See is nothing more than a tool by which to display its own political power. People invoke the name of God when going to war. They invoke the name of God when seeking salvation. Over and over, never tiring. When the key that saves them may be hidden in the very ones they are trying to forget." We see extreme hypocrisy among the clergymen, which Miura makes sure to underscore... A village priest, ironically, tells Schierke: "Relying on dubious superstitions like witches will not resolve our present state of affairs one bit." Does he really think that prayer will be any more effective? Believing in an invisible god is an act of purely supernatural and superstitious faith. How could it be worse or less valid to believe in the elemental forces of nature? Guts even asks him incredulously: "You're saying you believe in God but not in evil spirits?" However, it's with Farnese that Miura is the most direct and cynical. When Guts asks her if she has met God, she tells him no, but that he's in her heart. In response, Guts shuts her down with a tirade: "What a picture-perfect answer. Did you study in a convent? Long ago on the battlefield, a noble said nearly the same thing while he roasted women, children, an entire town... I ain't talking about some God like a hollow statue that ain't worth a damn. Confessin' is a waste of my time. I don't care about repentin'. You wouldn't understand a single thing I had to say. Just go and say a chant for me in some musty temple." His criticism is biting... But if you follow Miura's discourse, the worst crime of the Holy See's religion is having "disconnected" us from the forces of nature. That's exactly what young Schierke explains while contemplating the statue of the Sea God on the lost island: "As the doctrine of your religion spread throughout the world, the ancient gods were forgotten and faded into the depths of the Astral World. The old traditions must have still been passed down on this isolated island." Thanks to its remoteness from civilization, this island escaped the great cleansing carried out by the Holy See. By destroying and disparaging other myths, the monotheistic religion flushed the supernatural out of the

hearts of humanity, as the young witch again explains: "Long ago it was quite natural to believe in the existence of elves, but with the spread of the doctrine of the Holy See, of one universal world view, those who can see them have dwindled... So many of the elves who can no longer interact with humans have faded away to some place in the Astral World." Puck and Schierke explain that once upon a time, people went to wizards and witches for help and worshiped pagan deities. Basically, before monotheism crushed mythology, the two worlds lived together in peace because people were not afraid of spirits and, more importantly, they "believed" in them... This allowed the spirits to exist. The idea that belief enables an invention of the mind to gain enough substance to manifest is a recurring theme in the manga. For example, there's the Idea of Evil, created by humans, or the Qliphoth, supposedly formed from human nightmares. However, this idea is best represented by the elves. Farnese, while still wearing the blinders of her religion, is totally unable to see an elf flying right in front of her face. Puck, of course, is quite peeved by this, sad to be rejected in this way: "She doesn't see. She's not trying to. When it comes to me... to elves... she doesn't perceive us." As another little jab at the obtuse character of religious fanatics, Puck gives a long, eloquent monologue on closed minds, those who have let the flame of the supernatural go out: "For instance... when humans notice somethin', it stays in their memory. But if it's somethin' they don't care about, they don't remember, do they? [...] For some reason, lotsa priests are like that. Not so much in rural chapels, but when I go in big cathedrals, I'm not seen too much. And like in big cities. [...] Oh yeah, those who cling to the rigid world don't perceive elves." Miura implies here that the loss of belief in pagan supernatural figures has deprived the world of a more humanistic and peaceful way, with a narrow view of the truths of the world forced upon people. Flora explains this well: "The world doesn't extend in merely two dimensions. There exist profound depths within itself. This world could never be summarized by materialism or any single doctrine." In other words, the cosmic truth is too vast and too complex to be explained by a dogma that excludes all other beliefs. In a sense, the practice of witchcraft requires that you be able to demonstrate greater humility. Moreover, the old witch explains it thusly: "Accept the great mysteries and explore the entire universe from within your world, that is the way of magic." Miura implicitly tells us that witchcraft, contrary to the monotheistic religion, does not involve believing that you hold the truth and killing those who don't share that same vision. The witches succinctly condemn this principle of imposing one's own views on others when it comes to such mystical and personal beliefs: "Whatever different word you use to express them, the sun is the sun, and light is light. The mantras chanted may differ, but are not souls in want of salvation all the same? To divide and oppress people because of those differences is folly. God's name belongs only to God. It is not for man to conduct." In fact, throughout the manga, religious fanatics are presented as being incapable of opening their minds to cosmic concepts and forces because of the thought patterns they have boxed themselves into. We almost get the impression that they're "muggles," the term from the *Harry Potter* saga referring to humans who are incapable of performing magic and who sometimes cannot even bear its very existence. It's interesting to note that now that the Astral and Physical Worlds have become one, everyone will, of course, be forced to "believe" in the supernatural since it has entered the realm of reality. Miura also implies that magic is a more "positive" force than faith since it draws from the elements that make up life: "The four states inherent to the Physical World—solid, liquid, vapor, and energy—are all resonant with the workings of elementals in the Astral World, respectively, earth, water, wind, and fire." Thus, in order to invoke them and draw from their power, you must have a symbiotic relationship with these elements. You must connect to nature and the universe. As Farnese puts it, as she's progressing in her mastery of magic and preparing to invoke the Four Kings: "I feel how enormous the thing is of which I'm a part." Miura seems to favor this peaceful return to nature, with respect and humility, over the hunting of supposed "infidels" to be burned at the stake for heresy. Like everything else in *Berserk*, magic is presented in a complex, well developed fashion that's rarely over-the-top. Schierke, Flora, and Farnese practice theurgy, i.e. the invocation of benevolent beings; conversely though, others, such as the worshipers of the Great Goat, and by extension the Guardian Angels, instead practice the secret art of goetia, i.e. the invocation of demons. In a way, here we see the classic opposition between white magic and black magic. Flora can draw geometric symbols on your body to provide you with magical protection. She can enchant weapons by giving them the power of the elements, as she does with Serpico's Sylph Sword or Isidro's Salamander Dagger. Most importantly, witches can access the Astral World at will... However, while Miura seems to lean toward supporting "magic," he also gives us a warning: like any powerful force, in the wrong hands, it can bring terror and devastation. For example, when Void inflicts the Brand of Sacrifice, he also simply practices magic. So, magic can be a formidable weapon if used in service to evil. In the end, Miura does not pass judgment. He's not there to tell us what's right or wrong. His goal is to make us "walk in the shoes" of good and evil and to show us that things are not all black and white. The worst part of religion, according to Miura, may be its inaction, the passivity towards fate, as if faith means enduring—waiting and praying—while magic calls you to action: acting on what you can to change fate. This is perfectly illustrated by the village priest who, instead of accepting help from a witch, tells his followers to wait to be saved without defending themselves under the pretext that it's all just a case of God testing his faithful. So, sometimes, fanaticism is synonymous with fatalism.

ONE MYTH TO RULE THEM ALL

Apart from when a new "narrative technology" appears (such as virtual reality or the internet), these days, it's almost impossible to write a totally original story. That said, you can create a story that mixes so many borrowed original aspects that it creates the illusion of being like no other and gives off an air of novelty. In the case of *Berserk*, the visual style tends to be more willfully original while the story's content tends to be more "connected" to older stories. Whether you like it or not, whenever you write a story, you necessarily borrow, sometimes without even realizing it, from other, pre-existing narratives. With millions of stories written since humans first began telling them, you can be sure that whatever plot device, while it may at first seem innovative, has been used before. It's extremely difficult for the mind to come up with something it has never seen before. Then, there's the fact that there are also invisible rules to which storytellers conform. The result is that fictional plots resemble one another and obey similar storytelling conventions. In Greek mythology alone, you can already find practically all the story types and archetypal symbolic structures that exist. Furthermore, creating an entirely original story makes almost no sense because, for example, to create surprise in a novel, it's important that the reader first feel a certain familiarity so that they can then be better tricked. In 1989, when Miura began *Berserk*, it was already difficult to create something "never before seen" or a story "never before told." While the form of a story may be easily differentiated from others, its content often goes back to the same ancient sources used by every other story. To illustrate this point, let's look at the work of Joseph Campbell. In his book *The Hero with a Thousand Faces*, this American professor, who specialized in mythology, showed that the journey of all the great heroes follows the same, universal progression. After analyzing the structures and finding the common points in hundreds of stories, myths, legends, and religions, Campbell came up with a common, fundamental structure. From this, he theorized about the "monomyth," the idea that all myths are a variation on a single story. While his book received little recognition from his colleagues when it was published, it went on to be used later as a "bible" by creators who discovered Campbell's work. His research is too in-depth and extensive to be explained here without misrepresenting it, but the book is a gold mine. It tries to explore the other side of the myth, to understand the hidden structure behind the stories that humans have told over the course of millennia. To summarize, Campbell teases out the various phases that form the physical, psychological, and mystical adventure in a legendary story. He shows that all heroes go through stages, plot twists, dilemmas, challenges, and rewards. In this sense, *Berserk* is no exception to the rule: Miura's story goes through literally all of the steps enumerated by Campbell. In today's world, if you want to create something original, the most practical solution, other than trans-media remakes or adaptations, is to mix together seemingly disparate universes in a post-modern mash-up. Basically, you try to blend two distinct plot structures to create a new one. For example, *Shaun of the Dead* (Edgar Wright, 2004) combines a zombie film with a romantic comedy; *Westworld* (produced, among others, by J.J. Abrams) puts androids in a Western; *The Exorcism of Emily Rose* blends together a demonic possession film with a court film; the list goes on. If it seems like I'm going overboard with the examples, it's to highlight the idea that we are living in an age of references, re-creation, homages, revisions, etc. Starting from this same trend while trying to push the principle even further, Miura has given himself a crazy and ambitious challenge: to create a story that can "accommodate" and encompass any fantasy myth. In his series, the *mangaka* tries in a way to prove Campbell's thesis through reverse engineering: instead of showing that all myths tell the same story, he creates a tale that can fit all myths within it. Thanks to the mythological rules established in *Berserk*, there's no story or legend that can't find a place in the manga's supernatural universe. This is Miura's way of being original: proving that you can create a unifying, universal myth... In short, it's as if he's trying to write the monomyth. The *mangaka* uses many different devices to discreetly incorporate bits of existing universes into his series and, first and foremost, he incorporates bits of beliefs from real-life human cultures. For example, the sorcerer Daiba rides on a pterodactyl-like creature named Garuda. This name is no random creation: "Garuda" is a Sanskrit word for a man-bird from Hindu mythology who was said to be Vishnu's mount. It's simple, but effective because giving such a meaningful name to a creature so similar to its model shows that Miura has simply incorporated, almost as-is, a creature from a known religious myth. This is also the case with the tree that appears after the "Great Roar of the Astral World." The enormous tree of light connecting the heavens to the earth is a reference to the *axis mundi*, the earth's central axis, symbolizing the link between humanity and the gods. Depending on the culture, this *axis mundi* can come in different forms: mountains, as is the case with Mount Fuji; mythical structures, such as the Tower of Babel; and in Buddhism, particularly in references tied to the Kushan Empire, the *axis mundi* comes in tree form. What's more, Miura makes it very clear that he is trying to reference a universal symbol given that this is how he describes the tree that grows after the death of Ganishka: "Like the northern Tree of Myth, piercing the heavens and reaching to the ends of earth, like the eastern Tree of Sutra, where the sage meets enlightenment, like the western Tree of Ritual, signifying the reason of all creation... As if it were the origin rooted deep within all mankind, it was like the very essence of 'tree' itself." Thus, the author is very transparent about his intention to unify all of these cultural references. To do this, he draws on the folklore of various cultures, notably Irish Celtic culture. The name Skellig is a perfect example of

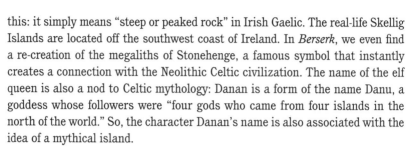

this: it simply means "steep or peaked rock" in Irish Gaelic. The real-life Skellig Islands are located off the southwest coast of Ireland. In *Berserk*, we even find a re-creation of the megaliths of Stonehenge, a famous symbol that instantly creates a connection with the Neolithic Celtic civilization. The name of the elf queen is also a nod to Celtic mythology: Danan is a form of the name Danu, a goddess whose followers were "four gods who came from four islands in the north of the world." So, the character Danan's name is also associated with the idea of a mythical island.

Miura works cleverly, using little touches of references from distinct sources. Elfhelm, on the island of Skellig, could in fact be inspired by the universe of J. R. R. Tolkien, who used this word as the name of one of his characters. The connection with *The Lord of the Rings* is no surprise in a series that aims to pay homage to the fantasy genre. Miura's borrowings from this groundbreaking series don't stop there: doesn't Guts believe that the trees talk, exactly like Ents, the forest spirits from Middle-earth? Elfhelm looks exactly like a peaceful village in the Shire: with a few Hobbits, you'd think you were in Tolkien's universe. On another note, when the Egg of the Perfect World tells his story, you can't help but see a parallel with the character Gollum. Like the wretched holder of Sauron's ring, one day, the Egg randomly came across a mysterious artifact, with which he became so obsessed that his appearance changed. While Gollum found the ring in the water, the Egg found his precious object deep in a trash heap he called home. Both were rejected by humans and ended up hiding deep underground, where they became crazy monsters... Their objects corrupted them to the point of turning them evil.

While Guts and his band are being guided to Elfhelm by the young wizards, just after arriving on Skellig, they suddenly enter an enchanted forest that's home to all of the classic magical beasts: unicorns, fairies, gnomes, goblins, fauns, etc. Miura is well aware that he's playing with clichés here, using our general image of fantasy creatures. He even has one of his characters comment on this: "This is amazing... Elfhelm indeed." Even the name Midland is somewhat reminiscent of "Middle-earth," the famous lands invented by Tolkien. Miura is a gracious host: he shows that all of these references can live together in harmony, and since Tolkien himself was inspired by Celtic myths when writing his novels, the relationship is consistent. Inspired by European mythology, the *mangaka* boldly continues his journey through Celtic lands, this time on the Scottish side: in *Berserk*, we find domesticated creatures called "brownies" that look like bipedal moles. We see them dusting in a house using feather dusters. Miura purposely, directly borrowed this concept: brownies are very well-known creatures from Scottish folklore. They were described as benevolent household spirits who perform chores for the family that agrees to host them; in exchange, the family gives them food. They even had the reputation for bringing good luck. This is yet another example, among the hundreds, showing that Miura loves the culture and history of myths and that his creativity is sharpened and stimulated by bringing together existing ideas to make them his own by stretching his imagination to its limits, the goal always being to write the ultimate universal story. In the manga, we also come across a kelpie, another character from Scottish folklore. Interestingly, Miura strives to stick closely to the mythical definition of this shape-shifting creature mentioned in numerous myths and legends. The kelpie was said to have characteristics of sea creatures, horses, and humans, living in streams and rivers, exactly like in *Berserk*. The *mangaka* also plays around with the classical fantasy beasts to the fullest extent possible: he includes trolls, dragons, elves, merrows, incubi, ogres, hydras, cockatrices, harpies, unicorns, goblins, golems, gnomes, and more. When Guts sails in a ship over several volumes? That's a great opportunity for Miura to explore all of the myths attached to the sea, as we saw with the Sea God. Similarly, just after Puck and the fortune-teller have left Rickert, she sees figures appear in her crystal ball: first Ketu, then Rahu. Once again, Miura did not make up these names: in ancient legends from the East, Ketu is a star that appears suddenly in the sky to frighten people; more importantly, it's also the descending lunar node, also called the "dragon's tail" in Indian astrology. Rahu, meanwhile, is said to be the star that steals the light of the sun and the moon; it is supposed to cause eclipses, as well as being the ascending lunar node. This "vision" appears in volume 12, right at the moment where the Eclipse begins... So, this reference is not without meaning and serves two functions. The first is to herald the advent of Femto—represented by Rahu, the bringer of eclipses—and to prepare the reader for what's about to happen; of course, only those who know the legend of Rahu would be able to make the connection with this obscure reference. The second function is to imply that the legends of our world actually make reference to the story of *Berserk*. So, there's a subtle way of "unifying" myths. This reminds me of the concept of syncretism, which is when elements from different beliefs are incorporated into a single religion. More broadly, syncretism implies that God may have a different name from one religion to the next, but by definition, it's the same God for all of us. Miura promotes the idea of a sort of syncretic mythology, creating a new body of myths from older ones. The rise and fall of Griffith can be seen, as we said in Part One, as an adaptation of the myth of Icarus, who, intoxicated by the joy of flying with his wax wings and feathers, gets too close to the sun and ends up falling into the sea.

These two stories evoke similar archetypal emotions. So, the *mangaka* discovered the mouth to the "canal of myths" and decided to have *Berserk* skillfully sail down it. The Astral World is the perfect representation of this in that it is home to every imaginary creature you can think of. From this one place, anything can come out. Another famous old work, already referenced in this analysis, incorporates different myths in the same way: Dante Alighieri's

Divine Comedy. In this epic tale, the hero is the author himself; the secondary character who accompanies him is Virgil, the author of the *Aeneid*, a mythological story that tells of the descent into Hell of Aeneas, a hero from the Trojan War and ancestor to Romulus and Remus. Virgil, a Latin poet who lived in the 1st century BCE, having already described the underworld well before Dante, "knows" the place well; thus, he plays the role of guide. That's exactly the same narrative principle that Miura uses: work within a pre-existing mythical framework and deliver a new, even more detailed understanding. While Miura enjoys hiding his references, Dante was much more blatant with them. In the story, he comes across dozens of historical and mythical figures, particularly as he travels through Hell. This is justified in his story since these people are dead or legendary: if you had to guess where you might find them, Hell would be a good bet. In no particular order, throughout the *Divine Comedy*, Dante meets Aristotle, Cleopatra, Achilles, Socrates, Saint Paul, Adam, Plato, the Virgin Mary, Moses, Noah, Caesar, Thales, and many others... The *Marvel Cinematic Universe* still has nothing on these Avengers of antiquity! Miura is clearly not the first person to strive to encapsulate all myths in a story that makes sense. When you see all that the author manages to effortlessly include in his story, it becomes clear just how skillfully his "*legendarium*" is constructed. *Berserk* is like a museum of stories, with a wide range of sources of inspiration, often leaving you impressed as a reader. For example, Miura pays homage to the plays of Shakespeare, specifically *Hamlet*, in the scene where Guts speaks to the freshly severed head of Vargas, screaming at fate to swear that, on his honor as a warrior, he will not end up like that.

There are also numerous references to fairytales and children's stories in different forms. Sometimes, the references are direct, as when Sonia, Griffith's devoted follower, talks to Schierke about her master, comparing her destiny to that of Hans Christian Andersen's *Ugly Duckling*. Miura also alludes to the Brothers Grimm and Charles Perrault with his references to captive or over-protected princesses waiting for their Prince Charming. We see this archetype in Theresia and also, particularly, in Charlotte. Griffith's way of entering the princess' room via the window is taken from stories such as *Rapunzel*, in which the prince, after facing many obstacles, finally manages to reach his beloved by climbing through her window. However, Miura does not simply reference or draw inspiration from existing stories: we can consider the story of the elves in the Misty Valley its own full-fledged fairy tale. Whether it's the adventures of Peekaf the Outcast or those of Rosine, these stories follow the same structure and classic morals of folktales, like an homage, more discreet this time, from Miura to the stories that are so important to our childhood. As usual, he mixes classic fairy tales with their more modern versions, such as *Peter Pan* (book by J.M. Barrie published in 1911). Don't you think Rosine and the elves who accompany her are a bit like Tinker Bell and the Lost Boys? Besides the refusal to grow up, embodied by a hatred of adults, when Rosine asks her elves what they should do with Guts, their response is decisive: "Get him! He's a liar! He's a lying grown-up. We always get the grown-ups!" Sometimes, you don't need to make a "clear" reference to a work for it to immediately come to the reader's mind. While reading this passage, I definitely thought of *Peter Pan*, even though I couldn't remember the title of Barrie's book. Finally, the last way in which Miura alludes to folk tales is by implying that the manga itself *is* a fairy tale: "We were now surely in the midst of some extraordinary tale." In support of this goal of creating a myth, we remember how much Miura focuses on the idea of making Griffith a legendary figure. Lastly, Miura presents the idea that his creatures are those described in folktales: "Although that is the realm of fable and folklore [...] The first night of winter, a pack of trolls attacked the village. Just like they had fallen out of a tale, they emerged from the darkness." Like something straight out of a fairy tale: there's the idea. We can almost say that the conception of Fantasia comes from a question that must have crossed Kentaro Miura's mind: what would happen if, after an event, all fantasy creatures suddenly came to life and entered our reality? "Amongst villages, cities, nations and peoples, for centuries, for millennia, stories have been told about them as if they really exist. People fear them, yearn for them, yet cannot catch or escape them. Thus have they gone on imagining this other half of the world and it now lies before their eyes. Mankind's desire." The intention is loud and clear: Miura wants to force those who believe in God to see the other forces that exist in this world. He knows that this confrontation between the real and the imaginary, between the Physical and Astral Worlds, will lead to a fascinating competition. As Isma puts it so nicely: "It's like the world's gone all bizarre ever since that strange wind blew through."

In addition to theater and folklore, Miura makes other tributes to literature. While he alludes to *Treasure Island* (R. L. Stevenson, 1883) while Guts' party is at sea, or the legend of the Man in the Iron Mask, a figure used many times in the history of literature, Miura returns most often, especially while Griffith is being tortured, to the work of H.P. Lovecraft, an American writer who shaped the horror aesthetic of the 20th century. While I've already described the most obvious homage to Lovecraft, in the Sea God segment of the story, there are other, more subtle references. First off, there's the appearance of the Idea of Evil, which is without a doubt inspired by one of Lovecraft's Great Old Ones. The God Hand has that dizzying, cosmic, terrifying dimension of a Lovecraft creature. Then there's the final form of Ganishka, which matches certain descriptions of Lovecraftian beasts: colossal, tentacular, and unspeakable. Above all, though, the structure of *Berserk* is very similar to that of a cosmic horror story in which humans find themselves powerless in the face of dark forces from another dimension that try to take control of reality. The scorn

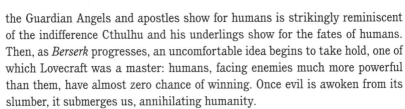

the Guardian Angels and apostles show for humans is strikingly reminiscent of the indifference Cthulhu and his underlings show for the fates of humans. Then, as *Berserk* progresses, an uncomfortable idea begins to take hold, one of which Lovecraft was a master: humans, facing enemies much more powerful than them, have almost zero chance of winning. Once evil is awoken from its slumber, it submerges us, annihilating humanity.

As I've already said, while Miura uses an abundance of references, they are just a starting point. He takes them, fits them together, and shapes them in his own way. In fact, if you type "beherit" into a search engine, you'll find more people who think that the word was invented by Miura instead of being one that predated *Berserk*. Miura transformed a forgotten word—beherit—into an iconic pop-culture term. Doesn't that show deference and a desire to pass on myths and ancient knowledge rather than random appropriation? If you look properly, you can see that the author's intention is quite far from simply trying to break a crude record for the greatest number of references. Perhaps Miura even sees in his monomyth something deeper and more psychoanalytical. There are two passages in the manga that point us in this direction. The first is when Guts is speaking with Vargas about the Count's beherit. He says to the old wise man that the object is a key used to open "another dimension that has manipulated the dark side of human history since ancient times." Could Miura be referencing the universal fears that lie in our collective unconscious? It's the idea that the imagination is a space shared by all of us to which we can connect through a dark corner of our minds. It's an idea—with zero scientific proof—that could explain why we find common elements in the works of authors who have never met, as if the stories that people believed they were making up were in fact just versions of a story hidden within all of us, symbolic of what drives us as humans. Miura often inserts the idea that it's by believing in the supernatural that it comes to life, as mentioned in the previous chapter when we looked at the concrete impact that believing in the supernatural can have on religion and our relationship with the world around us, as explained by a belief. In this case, we're looking more at the "universal" imagination and its life-or-death power over ideas, and thus over things. It's a bit like Robin Williams in the film *Hook* (Steven Spielberg, 1991): when he's sitting at the table in the Lost Boys' hideout, he first thinks that the boys are just pretending to eat food and are mocking him, but as soon as he begins to believe in the imaginary, the food appears before him. Isidro goes even further in a discussion with Flora, suggesting that, as a matter of logic, all you would need to do is no longer believe in the odious trolls for them to disappear. The witch's response is even more revealing in regards to the place in our brains in which imagination resides: "Things are not that simple. There is a thing called the subconscious that humans cannot themselves control." Finally, the Idea of Evil is the ultimate proof that our shared unconscious is real to a certain extent and that it is capable of creating abominations...

To conclude, if we don't want to come up with a whole new term to define Miura's spectrum of references, we could call it "total fantasy," a genre that comprises all sub-genres of fantasy, given that *Berserk* includes all of the fantasy creations you can think of: everything from dragons to devils, from zombies to Great Old Ones to unicorns, from biblical demons to legendary beings, in spite of them all being connected to very distinct eras and bestiaries. Getting so many different references to cohere so consistently is a real feat made all the more astounding by how this heap of borrowed ideas seems perfectly natural, never forced. There's a very humble and moving part of Miura's biography that could explain why he's so steeped in culture and how he's able to blend so many myths together. Here's what he says about when he began studying art:

"In an art class at my high school, I made close friends with all those who were interested in movies or music. However, I got to realize there was some kind of emptiness in me, in getting along with them. Meanwhile I was one of a group of five friends whose goal was to be a *mangaka*. All of them had their own specialty other than drawing manga, like playing the guitar for example. We influenced and introduced each other to things, saying things like 'this movie is great' or 'you should read this book... Otherwise, you won't be able to be a *mangaka*[1].'"

In another interview, he again references this time in his youth where, as an aspiring *mangaka*, he felt frustrated about his lack of cultural knowledge:

"The truth is that I sat at my desk drawing manga all the time and seriously lacked personal experience, and I felt insecure about that. Which is why I started thinking that I had better at least absorb as much of the stuff people recommend as possible[2]."

Here's a thought: what if Miura chose to absorb as much art and culture as possible to give himself some "substance"? In that case, *Berserk* could be viewed as a sort of personal diary of Miura's artistic feelings, stories that have moved him, and discoveries he's made. His manga could be, in a way, his personal art museum where he displays the works that have made an

1. Interview given in December 1996 in Kentaro Miura's studio, published in *Berserk: Illustrations File*. See Bibliography.
2. Interview conducted by Yukari Fujimoto, published in September 2000 and available on the website: https://mangabrog.wordpress. Translation by the blog author.

impression on him, works collected on a journey undertaken to explore other universes. To take this idea even further, it was by "absorbing" all of these creations that he discovered the world of the collective imagination. This incredible adventure that is *Berserk* was born of the frustration of a young man who felt that he lacked knowledge of culture and who, instead of getting upset or just giving up, threw himself headlong into the ocean of stories and myths in order to construct his own epic tale...

THE PUPPET MASTER

If you're not familiar with the album cover of Metallica's *Master of Puppets*, I encourage you to check it out as it's the perfect introduction to this chapter. It shows a cemetery filled with perfectly aligned headstones in the form of white crosses, much like the graves of American soldiers. In the upper corners of the image, hidden in the red sky, are two hands of divine proportions pulling on thousands of strings attached to the tombs. This instantly reminded me of someone controlling a puppet with invisible strings. That's what we call a "puppet master." Except that on the album cover, it's not puppets, but rather tombstones, that we see in the role of plaything, in spite of being decidedly inanimate objects. These hands would fit perfectly into Kentaro Miura's aesthetic given how his characters are so steeped in darkness and how he has them go through extreme evolutions. Indeed, the author seems to love having his characters swing from one state of mind to another and seeing how they react to his sometimes brutal plot decisions. Dr. Miura's laboratory of experiences is not a place where I would send even my worst enemy... As we've seen, Midland is a place that spares no one, a merciless world that, before long, requires that everyone be constantly on their guard. The *mangaka* is the master of life and death in *Berserk* and, of course, through what he makes his characters go through, he abuses his readers. As a puppet master with a divine aura, he has no problem making his puppets dance in a way so sinister that the audience knows to expect the unexpected and that their moral fortitude will be seriously tested. The moment when Guts accidentally kills Adonis exemplifies this idea because, at that point in the story, we "like" Guts and have forgiven his inhumane actions from early on in the story. And then he goes and fatally stabs a child, considered innocent by nature. This murder may have been involuntary, but given the state it sends Guts into, we understand that the Black Swordsman, because of this act, has a triggering experience in which, for the first time, his violence disgusts him and comes back to bite him. For us readers, it's terrible: we witness one of the greatest taboos, the killing of a child, and yet Miura, in the way he sets the scene, asks us to forgive the person who committed this act, Guts... which, over time, we will eventually do. Miura often plays the role of a mad amusement park operator, controlling a wild emotional roller coaster that constantly takes us on a plunge down into Hell. Of course, it's the Eclipse that takes the award for the biggest massacre of fictional characters by an author. For 13 volumes, we watched a band of characters fight, survive, love each other... and then we watched almost all of them suddenly be put to death. It appears that the puppet master isn't afraid to destroy his puppets so that he can start playing with new ones... However, the Eclipse plays another role in terms of conditioning the reader. Indeed, the Eclipse is a warning, as if Miura is telling his audience: "Have you seen what I'm capable of?" The message is that, with Miura, you should always expect the worst. The fear that such an event might occur again thus becomes a sort of Damocles' sword, putting the reader in suspense. An example from film, though one that came out after publication of the manga first began, uses a similar device. Wes Craven's *Scream* (1996) begins with a horrible scene in which Casey Becker (played by Drew Barrymore) is being hunted by the Ghostface Killer and ends up hanging from a tree by her own intestines. The scene is atrocious, nerve-racking, and gory, but above all, it serves as the opening to the film, thus conditioning the audience from the very beginning to see terrible things... It makes the viewers ask themselves: "If this is just the beginning, what's it going to be like later?" Yet, no scene throughout the rest of the film gets anywhere close to this level of horror and violence. However, because that scene is etched in our minds from the beginning, each time the killer appears, we feel our terror rise out of fear that the opening scene will be reproduced. Similarly, even as *Berserk's* tone has "softened" and ordinary fantasy has gained the upper hand over dark fantasy, I have still had a little voice in my head telling me that Miura is preparing a nasty surprise for us, a new event even more destructive than the Eclipse. Thus, the genius of the *mangaka*–and of Wes Craven–is in perfectly controlling the way in which he plays with his audience's fear and fascination with horror.

Not content to just play with our visceral fears, Miura is also very gifted when it comes to creating personalities that "divide" his readers. This is the case with Griffith, of course. While most readers begin to hate him from the Eclipse onward, as the manga progresses, others actually end up trying to excuse his actions: to achieve his goal, he had to agree to sacrifice his loved ones. If his goal is noble and ultimately serves the greater good, is his sacrifice really so reprehensible? Also, since his "rebirth," those who like the early Griffith see him being his best self again, as Miura depicts him as a god on earth, as if to further heighten the uncomfortable feeling that comes with his return to Midland. Changing tone, Puck and Isidro are also divisive for displaying too much humor and being annoying at times. I think that Miura is well aware that each character has their fans and what he does to those characters will have an impact on his readership, so no movement by the puppet master is without meaning. The *mangaka* was also smart in creating many "fragile" characters who are indecisive and racked by doubts. For example, for a long while, Guts doesn't know what to do with his life and we don't know what he'll do next. Additionally, we're constantly afraid that he will descend into madness because of his armor... All of the characters are walking on a tightrope from which they risk falling. Farnese is constantly questioning her faith, while Casca first doesn't know who to love, then doesn't even know who she is. These characters on the edge are easier to shape and turn on their heads than a very distinct protagonist anchored by a strong personality. We've already seen this: Miura likes to jerk his puppets around. That's why it's not unusual to witness a character do an "about-face," making a 180-degree turnaround. There's Griffith's sudden betrayal, of course, but also the King of Midland's bout of insanity. Along the same lines, Rosine, in spite of having the best intentions, completely changes once she becomes an apostle. Like her, all those who use beherits to become apostles make this moral U-turn and their victims thus see their loved ones transform into executioners in a snap. While the fate of these characters is often tragic and "preventable," it is also... ironic. The most striking example is Casca, who, as a girl, is saved by Griffith, who later becomes her torturer. The Falcon, meanwhile, spent years and years climbing the ladder of power, only to see everything collapse because of a little fit of jealousy. We also see this irony when the Skull Knight, believing that he's saving the world with his magic sword, actually helps the antagonists carry out their plan. Many episodes in the manga have the flavor of dark humor brought about by this feeling of irony, in which karma plays tricks on those that have gotten on its bad side or bad luck hinders the best intentions. For Miura, it's also a way of delivering little parables about life. The character that best represents this turning of tables occasionally brought about by the irony of fate is Farnese: she spends her life burning witches at the stake... only to end up becoming one herself. There's a particularly interesting dialog on this subject at the exact moment when Flora meets Farnese for the first time at the Mansion of the Spirit Tree. "My folk were not among those whose lives you took." So, the tragic irony: Farnese only killed innocent women. However, it's Miura's way of showing how peaceful and wise Flora is, as she forgives Farnese: "Even if they were, the fault would collectively lie upon the servants of your deity. I do not seek retribution from you as an individual." Thus, it's doubly ironic because Farnese was wrong in her judgment and wanted to kill people who are actually more evolved and empathetic than she is. The irony is so strong that the young woman chooses to completely change her views of morality and the world. She is one of a few characters in the manga to find a form of redemption, to choose a better path for themselves and for others. She questions everything she has been taught and indoctrinated to. She forces herself to face a frightening new world. She learns to fight and ends up joining the cause she had always battled against. In this way, she demonstrates a radical change in her mentality and begins to let empathy guide her. This change in Farnese is completed when she eventually manages to perform magic, as if nature and the elements have finally accepted her. Nina and Guts are also among the characters who evolve in the right direction; Jill manages to find the strength to fight in spite of the pain and tragedy she suffers; and even Schierke ends up seeing the point in helping humans, in spite of their nature. All of these characters who pull themselves away from the dark side are lights that shine in the darkness of Midland. Miura is an alchemist who plunges his inventions—his characters—into different storytelling baths, then describes to us what happens, trying to imagine how humans might react in response to the wildest and darkest possible events. The *mangaka* also loves to deconstruct his characters, by which I mean that he starts with a cliché, then proves it wrong, as we see with Guts and Griffith. From being boorish, violent, chauvinistic, and nihilistic—so stereotypical of the "badass" heroes of the 1980s—Guts evolves into a more sensitive, benevolent human who fights for a noble cause. The author even has him "cry" on two occasions, proof that the Black Swordsman has opened up some of the gates to his emotions. Conversely, Griffith, who resembles in every way the idealized image of the heroic white knight, is actually hiding his vile, hardly human character. Miura even deconstructs Casca, having her swing from strong woman to defenseless victim, then spending a ridiculous amount of time trying to rebuild her character. The metaphor of scientific experimentation in a storytelling laboratory is apt. We can tell that a character's transformation in a given environment is something that fascinates the author and there are a few passages in the manga that seem to create a "mise en abyme" with the divine aspect of a story's creator: while being held deep in the dungeons, Griffith remembers his past and says this, which fits perfectly with the author's position: "Thereby, have I grasped the hearts of so many in these hands." With his pen, Miura has grasped the lives of so many. There's a detail that I like to think of as subliminal proof of this theory. Indeed, it's commonly believed that Miura lent his own face to the character Pippin and, from the few photos one can find of the *mangaka*, there indeed seems to be a certain resemblance. Interestingly, Pippin is the only character to touch Guts, even though Guts hates physical contact because of his past. Still, Pippin drags Guts to go have a drink with the band, unable to do anything to stop him. Perhaps it's a way of signifying that only Miura—and thus Pippin—is allowed to touch Guts, whether he likes it or not. In fact, while we don't know who the fictional father of the Black Swordsman is in the manga, we do know his true father: his name is Kentaro Miura. What's more, it's interesting to note that Pippin is sacrificed during the Eclipse, as if the author were saying goodbye to himself along with everyone else. Given that the merce-naries in the Band of the Falcon were inspired by Miura's friends from high school, maybe that's a sign that with the Eclipse, Miura abandoned the biographical aspect of *Berserk* to focus purely on mythology, having made peace with his past. The *mangaka* no longer had doubts: he had become a real author and could take us into the depths of darkness. He could finally become the dark, demiurge puppet master. Miura knows this: while the theater of human trials and tribulations may put on a tragedy, it will be a fascinating spectacle if it's well written. The idea that there's hidden beauty in the dramatic horror of existence reaches its culmination in the words of Slan during the Eclipse, as the reader watches in horror the ordeal suffered by Casca and Guts. The Guardian Angel offers these troubling words that seem to move her: "Such beauty... It touches me. Love, Hatred. Pain, Pleasure. Life, Death. This is to be human. This is to be evil." As if beauty could come from the very darkest places in the human soul...

THE STYLE OF KENTARO MIURA

Talking about "style" when it comes to art is very tricky. First of all, by nature, everyone has their own style. Some artists start by copying other styles or trying to imitate the greats, but even in that case, they end up adding their own personal touch, a little something that makes their work different. However, in most cases, an artist tries to develop a style that will differentiate them from all others, that will make them unique. A style is a particular way of creating something, one that gives the work a particular aura... Let's be clear: no one style is better than any other. Art history (the conventionalist side of it) has tried to make us believe the contrary, trying to label some works as beautiful and other works as ugly, but the truth is much more complex. A drawing in the vein of "outside art" may be more moving to some than a painting from the 16th century. It all depends on what the viewer feels, what their personal tastes are. One's artistic sensibilities depend on perceptions and they are different for each individual. Following this logic, an image presenting a scene of horror can be unspeakably beautiful, as Miura suggests in a bit of dialog: "This scene which should be only gruesome, however instead it was like an inimitable painting." This is the *mangaka*'s visual challenge, part of his style: he wants to make us experience the worst-imaginable horrors through his visions, each more virtuosic and magnificent than the last. Many people refuse to read *Berserk* thinking that it's violent, brutal, and thus of no interest, as if violence precludes the beauty and finesse of a subject. Believing that art must be "pretty" and must only show "beautiful" things is a serious mistake. When Caravaggio painted *Judith Beheading Holofernes*, he created a painting of indescribable richness, in spite of the fact that it shows a terrible scene of decapitation. While Miura is lauded by many fans, he is far from being truly recognized for his true genius. Continuing with the unfounded clichés tied to art, saying that one style is superior to another implies that certain artists use the right techniques, while others use the wrong ones. In reality, the situation is much more complex than that. No creation comes into existence without a lineage of techniques and influences. Some seem to think that the ability to evoke emotion is derived only from knowledge of artistic techniques. Wrong again. A professional artist can create a flat, soulless drawing, while an amateur can produce a masterpiece. In the end, it's the viewer who determines whether something is "good" or "bad," but nothing gives us the right to judge a style or assign it a rating. Thus, accordingly, I will only give you my appreciative opinion on Miura's artistic choices; I will not pillory works that I believe to be less "meticulous" in appearance. This precondition is very important because, when it comes to art, it is essential that we bear in mind that all art forms, whether major or minor, can move us, as long as there's an aesthetic intention and a desire to convey an emotion. Each *mangaka* has their own artistic sensibilities. As long as their style serves the story that they're telling, that's what matters most. For example, *Blame!* by Tsutomu Nihei presents a style of drawing that's cold, at times muddled, and hatched, with empty spaces and lines that fade away before they're finished. We could say, exaggerating a little, that his drawing style is almost like sketching, and yet it's incredibly powerful, totally serving the subject and setting of his story: an unfinished city that has fallen into ruin and stretches out infinitely... So, it's all a matter of stylistic consistency and originality. When you decide to analyze the style of a drawn work—animation, comics, or manga—you have to take into account various elements. At random, these include lines, visual style, composition, lighting, scene cutting, backgrounds, details, the degree of realism, the meaning of the setting, etc. There are so many visual parameters that come into play in this type of art form that it quickly becomes dizzying in its complexity. Add to that the number of pages drawn by Miura and it'll send chills up your spine. Thus, Miura has spent an astronomical amount of time composing these tens of thousands of images. Already remarkably talented from the get-go, the *mangaka* never stops improving, taking on greater and greater visual challenges, such as the battle with Ganishka or the appearance of Falconia, in which he unveils complex architecture never before seen in the manga.

So, how can we define Miura's drawing style? He has clear, precise lines. Each form is finished. Each line is well connected to the others. While clear lines can sometimes be seen as cold, Miura manages to avoid this pitfall thanks to his use of hatching. He uses this technique of fine, parallel lines to give volume to his drawings, to create light and shadow, to create different materials and textures, etc. His way of using hatching is very similar to traditional engraving techniques, such as those you would find in the works of Albrecht Dürer and Gustave Doré. While his hatching is generally clean and delicately placed, Miura does not hesitate to disturb these lines when the drawing must express anger, horror, or violence. The most common example is when Guts enters the Berserker Armor trance: the hatching shifts and begins to vibrate, as if Miura began drawing in a state of rage, allowing us to feel the character's state of mind thanks to the technique used to represent it. The hatching becomes the most effective vector for conveying a visceral emotion. As such, there's no need for words to understand Guts' physical and psychological condition. However, the most troubling instance of this tortured hatching is the first time we enter Mozgus' torture chamber. The page appears to have been scratched with feverish hatching, as if to express the endless suffering of the poor souls trapped in this space, an oppressive atmosphere exacerbated by the unlucky, dirty appearance of the scene as a whole. It's not said outright, but the eye understands perfectly thanks to the style of drawing: this room exudes suffering and madness. However, it's when he uses hatching to express speed and movement during combat that Miura's skill is at its most breathtaking. Thanks to his mastery of these movement lines, he manages to create incredibly dynamic, prodigiously legible scenes in spite of the complexity of certain battles. The hatching communicates the extreme speed of blows while highlighting their trajectory. Thus, the eye is able to much more easily understand what's happening in battles in spite of their violence and fast pace. At times, Miura even goes as far as to have Guts appear in the same panel four times, in different places, with everything connected by movement lines. It's as if the Black Swordsman is moving faster than the *mangaka* can draw, or as if someone were taking a long-exposure photo and the subject kept moving during the shot. However, his perfect mastery of hatching is far from Miura's only visual strength: all of the indomitable, combatant savagery is accompanied by rivers of blood. To depict it, he uses his darkest ink and draws fountains of blood with varying trajectories that shower the entire panel. If you look closer, you can make out dots of ink that Miura made with little, purposeful splashes while inking. They give an even more realistic element to these scenes of extreme violence. The author's drawing is always meticulous. Each detail in the image, even those that are purely decorative, is treated with the same importance. The *mangaka* likes each image to be realistic and natural, even when it shows improbable things. The proportions of people and architecture are always true to reality down to the smallest details. Even the monsters are drawn "seriously." Even though Miura's style is characterized by this purposeful naturalism, he does not limit himself to this approach. He knows how to change it up to make us laugh, like with his *chibi* drawings, or to use much freer, wilder lines when the scene requires it. And then, there's all his work based on photographs when he wants to draw inspiration from real life. To give a concrete example, in Elfhelm, when Schierke and Farnese use the mushrooms to enter Casca's unconscious mind, we get the impression that Miura consulted an encyclopedia of fungi and that he actually worked off of meticulously chosen, real-life models. One could say that all of Miura's talent lies in his very particular drawing style because he manages to take ownership of all of the models from which he takes inspiration. He makes them so personal, aesthetic, and, above all, coherent within his story. *Berserk* is also a journey into the author's learning and discoveries: we can tell that he is constantly educating himself artistically and he incorporates bits of that visual learning into his work, as one would add an ornament to the ideal Christmas tree. While he borrows a lot from real life and from culture, he has such a talent for blowing us away with his art that the reference is forgotten. All of the external influences found in *Berserk* become *Berserk*. Miura has nothing to prove anymore: he has demonstrated his mastery in every way. Sometimes, artists have pet peeves: things they don't like to draw, things that bother them, or things that they have trouble depicting faithfully. That's not the case here: Miura is capable of drawing with perfection ballrooms filled with gilded objects and nobles in formal dress and then, a few pages later, bloody, epic battles. Even the architecture is meticulous and coherent, showing excellent mastery of perspective. He brilliantly depicts the elements and nature: raging seas, menacing clouds, peaceful countryside, lush vegetation, etc. Bodies, too, are skillfully drawn: in the series, we find every type of body and face. If you just try your hand at drawing, you'll realize the insane mastery of Miura as an artist. *Berserk* is a cathedral with a thousand details and expert embellishments that Miura has been constructing for thirty years now, and it's with his pen that he maintains this edifice like no other. From a technical point of view, we know that when it comes to a pictorial creation, lines alone are not enough, and Miura also shows mastery of contrasts and lighting of his scenes. These give his drawings all of their volume and depth, with the artist playing subtly with chiaroscuro and darkness. Finally, while his lines may be skillful, that's not enough to make a good panel: the artist absolutely must consider scene-setting, framing, and composition. To borrow a film term, the *mangaka* must consider his "camera angle." No surprise here: this is yet another area where Miura excels. Perhaps it's worth noting a biographical aspect from Miura's childhood here: his father was a storyboarder in advertising. In a joint interview with editor Kazuhiko Torishima, Miura opens up and says that, as a child, he was aware of the nature of his father's work.

"I had lots of opportunities to see his work before he submitted it, so of course I was conscious of it. His drawings would end up on TV commercials, so that's how I got to know about the work he does[3]."

---

3. Joint interview with Kentaro Miura and Kazuhiko Torishima for the magazine *Young Animal*, published by Hakusensha. English translation from the website *Crunchyroll*.

More interesting still, this is how Miura got a taste for the scene cutting that comes with creating a manga. While a storyboard is often more functional than aesthetic, it is very similar to a manga or a comic in its form. According to Miura, it's even what pushed him to start drawing manga.

"Storyboards are made to convey meaning by pictures alone, so of course I could. I think my paneling style might have taken inspiration from my father. I'd stopped doodling at preschool, and in elementary school, I began drawing manga[4]."

Not only does Miura know how to use cinematic framing and scene-setting, he also takes full advantage of all of the complexity of point of view permitted by drawing, including things that you could never do with a camera. Today, only 3D is capable of rivaling what you can do with a comic strip or, in this case, manga. A cinematic example: at the beginning of a chapter, Miura shows a bird flying over the ocean. That bird then crosses paths with a sea monster that very nearly devours it. Having escaped death, the bird continues its flight until it perches... on our heroes' ship. In this way, using this bird-camera, Miura shows us that a sea creature is on the prowl near our protagonists, and he does so without interrupting the action and with the grace of a bird; all of that, of course, without any dialog. However, there is another scene that perfectly illustrates Master Miura's strengths for scene cutting and narration through images. In volume 18, a two-page spread depicts the poverty-stricken area around the Tower of Conviction. We overlook a camp of destitute people. Without a word, for ten panels, the *mangaka* manages to depict the most extreme poverty. A bird's-eye view shows us the camp from high above: we see dozens of makeshift tents sheltering people who are frozen and hunched over, huddled around a dying campfire. A closer shot shows us these poor wretches in more detail. In the foreground are two old people; behind them are young children hugging their knees to their chests, their faces emaciated. Some are lying on the ground, having fallen over from fatigue; others are trying in vain to sleep while crouching. All of those whose eyes we can see have a blank stare, as if there's no one left inside these shells of skin and bone. We don't see a single man in the prime of his life: all those in fighting condition have gone off to war. The next panel shows women sitting in a tent, warming themselves around a small fire and seemingly waiting for death to come, resigned. We then see an exhausted mother trying to breastfeed her baby while her two other children tug at her sleeves, likely asking for food. Two women look at each other with the grave air of those who have lost all hope. The next panel shows

4. *Ibid.*

empty dishes strewn across the ground and we understand that there's nothing left to eat. As if the despair had not yet reached its peak, the next panel shows children with sticks using the little strength they have left to hunt something on the ground. The next "shot" is terrible: young children fight, seemingly enraged, over a rat that they've finally trapped... hoping to eat it. The ninth panel shows another view of the children's fight, in which they occupy the foreground. In the background, very small, Miura draws a silhouette pulling a hand cart. As if the camera is moving between the children to zoom in on the background, we then find out what the cart is carrying: the lifeless bodies of elderly people and children who have died of hunger. Managing to show so many things and communicating so many emotions in just ten frames—without using any text—is a stroke of genius. And those are just ten frames out of tens of thousands drawn by Miura. For each of them, the framing is well thought-out and the boldness is constant. It demonstrates the author's power and inventiveness in terms of visual composition. If his visual style is beyond reproach, his way of enhancing it with scene-setting must be even more so...

A DARK SIDE TO ART HISTORY

Of all the possible ways to understand *Berserk*, there's one that really spoke to me: an artistic understanding. I have been moved by the aesthetic vein in which Miura creates his manga because he references artists whose work I have admired since my childhood. It seems that the things that have left an impression on Miura have affected me in just the same way. In his manga, he makes direct reference to works of art and the universes of certain artists who, of course, were chosen for a particular reason: Miura has positioned his manga in a specific artistic lineage that does not draw inspiration from just one period or aesthetic movement. Thus, this lineage cannot be clearly placed in the chronology of art history. So, this chapter will focus more on a personal theory, but based on the artists that Miura references, we see a "dark throughline" appear. If we want a term that encompasses all of the works I'm referring to, we can talk about "the uncanny"[5] or "dark art." Before we look closer at their work, here is the list of artists, in chronological order, referenced by Miura: Hieronymus Bosch, Francisco de Goya, Gustave Doré, Edvard Munch, M.C. Escher, H.R. Giger and, to a certain extent, Clive Barker,

---

5. A term that comes from the founder of psychoanalysis, Sigmund Freud, who used the word as the title for one of his essays (*Das Unheimliche* in the original German, 1919). It refers to an uncomfortable feeling one might feel toward certain everyday things or objects. Borrowing from the works of Ernst Jentsch, a German psychiatrist from the late 19th century, Freud illustrated this psychoanalytical concept using the works of numerous German Romantic writers, particularly E.T.A. Hoffmann.

since he was also a painter and designed his creatures himself. What these artists have in common is that they have explored a certain form of the fear of the abyss while trying to probe the darkness of the soul or of perception. Additionally, most of them have opened up new pathways into the dark side of the imagination, inspiring thousands of artists. Some references are just nods to their works: in the case of Munch, it's just a scared Puck who adopts the same pose as the figure in the famous painting *The Scream*. In other cases, the homage is vaguer. This is the case, for example, with Francisco de Goya, a Spanish artist whose works included some famous, fantastical paintings on the subject of witches' Sabbaths.

✹ *His two most emblematic paintings, whose aesthetic Miura has aimed to reproduce, are* Witches' Sabbath *and its even more famous variation* Witches' Sabbath (The Great He-Goat).

❀ *Francisco de Goya y Lucientes* – Witches' Sabbath (The Great He-Goat)

Alongside *Devilman*, these two paintings are the very source of inspiration that led Miura to imagine a story arc centered on witches' Sabbaths, which were still a source of fantasy in Goya's time. In *Berserk*, there's no panel that identically reproduces one of Goya's images. However, when you look at one of the Spanish painter's works, you can easily imagine the *mangaka* saying to himself: "What would happen if this painting came to life?" The homage to Goya is clear as day, but has not yet been made in a direct reference.

When it comes to Giger, the nod is more discreet, but still very much present. This Swiss painter has become world-renowned thanks to the Ridley Scott film *Alien* (1979). The success of this movie brought Giger's work to Japan. Much more open to extreme imagery than other countries, Japan was very receptive to Giger's dystopian worlds and sexualized, mechanical bodies. He had tremendous influence on mangas such as Kazushi Hagiwara's *Bastard!!* and Tsutomu Nihei's *Blame!*, and there's no doubt that this hard-to-define artist made an impression on Miura too. Giger opened doors to the dark side that had never before been touched in the art world. He brought to life a totally coherent and personal universe that projects both terror and beauty, such that it's impossible to be indifferent toward his work. Miura hid a reference to Giger in his demonic pantheon by giving the Guardian Angel Conrad a face borrowed from one of the Swiss artists' paintings. The very first monster we come across in the manga, the very same one who later kills Corkus, is a creature that Giger would have been proud to call his own, and her resemblance to the monster from the film *Species* (Roger Donaldson, 1995), which Giger designed for the movie well after that first issue of *Berserk*, is uncanny in hindsight. Giger was already a specialist in monstrous, sexual, archetypal, feminine figures when Miura discovered his work, which likely explains this coincidence. Since Giger was working in a space much closer to science fiction, that's probably why Miura did not include more references to him in his manga, given the time discrepancy between their work. That said, Giger and Miura have produced works with similar themes. For example, Giger represented Baphomet a number of times in his paintings, such as *The Spell II*, *The Spell IV*, and *Baphomet*.

197

Both creators share a passion for Lovecraft: Giger's first catalog of works, published in 1977, was called *Necronomicon*, named after the fictitious book of necromancy so emblematic in the mythology of Lovecraft. Giger, the King of Cyborgs, was, like Miura, fascinated by death, magic, the occult, pentagrams, and sexuality, not to mention depictions of the Devil... Giger, too, worked on the subject of nightmares and his series of drawings entitled *Shaft* evokes a terror quite similar to the bad dreams that Guts has with the fetus and the eye in the labyrinth. Similarly, when Schierke and Farnese journey into Casca's unconscious mind, they come across creatures whose torsos look like gorillas, but whose heads, arms, and legs take the form of menacing, muscular phalluses, echoing certain paintings by Giger, who also liked to use this sort of imagery in works tied to the unconscious mind and terror, desire, or sexual angst, such as his women with phallic appearances. The parallel may seem random, but Miura and Giger are the only artists I know of who have depicted things like this without it seeming ridiculous or vulgar in the way it makes sex terrifying. So, even if the temporal dimensions of their respective images are far apart, both artists share a real artistic lineage. Thus, the homage that Miura pays to Giger via Conrad is not so surprising because any of the hellish and inhuman universes that appear in Giger's paintings could easily be the dimension in which the God Hand lives when it's not in the Physical World. The ceremonies initiating new apostles give the same impression of timelessness and vertigo as Giger's paintings.

❂ *Gustave Doré – Fay ce que voudras – Illustration of Rabelais' Gargantua and Pantagruel*

Continuing to pay homage to the pioneers of fantasy who influence him, Miura left some clues about his love for French engraver and painter Gustave Doré. As a first point of uncanny resemblance, Doré made illustrations of works to which Miura makes direct reference: we already know about the

Divine Comedy and *Paradise Lost*, but it's also the case for the Bible, Rabelais' *Gargantua* (the origin of the phrase "Do what thou wilt"), and folktales like those by Charles Perrault.

A bit like Giger, there's an uncanny resemblance between the fantasy themes of Gustave Doré and those of Miura, not to mention the *mangaka*'s visual style. I've already mentioned that his style is quite similar to that of engraving and it's precisely the similarity to Doré's style that creates this impression. Miura's hatching, his ability to manage lighting and depth, his way of magnifying the bleakest visions: these are all aspects that seem to fit into Doré's lineage. When you review the works that Doré illustrated, you get the impression that he represented all sides of fantasy in his time, a point shared with Miura. From *Don Quixote* to the *One Thousand and One Nights*, Doré explored very diverse influences from multiple cultures... Much like Miura with *Berserk*, Doré's way of adding a legendary touch sometimes made his illustrations just as famous as the works they represent. In both virtuosos, we find the same desire to explore every nook and cranny of the "classic" imagination, showing that they can take on anything. In regards to the homage to Doré, it's much more obvious on certain pages of the manga in particular. I've already mentioned *Satan Descends upon Earth*, to which Miura paid tribute with Zodd flying through a dark sky; however, that's not the only example.

❈ *Gustave Doré* – Satan Descends Upon Earth

A full page of the manga shows Casca in the foreground, her back to us, facing the Tower of Conviction in silhouette, as if it were backlit, and surrounded by tents full of starving refugees. The composition of the image and the shape of the tower are borrowed from an illustration by Gustave Doré, *The Confusion of Tongues*, from his illustrated edition of the Bible.

❂ *Gustave Doré – The Bible – The Confusion of Tongues*

Both towers are covered by the same tormented clouds; however, instead of a camp of impoverished people, Doré showed the workers building the Tower of

Babel. In another, more subtle example, Miura borrows from another fantastic image by the engraver. At the very beginning of volume 34, a two-page spread shows two peasants laboring in a field. They've stopped working because, in the distance, they see something that seems incomprehensible to them. What they see is Ganishka in his final form before he's transformed into a cosmic tree. The subjects and the composition of the image are most likely inspired by another illustration Doré did for the Bible: *The Return of the Ark to Beth Shemesh*. The way Doré's image is put together is similar and although its peasants are Middle Eastern and harvesting wheat, they too are in the foreground and stop their work to admire a fascinating scene in the distance. In the engraving, it's the Ark of the Covenant that shines in the distance with a divine, reassuring light... Miura, on the other hand, continuing with his inversion of biblical values, shows his peasants a monster with a Lovecraftian aura. By relying on old engravings illustrating a holy book, Miura kills two birds with one stone: he subliminally infuses his images with a biblical dimension while showing his respect for an artist who has inspired him.

The next visual artist from whom Miura borrows certain "visions" is none other than the great Maurits Cornelis Escher. This highly talented Dutch creator of engravings and drawings was passionate about mathematics and the concept of infinity. He went down in 20th-century art history for creating unforgettable, iconic images combining optical illusions, mathematical curiosities, fractals, and other elements. In addition to producing highly technical and precise images, Escher succeeded in imagining an extremely rich universe, sometimes verging on fantasy. Anyone who's seen his world-famous lithograph *Relativity* (1953) would immediately recognize that it was borrowed for the first appearance of the God Hand in the manga.

❁ *Escher* – Relativity

Miura absolutely does not hide this: he deliberately borrowed this idea of an impossible labyrinth from Escher, with the many stairways obeying contradictory gravities. This work by Escher has been referenced a thousand times, from *The Simpsons* (Matt Groening) to the film *Labyrinth* (Jim Henson, 1986) to *Chrono Cross* (1999): as soon as you see those odd staircases, it's definitely an homage to Escher. However, where Miura's references to Escher get interesting is that he doesn't limit himself to this universally recognized image; he also references another Escher image, but this time more discreetly. When Griffith is locked away in the King of Midland's dungeon and is delirious from the tortures inflicted on him, he has a hallucinatory vision: he hears the God Hand calling him from their strange dimension. We only see them very briefly, at the end of the vision, but they're shown in a setting that leaves no doubt that Miura borrowed it from Escher's 1946 work entitled *Another World (Other World Gallery)*.

❀ *Escher – 1946* – Another World (Other World Gallery)

Several points tell me this: both images show the inside of a strange, square-shaped tower open on all sides with vaulted archways oriented in different directions. If you place both images side by side, you'll also immediately notice that they have identical vanishing points so that the tower seems to rise (or descend) infinitely. No way that's coincidence. To drive home the reference, Miura positions his Guardian Angels so that they follow the same principle of different gravities in a single space that we see with the placement of the harpies in Escher's image. The image is spellbinding in the manga because it shows us the God Hand in a setting that does not seem to follow the same laws as our reality, signifying that Miura intended to reproduce this sensation of infinity and loss of bearings that Escher was able to depict like no artist before him. Another fantasy pioneer in Miura's lineage. However, the best part about these two references to Escher is the idea that Miura wanted to connect with two distinct Escher works in order to create a single space-time in which to anchor his story. The Dutch artist's images often seem to be taken from a dream... Instead, Miura saw in them a nightmare and, more than an homage, we can say that he offers an exaltation. I think that the *mangaka* would be happy to learn that he introduced thousands of young readers to Escher's work thanks to his aesthetic choices. However, beyond simply passing on the images, he delivers another message: works of art are lasting universes that slip away from their creators; any other artist is then free to explore those universes. Miura loves these works so much that he wanted to "put some Escher" into his ideal opus: *Berserk*.

The final homage, which is the craziest and most moving, is paid to the very first explorer to have opened the strange gates to Hell through art: Hieronymus Bosch (around 1450-1516). Of course, Bosch is neither the first nor the only one to have painted terrifying scenes or visions of Hell. However, the iconography that he created is still so present in people's minds to this day that is has remained a reference... This may seem difficult to prove, but Bosch painted images that are so crazy, so absurd, and so disturbing that he is now considered one of the founders of the fantasy genre. As a forerunner, he left his mark on his age in history thanks to his innovative style, to the point that he was imitated numerous times. However, over the course of centuries, his work fell into relative obscurity as aesthetic tastes changed. It was the surrealists, in the early 20th century, who rediscovered Bosch's work and joined his lineage. Thus, Hieronymus Bosch returned to the forefront of the art scene, restored to his rightful place as a master and uncontested genius. I'm telling Bosch's story because Miura makes reference to his work in the most blatant and direct way possible. At the end of volume 34, just after the two-page spread with dragons in which Miura names the realm of Fantasia, we find four more sublime and troubling two-page spreads, each one representing a different Guardian Angel. Slan is depicted in a sort of tunnel of flesh made up of abstract, sexualized female bodies; Conrad emerges from a heap of rats that, by the thousands, form his face; the spread representing Void simply shows a close-up of the Guardian Angel's emblematic brain; but without a doubt, it's the two-page spread for Ubik that grabs our attention. To represent the "ideal" environment for this Guardian Angel, Miura simply borrows from a Bosch triptych called *The Garden of Earthly Delights* (1494-1505). These three paintings have to be the painter's most famous. The triptych consists of three panels: the Bible's Paradise, Purgatory, and Hell.

❆ *Hieronymus Bosch – Detail of Hell* – The Garden of Earthly Delights

Unsurprisingly, the piece borrowed by Miura comes from the most disturbing panel of the three: the one representing Hell. In it, Bosch depicts a load of creatures, as vile as they are original, participating in an infernal spectacle. Even if the reader isn't familiar with the original painting, they'll notice that the bestiary presented is different from the style of creature typically seen in the manga. In the middle of the beasts in the foreground, who are of relatively normal size, is a giant, chimerical creature: it consists of a man's torso and head, walking on its arms. Within his hollow, open torso, we see a strange banquet taking place, with people seated at a table lit by a single candle. There, tiny and yet frightening, we see Ubik, sitting at the table, surrounded by figures from the Bosch painting. It's interesting to note that, of all of the characters in this scene, Ubik is the only one who is not copied from *The Garden of Earthly Delights*. This is without a doubt one of my favorite passages in the manga because what it suggests is absolutely magnificent. Indeed, Miura gives us the idea that he could find no better image to represent the ideal setting for his Guardian Angel. Ubik is in Bosch's Hell: that's the one and only place for him. The *mangaka* reveals to us that this image haunts him. It is so powerful in his mind that he can't help but dutifully reproduce it out of deference for the visions of the Dutch master, like an homage to an artist whose visionary originality will never really be outdone by anyone. Miura "believes" in Bosch's Hell and gives it substance by including it in his myth. Bosch, who was at the apex of his art career at the start of the 16th century, had an approach to chimerical creatures similar to that used by Miura in creating his apostles: demonic, absurd creatures that are half-human, half-animal. Miura pays tribute to this founder of the dark art movement, the first artist to have depicted such surreal, never-before-seen universes. There's another homage to Bosch that took me much longer to find and that I've never seen mentioned by anyone: during the Eclipse, in the second half of volume 12, a two-page spread shows the Band of the Falcon in the foreground, with their backs to us, facing gargantuan abominations. There's just one speech bubble, containing a single word: "Despair." On the right-hand page, just above Casca's silhouette, we see a strange creature that's curiously less menacing than the others. It has a narwhal-like head, two deer's feet, and dragon's wings. I had never paid this beast any attention in the various times I read this passage, but once I noticed it, an odd feeling of déjà vu washed over me. Being a big fan of Bosch, I soon realized that I had seen this chimera in one of his paintings. After a bit of searching, I managed to find it. This creature can be seen in the triptych *The Temptation of St. Anthony* (around 1501). In the center panel, on the left-hand side, you can see a man with a tree trunk on his head holding onto this beast by its horn and a wing, marching toward St. Anthony.

✿ *Hieronymus Bosch – Detail of* The Temptation of St. Anthony

So, it seems that Miura must have spent hours poring over Bosch's paintings —or at least this one—and wanted to discreetly make reference to them in his own work. This monster appears in volume 12 and the two-page homage to Bosch appears in volume 34, which means that even before Miura chose this aesthetic and ambiance for Ubik, Bosch's influence was already hiding discreetly within *Berserk*.

The "temptations of St. Anthony" refers to St. Anthony the Great, who is often considered the founder of Christian Hermeticism, a concept by which a person withdraws from society for a certain period of solitude in order to get closer to God. What makes St. Anthony so interesting for this analysis is the demonic and tempting visions to which he fell victim during his retreats. This is why the poor hermit has been depicted praying in a landscape infested with demons and abominations competing for who can be the most perverse and obscene. Such depictions were used throughout the Middle Ages and Bosch himself produced several versions. At a time when freedom of expression was limited by the Church, the portrayal of such a scene allowed artists to let their creative juices flow with the figures they wanted to create. They could even imagine the most diabolical imagery thanks to the Bible and its very peculiar visions... So, quite naturally, the depictions of St. Anthony being assailed by monsters proliferated. Miura must have been moved by this hermetic figure tormented by monstrous visions because Guts suffers a similar fate after he's branded with a mark that transforms him into a fighting St. Anthony when night falls. So, in his own way and through the manga, Miura perpetuates the tradition of depictions of St. Anthony...

As we've seen, behind its official story, *Berserk* hides an invisible dialog between Miura and certain artists, most of whom are deceased. The *mangaka* references these artists because he believes that they have enriched our imaginations by breaking the mold. They proved that "something else" could be done with art. Miura makes such powerful references to these pioneers of fantasy in art because they are the only family of artists in which he fits. This idea that certain creators pave the way for others is foundational in art history. For example, most fantasy writers have followed in the footsteps of Tolkien, while modern horror authors have been inspired by the writings of Poe and Lovecraft... and hundreds of artists draw and will draw thanks to inspiration from Kentaro Miura. *Berserk* is a masked homage to all those who have opened the forbidden doors to the dark side of art. These artists laid the groundwork for the unique story that Miura would tell.

THE VAMPIRE'S LAIR

When you cherish a story and are passionate about analyzing it, it's not unusual for your interest to go beyond the work itself: you want to know all there is to know about the author too. Basically, you want to untangle the threads of the story's creation and better understand the artist so that you can better understand their work. You want to understand the workings of the intimate machinery that inspired their visions. This is particularly true when the work in question is dark or disturbing... It's the "you have to be crazy to write that" syndrome. This is an understandable cliché: sometimes when a work of art disturbs us or we don't understand it, we mock the artist rather than questioning our own reactions and trying to understand the artist's approach. The author who plunges us into darkness can actually be more balanced and sane than one who only looks toward the light and refuses to acknowledge the dark side. Clive Barker lends support to this argument with this bit of advice that he gives to creators: "Be regular and orderly in your life, that you may be violent and original in your work." This adage fits perfectly with the rules that Miura follows. Indeed, the amount of work and investment needed to produce–singlehandedly–a series like *Berserk* requires a very special lifestyle that few people would adopt. Here's Kentaro Miura's unbelievable schedule, as he described it in an interview:

"As for my usual daily schedule, I get up around 7:00 – 8:00 PM. I start to work around 8:30 – 9:00 PM. I work and then eat. And then I work again until the next break at 3:00 AM, when I take one meal. Hmm, until 3:30 AM, while eating, I watch a video that I recorded on that day. And then I get back to work. After that, I have my last meal at 6:00 AM and work until around 12:00 PM. Until 1:00, 2:00 or 3:00 PM at the latest and until 11:00 – 11:30 AM at the earliest. It's my normal working routine[6]."

It's precisely because of this interview extract that I named this chapter "The vampire's lair." Consider this: Miura gets up to work as night falls, under the pretext that he doesn't like to draw in natural light... The *mangaka* even jokes about this when the interviewer expresses surprise about the fact that he never sees the light of day:

"I see the morning sun through the veranda. I come out to the veranda and the morning sun is so bright that it dazzles my eyes. I can concentrate best on my work under the light of this lamp. I don't see the sunlight. I'm a vampire[7]!"

But instead of using sharp fangs to bite humans, he uses a pen to make fictional characters suffer. Hidden away in an office he never leaves, Miura

---

6. Interview given in December 1996 in Kentaro Miura's studio, published in *Berserk: Illustrations File*. See Bibliography.
7. *Ibid.*

works while the rest of the world sleeps, as if Midland only comes to life once Japan has gone to bed. In fact, the *mangaka* is not so different from St. Anthony: he lives like a hermit, a recluse monk. There's a dialog between Guts and Rickert that can take on a second meaning. When Rickert asks the Black Swordsman where he disappeared to for a year, the latter responds: "I went into the mountains and swung this sword." So, if Guts went away to be with his sword, could Miura be using this as a metaphor for his pen and his own solitude? The *mangaka* seems to use Rickert to make fun of his own lack of sociability: "Mountain training... Practically was a deserted island. Wow... That's pretty old-fashioned." You might think that I'm reading too much into this—and that's very possible—but there's something Miura said in an interview that calls us to do this "autobiographical" reading of *Berserk*, meaning that we should consider the possibility that the author has hidden bits of himself in his manga:

> "I have a pet theory: If you can't think of your own personal history as a story, you can't become a manga artist[8]."

So, Miura leaves little doubt in our minds that he has infused his story with an intimate, personal touch. The author has also revealed that the love-hate relationship between Griffith and Guts is inspired by his own past. When he was young, he realized that he would never become a *mangaka* if he remained in a normal high school, so he enrolled in one with an arts program. It's likely that Miura's mother encouraged him in this choice (and influenced his preferences) because she herself was a professor of art history. That's when teenage Kentaro met Koji Mori (author of the manga *Suicide Island*) and they developed a complex relationship that was a blend of admiration and jealousy. Miura confesses that he practically suffered from his fascination for his friend and future competitor.

> "It actually made it hard to be normal friends with him. He was so awesome that if I didn't stay away from him, he would dwarf me. I didn't like my options, so I fought back the only way I could, which was to keep working on manga. [...] That was actually the inspiration. But sometimes I would be Guts, and sometimes I would be Griffith. It's probably something that happens a lot in guys' relationships[9]."

8. Joint interview with Kentaro Miura and Kazuhiko Torishima for the magazine *Young Animal*, published by Hakusensha. English translation from the website *Crunchyroll*.
9. *Ibid.*

Knowing about this autobiographical aspect, the relationship between Griffith and Guts can be understood differently. Some of the dialog between them even takes on a new flavor, like this speech from Griffith about friendship: "To me a friend is something else. Someone who would never depend upon another's dream, someone who wouldn't be compelled by anyone, but would determine and pursue his own reason to live, and should anyone trample that dream, he would oppose him body and soul... even if the threat were me myself. What I think a friend is is one who is my 'equal.'" This kind of surprise is the kind of reward you get by reading up on an author. You rediscover their work in a new light and some elements of the manga become even more meaningful. Miura is quite a reserved person, having given only a dozen interviews in thirty years, none of which have been on camera, and there are almost zero photos of him. Although he's been quite open in these conversations with journalists and fans, it's not much in comparison to his 9,000 dense pages teeming with ideas and influences. In that sense, could it really just be random that, in the manga, Miura lent his appearance to Pippin, a character who never says a thing and keeps his eyes almost shut? The *mangaka* speaks to us much more through his work than through question and answer sessions. Miura is discreet and seems uncomfortable with the idea of opening up when it's not by way of his creation. At the end of *Berserk: Illustrations File*, he wrote a note to conclude the book. In it, addressing his readers, he confessed that he was afraid of doing a bad job of responding to an interviewer and showing off his never-before-published drawings from his youth... Basically, taking us behind the scenes and showing us who Miura really is.

"I'm not very articulate, so I ask myself, 'have I properly expressed what's on my mind? Have I avoided any pointless digressions?' By nature, *mangaka* only examine themselves through manga. Revealing yourself through your work is all fine and good, but it's unseemly to sell pieces of yourself elsewhere. You entrust them to your readers through your works. That's what I think... That said, I've done it, for better or for worse. Pretty much like: 'OK, I'll go along with it! Look, this is me!!' If there are people who have enjoyed that, then we can say that it was worth it. We'll have to wait for the next time I make a fool of myself like that, years from now... That will be proof that *Berserk* is continuing to thrive[10]!"

While demonstrating humility, Miura affirms that he has included pieces of himself in his work. We can see this intimate connection at play in volume 3:

10. Interview given in December 1996 in Kentaro Miura's studio, published in *Berserk: Illustrations File*. See Bibliography.

when Guts abandons Theresia to her sad fate after slaying her father, the Count, he hides his face so that Puck can't see that he's crying. However, these tears are not for Theresia: at that very same time, the magazine that would initially publish *Berserk* each month, *Animal House*, had just announced that it was going out of business. After finally getting his own series, Miura saw his dream slipping away from him. Thus, it was not Guts crying, but rather his creator crying through him. Thankfully, publication began again in the magazine *Young Animal*, the successor to *Animal House*, and so the story was able to continue. Moreover, it was after that momentary pause that the *mangaka* picked up Guts' story from the time of his birth. While initially certain characters were based off of Miura's life experiences, he soon expanded his vision:

"In the beginning, about up to volume five, I was still writing stuff that I had thought of when I was in college. So my real life was reflected a lot in the stories in the beginning. And after a while, I started to see the bigger picture[11]."

How can a recluse who works at night expand his vision of the world? First, thanks to research through books and images, which are the sources Miura mainly works with:

"I do have a huge pile of pictures that I use as reference. I use a collection of photographs from different countries... but it's actually easier to find the pictures of armor or landscapes in Japan. So, whenever I need some pictures, I'll go find it by myself or ask somebody to get it. So the collection is really big now. [...] Pictures are the best reference for a cartoonist. It's all about how something looks[12]."

That's the crux of it: how something looks; in other words, how does the *mangaka* see things? For Miura, in addition to the images used as references, books are also sources of discoveries. I tried to learn more about these books while doing my research for this book you're reading because I felt like if I could identify some of the books from his library, I could learn more about his influences, about what he's seen and read in these books of images. On the Web, I saw an old photo of the library in his office, but it was too blurry for me to read the titles... Then, on a trip to Japan, I bought the *Berserk Official Guidebook* which included some photos of several sections in his library. I felt a mixture of joy and frustration because I was finally able to see the spines of some books, but most of them were in Japanese and the titles were written

11. Interview given for the North American release of the *Berserk* anime series, as an audio supplement for the zone-3 DVDs. See Bibliography.
12. *Ibid.*

so small that they were practically illegible... Still, I was able to identify some interesting works by taking zoomed-in photos and straining my eyes to read the minuscule text. I was excited to find an anthology of H.R. Giger works, a book on Hans Bellmer, and more, because this confirmed my intuitions with facts. So, I made a list of the books I was able to decipher and consulted them. From this work, I discovered that Miura is interested in everything and researches the themes that he explores. I'm not going to list all the 39 titles I identified because that would be obnoxious, but that list includes a bit of everything: books on Italian and Roman architecture, others on art and photography; many works on human and animal anatomy, sea creatures, insects, etc., as well as many volumes connected to military and medieval traditions. In this work library, you find a book on facial expressions between illustrated works on dinosaurs and on tanks. Miura draws many of his inspirations from this enormous repository of diverse artistic and historical sources. There are even a number of books on "concept artists" who have developed universes for movies and video games. This "documentary maker" aspect of the *mangaka* explains both his broad knowledge and his meticulous nature by which, for example, he would amuse himself by representing all phases of the moon in his manga. This documentary-like style makes each drawing detailed and convincing as Miura only invents that which does not already exist. Everything else is faithfully reproduced, even if time periods are mixed together. Besides these inanimate images, Miura also draws inspiration from television, which he has chosen as his main source of contact with the outside world. That said, most often he just turns it on to listen to the sound while he's working.

"But I live in isolation, watching the world only on the news on TV, so I start to see the bigger picture. I can look at the world from another angle. I'm not talking about one specific event. If I see news about war in another country of if there's a massacre somewhere in Japan, I just look at the world objectively. Religious cults or acts of atrocity have been the topics of the news recently. When I hear those stories, not that I want to find some kind of answer, but it makes me want to visualize what's happening. I just want to see it in my world in my own way. The idea becomes clearer and polished in the process[13]."

It's fascinating to find out that, in the end, Miura has a worldview that passes through warped lenses. What he sees of the world is the way in which the world sees itself. Perhaps this explains his apparent misanthropy... Other than a few sparks of hope, his vision of humanity overall seems to be quite pessimistic, or at least it has been to this point. Still, it would be a mistake

13. *Ibid.*

to see in Miura a simplistic loathing of humanity, as is proved by his attitude in interviews: in them, he seems to actually be very affable and kind, gladly and humbly opening up. In addition, *Berserk* exudes a love for all of humanity's complexity. I think that Miura is fascinated by the human capacity to rise to the highest highs and sink to the lowest lows. He is constantly showing that life is fragile and that there are many dangers, but in spite of it all, he holds a bit of hope in the palm of his hand. It's likely that Casca will finally put herself back together; Farnese came back to her senses and freed herself from her dogmatic shackles; Guts is managing his anger better; Schierke has liberated herself. Statistically, there seems to be more hope for the women than for the men, but the fact remains: not all of *Berserk* is shrouded in darkness; a few lights glimmer in the night. This makes Miura a heretical vampire: part of him believes in humanity.

Finally, my intuition tells me that in his manga, the artist delivers some quite intimate messages about his drastic life choices brought about by his career as a *mangaka*. In the following monologue, Griffith talks about his vision of "dreams" and if you replace the word "sword" with "pencil," the meaning of the speech becomes "manage to make a living from one's art." You can really see Miura's basic ambition and the power of his motivation: "Perhaps he must come upon one other precious thing. [...] For no other's sake. To accomplish it for him... For himself. A dream. One who dreams of world domination. One who devotes his whole life to the thorough tempering of one sword. If there is a dream which takes one his whole life to find, there are also dreams which, like storms, devour tens of thousands of other dreams. With no relation to social status, class... background. Whether it suits them or not, people yearn for a dream. Sustained by a dream, hurt by a dream, revived by a dream, killed by a dream. And even after being abandoned by a dream, it continues to smolder from the bottom of one's heart... probably until the verge of death. A man should envision such a lifetime once. A life spent as a martyr to the god named dream... Ultimately to be born, and to then simply live for no better reason. I can't abide such a lifestyle." When Miura was young, he identified his strength very early on: drawing. And his mission? To be good enough at drawing to make a living from it. In sum, the *mangaka* answered Griffith's question: "That's what I want to know! What is my place in the world? Who am I? What am I capable of? What am I destined for?" While there's a rather heroic side to Miura's all-consuming ambition for excellence, there's also a dark side to this lifestyle because of the sacrifice it requires. To live this way, you have to distance yourself from society. Farnese's mother tells her exactly that: "When it comes to your feelings, you are artistic... so much so that you can't abide this world." However, Miura implicitly tells us that even if the profession of *mangaka* is difficult and the opportunities are hard to come by, personal fulfillment must be pursued at all costs. Guts meets a man who says that he doesn't like mercenaries like him because they're merchants of death. The man then tells Guts about his nephew who died for having chosen to become a mercenary. The nephew died in anonymity, never having had a family of his own. The Black Swordsman responds to this point blank: "He died doing what he wanted, no matter what, right? The bastard died happy. We only have one life to live. There's nothing after that." Here the *mangaka* explains his frame of mind. He prefers a life of misery filled with passion over a "normal" life without passion. That's exactly the kind of mindset you have to have if you want to make a living from art because success most often comes after a long, lonely dry spell. It's touching to see that Miura listened to young Kentaro by pursuing this teenage dream of becoming a *mangaka*.

"To please others or to receive praise by drawing was the happiest thing in my youth. I guess 'old habits die hard.' My family moved quite often at that time. My drawings enabled me to make new friends in the schools I shifted to. Now that I think of it, it was a time when I already established my identity as a drawer in a way[14]."

Like Griffith, Kentaro committed himself to a cause, a quest that gave him a reason to get out of bed each morning—or rather, each evening—with all the passion of a child with a dream. Anyone who has tried to become an artist knows the price you have to pay. How many do you think have given up after years of struggling and still remaining in obscurity? Those who succeed in the arts—no matter the medium—are people who have held out longer than everyone else, who have failed numerous times, but have always gotten back on their feet. Miura seems to love Griffith because he understands his dream. He understands his sacrifice. He knows the price one must pay to become master of their domain. Miura lives through *Berserk*. There's one last quote from Griffith that I can't help but see as an allegory for Miura's success and his feeling of relief at having escaped anonymity: "That is how I have achieved everything so far. There were days when I had not even a slice of bread to eat. But now I can even talk like this, to you, the princess of a whole kingdom." Are we, the readers, that princess whose attention Miura yearned for? The worst fate for a *mangaka* is to no longer be read and for their adventure to end... From Miura, we get the feeling that he is immensely relieved to have achieved his childhood dream.

14. Interview given in December 1996 in Kentaro Miura's studio, published in *Berserk: Illustrations File*. See Bibliography.

THE LONELY GOD COMPLEX

It's hard out there for a god. When you create a universe, you necessarily fill the role of virtual deity with absolute power over the world you invent. You're a bit like the God of Genesis in the Old Testament: the Creator establishes laws and experiments with different creatures. When the artist is in front of a blank sheet of paper, when they create their story, they experience that absolute power: they can do whatever they want insofar as they can put it into words and drawings. It's a terrifying exercise at first, but once you have more of an idea of where you're going and what message you want to send as a creator, the process of creation becomes intoxicating. You can invent whatever you want; you can follow your fantasies and desires. To Miura's credit, he has never stopped showing us that he honors his status as a creative demiurge: we sense that he is free, has no limits, and lets his creativity run wild. However, that divine power comes at a price: the creator must give up something in exchange because for any god to exist, people must believe in it; similarly, a *mangaka* without any readers will have to call it quits. Although the artist must love their art and create images that they want to see, they are not totally alone in the creative process. Readers enter into the equation. When a creator writes a "one-shot" manga, an entire story contained in a single volume, the reader takes it for what it is. The reader holds in their hands a complete story. It elicits no expectations, hopes, or fantasies from the reader because they can read it from start to finish in a relatively short amount of time. Conversely, when an artist creates a series, with events playing out in the long term and released episodically, things work quite differently. To follow a story published over a number of years, the reader has to make a commitment. When you watch a movie, it makes for a nice (or not so nice) evening, but it's a short-term event; the whole goal is to have a good time and walk away with fond memories of the film. The case of *Berserk* is very different: Japanese readers who began following the manga in 1989 with its pre-publication in magazines have spent the last 30 years reading it. So, a reader who was 18 when the manga began is 48 years old today... When you think about it, it makes your head spin and it's the proof that *Berserk* is the life's work of Kentaro Miura, first and foremost, but also of his readers who have been there since the beginning. To that point, it's not unusual to read or hear from fans of the series who fear that the *mangaka* might not be able to finish his manga: he might die of old age before completing the story. This shows readers' deep attachment to the story and demonstrates the almost legendary status Miura has achieved. To have readers following a story over three decades, especially one presenting such powerful, dramatic events, necessarily means that you have demanding, committed, detail-oriented and at times fanatical readers, hence the term "fan." Miura sets the bar so high with his story and evokes so many intense and contradictory feelings in his readers that they cannot remain indifferent. They eagerly await each new volume of *Berserk*. Miura has at times pushed back the releases of certain episodes simply to save himself from cracking under the workload and the pressure that he must feel from his audience's expectations. To really understand, you have to put yourself in his shoes. While I don't know Kentaro Miura personally, I can still have a good idea of what he goes through. He works like a madman and his entire life revolves around *Berserk*. Producing 9,000 pages over 30 years requires a monastic lifestyle that would verge on austere if it wasn't for the fact that Miura does it out of passion. You also have to imagine how much "behind-the-scenes work" goes into each page, which we don't really think about when we devour that page in the span of 20 seconds and then move on to the next. Each published page we read is made up of many hours of work and hundreds of decisions. Miura is constantly making thousands of choices. That's true for any artist, but a *mangaka* who handles both the story and the illustrations has double the work because they first have to come up with the plot. For example, as soon as Miura introduces a character, he has to decide what their fate will be, what will happen to them, and how he is going to depict them. He has to come up with his text, the setting of the scene, how to cut up the scene, and then draw all that. He first gets his ideas down on paper, then he does some preparatory sketches to flesh out those ideas, which adds to his workload, but goes unnoticed by the readers. On top of that, with each choice he has to make, he is confronted with hundreds of possibilities. He has such broad knowledge of film, literature, and art that he knows perfectly well when he borrows something, when he pays tribute, or when he creates something novel. Then comes the final drawing and inking. This is where he fashions the smallest details and chooses each visual element with pathological meticulousness. Thus, each frame requires hours of work. Just imagine how many hours it takes to produce a 200-page volume. Still, readers sometimes tend to think that the author they love so dearly is a machine. And it's hard to blame them because the artist's fragile side is so hidden, often by the creator himself. Nevertheless, when you create a story like *Berserk*, you must be racked with paralyzing doubts. You know that your audience has very high expectations and that with each decision, you risk disappointing them. In that context, Miura must have needed quite a bit of courage to write volume 13, knowing how his readers would react. Even so, he continued on and those who kept reading *Berserk* have become big fans of Miura. He started something so horrific and so powerful that thousands of people are eager to find out how the story will end.

"I actually don't think I could let such a long, grim story end with a grim ending[15]."

This cryptic phrase shows that Miura is thinking about how to end his story and that he is well aware that he is not totally free in his choice. The statement reveals that even if he wanted to give *Berserk* an unhappy ending, that could be a hard pill to swallow for his readers who have fanatically followed this story for so many years. The author himself knows that this epic is his life's work and that, to a certain extent, it's greater than him. Millions of people have become invested in the series: he has to do right by the cathedral he's been building. When journalists ask, Miura admits that he would like to work on other projects, particularly related to science fiction, but he can't indulge himself.

"Besides, I want to do my best on my current work above all. *Berserk* is my first good serialization. I'll be sad if I can't complete it while I set about doing other works[16]."

Miura has done such a good job playing the part of a god of creation that his believers expect answers from him. He has raised so many questions and introduced so many mysteries that his readers are dying to know what the next truth he reveals will be. Everyone wants to know who Miura will have win out... Will it be Griffith? Guts? Casca? His readers expect that the author will conclude his series with a revelation of major moral significance. I personally don't think that's a good idea: Miura raises so many questions specifically because he does not have the ultimate answers to the mysteries of our existence. There's a final theory that came to me the last time I read *Berserk*: what if Kentaro Miura were the true god of *Berserk*? Could we even say that he is the Idea of Evil? What we can say for sure is that there's yet another meta-discourse to be found in the series, this time on the idea of the god-artist. In the manga, causality represents the choices to be made by the *mangaka*; it represents the plot. Is it because Miura is afraid that his inspiration will fail him that he made causality such an evil force? He alone knows the truth of this story; he alone knows how it will end; and if he makes choices that disappoint, he alone will have to bear that burden forever. Miura embodies causality, that mysterious and invisible force that brings about such sad fates for his characters. Just like causality, Miura has a plan for them.

15. Interview conducted by Yukari Fujimoto, published in September 2000 and available on the website: https://mangabrog.wordpress. Translation by the blog author.
16. Interview given in December 1996 in Kentaro Miura's studio, published in *Berserk: Illustrations File*. See Bibliography.

From a character's first appearance, he knows where destiny will lead them. We've seen just how dark a series *Berserk* is... Is Miura's heart that organ of darkness floating in a vortex, listening to news stories about massacres, then infusing his own story with that violence? It's a bit like the Skull Knight, who appears suddenly in the night to save the hero at the last minute: Miura alone will be able to save Guts because the Black Swordsman and his party now face so many powerful enemies that it's hard to see how they can survive. There's Griffith and his army, his band of demons, Nosferatu Zodd, and, of course, the Guardian Angels of the God Hand, as well as all of the apostles of Midland... Unless some miracle enters into the plot, the outcome looks very dark. Still, the *mangaka* suggests that a happy ending is possible... What's clear is that some people will definitely be disappointed because readers are very divided: some are on Team Guts, others on Team Griffith, and others still on Team Casca. An ending that's too happy and "naive" will also not do justice to the series. Miura faces a serious conundrum. Does he already know the precise ending to his tale? If so, since when? Has he kept the pages containing the final arcs of his story under lock and key? Is it as he says in the manga: "Everything has been determined"? The nerve it takes to write a passage like volume 13 proves that Miura is capable of anything. No matter what he decides, I trust that he will surprise us. I would even prefer a mixed ending because if Guts wins and kills Griffith, what will happen to Midland? Will it just be a chaos of trolls and demons? That's not exactly what one would call a happy ending... On the other hand, if Guts dies and Griffith comes out as the victor in this epic, he may bring a certain peace to Midland, but will have committed the worst atrocities to achieve that... Perhaps Casca will surprise us. Maybe even Gusca, the trio's offspring, will turn out to be the key that opens the door to the grand finale. I hope that Miura will at least create an ending that pleases him personally, that he can write the conclusion that excites him the most, even if it disappoints every single one of his readers. It would be senseless to write the ending while only worrying about what readers want. The best way to lose your way is to follow something other than your own vision. To this point, and to our great joy, he has followed his own path, having us sail the raging seas of his imagination. That voyage has been one of the most incredible I've ever had the privilege to go on. Even though I don't know how the journey will end, I do know that *Berserk* is a trip from which I'll never return...

BERSERK

WRITTEN IN DARKNESS

CONCLUSION

O F ALL THE FEELINGS I have for Kentaro Miura, the strongest is gratitude. If one day I were lucky enough to meet him, I think that the only words I would be able to stammer out (holding myself back from assailing him with a thousand questions) would be... thank you. Thank you for giving so much of yourself over the past thirty years in order to offer us a story so deep, so dark, and so free that it almost becomes frightening. Singlehandedly producing such a series is a real feat. He may not be totally unique as a *mangaka*, but few artists have dedicated themselves like him to such a long, dense, and extensive adventure. As Gaston says: "And we got pulled into the middle of some crazy story someone wrote." I hope that thanks to this book, you know a bit more about the author of this "crazy story" and that I have been able to put into words all that I have felt while reading the series. The scariest thing for me is to think about all the things that I read too much into or that I forgot to mention. You could spend years studying *Berserk* for a doctoral dissertation and never be done. As I said in the introduction, *Berserk* is an indomitable series and we can only hope to uncover a fraction of its secrets. However, what's fascinating is that Miura does not have total control. He may have made thousands of decisions, but certain choices are guided by his unconscious:

"There are things I have consciously taken inspiration from, but there are others that have fallen deep into my consciousness and come back to me out of nowhere much later."

When I started this book, I was worried about analyzing a series that's not yet finished, but given the purpose of *Berserk* and given the secrets it still holds, in the end, I'm content with this state of affairs. I'm even almost convinced that once we know the end, we will be filled with more sadness than joy at discovering how the story lines play out. It's not the opening of a treasure chest that makes the adventure; it's all the twists and turns along the way to that chest that will stick with us. Even if *Berserk* were to never end, for me, it has already achieved its objective. *Berserk* has become an integral part of our collective unconscious. I even think that over time, we will increasingly recognize the genius of Miura, the consummate artist, who demonstrates incredible mastery both in the way he comes up with stories and the way he translates them into images. By so masterfully inviting us to dive into the waters of eternal stories, Miura has helped me finally understand this quote from Clive Barker:

"That which is imagined can never be lost."

WRITTEN IN DARKNESS

BIBLIOGRAPHY

Miura, Kentaro, *Berserk*, volumes 1 to 40, published by Dark Horse Comics.

WORKS FROM WHICH PASSAGES ARE CITED

- Gabriel, Richard A., *No More Heroes: Madness and Psychiatry in War*, Hill & Wang, New York, 1988.
- Hume, David, *An Enquiry Concerning Human Understanding*, Flammarion, Paris, 2006.
- Institoris, Henricus and Sprenger, Jacob, *The Hammer of Witches: Malleus Maleficarum*, coll. Atopia, publisher Jérôme Millon, Grenoble, 2005.
- *The New Testament. The Book of Revelation*, United States Conference of Catholic Bishops, 2020.
- *The New Testament. The Gospel According to Matthew*, United States Conference of Catholic Bishops, 2020.
- Sallmann, Jean-Michel, *Les Sorcières, fiancées de Satan*, Gallimard, Paris, 1989.
- Sturluson, Snorri, *Histoire des rois de Norvège - Heimskringla*, coll. L'Aube des peuples, Gallimard, Paris, 2000.
- Zheng Xu, *Story of Three Sovereigns and Five Emperors*.

MAIN WORKS CITED

- Alighieri, Dante, *The Divine Comedy*, Gallimard, Paris, 2010.
- Campbell, Joseph, *The Hero with a Thousand Faces*, Pantheon, New York, 1949.
- LaVey, Anton, *The Satanic Bible*, Avon, New York, 1969.
- Lévi, Éliphas, *Dogme et Rituel de la Haute Magie*, Bussière, Paris, 1990.
- Lovecraft, Howard Phillips, *The Shadow over Innsmouth*, Visionary Publishing Company, Everett, 1936.
- Milton, John, *Paradise Lost*, Gallimard, Paris, 1995.
- Tolkien, J. R. R., *The Lord of the Rings*, Allen & Unwin, United Kingdom, 1955.
- Tzu, Sun, *The Art of War*, coll. Champs classiques, Flammarion, Paris, 2017.

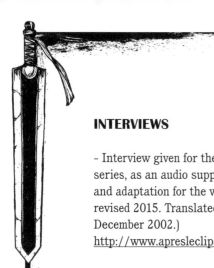

INTERVIEWS

- Interview given for the North American release of the *Berserk* anime
series, as an audio supplement for the zone-3 DVDs. (French translation
and adaptation for the website *Berserk : Après l'Éclipse* by Lady, 2006,
revised 2015. Translated by ZKK from the DVD audio track for *SK.net*,
December 2002.)
http://www.apresleclipse.net/auteur_interview_2002bis.php

- Extract from an interview given by Miura when he won second place
in the Tesuka Osamu Cultural Prize in 2002. (French translation and
adaptation for the website *Berserk : Après l'Éclipse* by Lady, 2015. According
to the translation from the Japanese by Puella for *SK.net*, February 2003,
with help from the Italian translation from BChronicles.)
http://www.apresleclipse.net/auteur_interview_2002.php

- Interview of Kentaro Miura by David Castellazzi - originally published in
Jappamondo n° 3 and subsequently republished in *Scuola di Fumette* n° 8 in
February 2003 in the body of an article on *Berserk*. (French translation and
adaptation for the website BAE by Lady, 2006. Source of the *BerserkChronicles*
[Italy] text.)
http://www.apresleclipse.net/auteur_interview_2003.php

- Joint interview with Kentaro Miura and Kazuhiko Torishima for the
magazine *Young Animal*, published by Hakusensha. English translation
from the website *Crunchyroll*.
https://www.crunchyroll.com/fr/anime-news/2016/08/18-1/interview-
avec-kentar-miura-dans-le-young-animal-partie-1
https://www.crunchyroll.com/fr/anime-news/2016/08/19/interview-
avec-kentar-miura-dans-le-young-animal-partie-2

- Interview given in December 1996 in Kentaro Miura's studio for the
artbook *Berserk: Illustrations File*, French translation by Anne-Sophie
Thévenon for Glénat, 2009.
http://www.apresleclipse.net/auteur_interview_1996.php

- Interview of Kentaro Miura for the *Berserk Official Guidebook*, translated
into French by the publisher Glénat in 2017.

ACKNOWLEDGMENTS

BEFORE making some more personal acknowledgments, I wanted, first and foremost, to thank all of the community websites and other forums for the passionate, very active fans of *Berserk*. This book would not have been possible without their help: all sorts of archiving and categorizing, fascinating theories, impassioned debates, and more. These various websites are excellent resources for anyone trying to better understand this story, which can be cryptic at times. So, above all, thank you to these websites for their help and their passion.

http://www.apresleclipse.net/
https://www.skullknight.net/
https://berserk.fandom.com
https://tvtropes.org/
https://www.reddit.com/r/Berserk/

I would also like to thank everyone who conversed and interacted with me via different networks while I was writing this book and asking certain questions for it. Thank you for your energy and goodwill. You helped me get through periods of doubt with a smile on my face. Such doubts are common when writing a book, especially one on such a complex and frightening series with a very devoted fan base.

Finally, from the bottom of my heart, I would like to thank certain people, both near and far, who helped me in writing this book. First, I would like to thank Mehdi for this wonderful, complex gift: thank you for your trust and kindness. You were able to offer me reassurance and helped me out big time in what was a new adventure for me. Thank you for your advice and your thorough revisions. In addition, I would like to thank everyone at Third Editions. It's a real pleasure to see people with such passion.

I would also like to give special thanks to Sinpiggyhead for his amazing cover art. Seeing his art reassured me. I said to myself, "if people don't like what's inside, at least they'll have a beautiful piece of art." Paying tribute in your own way to Miura's genius is no easy task, and yet... I am proud to have my words wrapped in his artwork.

I would also like to thank certain people who have supported and motivated me during this period of writing, which has at times been lonely, and who have offered me their knowledge: thank you to Benjamin "Benzaie" Daniel for our conversations on the series, for being there for me, and for lending your support to this project; thank you to Da French Phenom for your general knowledge and for your assistance with Japanese references I was unfamiliar with; thank you to Benoît "ExServ" Reinier for your kindness and advice on how to approach such a project; thank you to Sullivan Rouaud for our conversations and for giving me the energy to finish, which was a big help; thank you to Frederico A. for our conversations on *Blame!* and on this book.

Finally, thank you to my friends Patrick Baud, Gilles Stella, AL9000, the three Melissas, JB, Ambroise, DollyWood, Colorblind, Stooloots, and Orion Mega, as well as everyone else who has supported me and given me the joy of friendship. There are many more people with whom I have discussed this subject and who I could thank, but unfortunately, I can't name you all.

My final thank-you is for Alexandra, the love of my life. Thank you for your patience and encouragement throughout this journey, which has been hard at times. I couldn't have done it without you. Lastly, little Isaac, this book is for you, when you're old enough. I can't wait to share *Berserk* with you, that your mind may open up to adventure, to the beauty of darkness, and to the journeys that art can take us on...

Also available from Third Éditions:

Legal submission: November 2020
Printed in the European Union by TypoLibris.